Solve IT!

FOR WINDOWS

Version 3.1

Management Problem Solving with Excel
and Access and the World Wide Web

Kenneth C. Laudon
New York University

Jane P. Laudon
Azimuth Corporation

Kenneth Rosenblatt
Azimuth Interactive, Inc.

Spreadsheet and Database Cases for Excel and Access with Internet Web Cases

Download student files from the Web!
(see last page for details)

INTERACTIVE

New Directions in Learning

Visit us online: http://www.MySolveIT.com

Azimuth Interactive, Inc. ©2003

Azimuth License Agreement

Carefully read the licensing agreement before using the Student Data Files or case book. By using the data files and case book, you accept the terms of this agreement. This package contains valuable proprietary materials of Azimuth Interactive Inc. ("Azimuth"). Azimuth retains the title and ownership of the software, including all patent, copyright, trade name, trademark, and other proprietary rights related to the software. All written materials are copyrighted.

Permitted Uses

The data, programs, and case book included in this package are licensed only for individual use on one or several computer systems by the original purchaser. You may make a single backup copy of the files to support your use of the package.

Prohibited Uses

You may not make the software, or any parts of the package, available to other persons by copying, translating, lending, leasing, or selling. This package may not be re-sold as a "used book" and to do so is a violation of federal copyright and software protection laws. The Student Data Files may not be placed on a network of any kind without permission of Azimuth.

Limited Warranty

Azimuth warrants that the book and data files on which the software is distributed are free from defects in materials and workmanship for a period of 90 days following original purchase. If you experience a problem, return the case book and sales receipt to Azimuth through your local bookstore. You must have evidence of purchase. A replacement unit will be shipped promptly. Azimuth makes no other warranty express or implied

Trademark Acknowledgement

IBM is a registered trademark of International Business Machines Corporation.
Windows 98, Windows 2000, Windows Me, Windows XP, Office 97, Office 2000, Office XP, Microsoft Word, Access, and Excel are registered trademarks of Microsoft Corporation.

Copyright 1992-2003 Azimuth Interactive Inc.
Printed in the United States of America
Azimuth Interactive Inc.
23 North Division Street
Peekskill, New York 10566

ISBN: 1930581-99-8
2003

Table of Contents

Preface to Solve it! 3.1 for Windows

Solve it! was created by the authors based on their experience teaching information systems and management courses at New York University's Stern School of Business and at other universities around the world. Business students in all areas of study need to learn how information technology can be used to solve business problems. This is true of not only of finance majors, but also of majors in management, operations, marketing, accounting, and information systems.

In introductory courses students learn basic computer literacy and develop hands-on experience working with productivity software—spreadsheets, databases, project managers, and word processing. These are still valuable skills but obviously much more is needed in today's business marketplace. What comes after basic computer literacy?

Solve it! builds on basic computer literacy skills. We focus much more on problem solving and critical thinking skills rather than teaching key stroking skills. We believe the most effective use of the new productivity software suites like Microsoft Office results from students learning how to use the software to solve some of the traditional problems in business. Students need to solve problems by exercising their own judgments. Students learn problem solving skills by actually solving problems.

Solve it! began in its early test versions as a collection of cases and a case service. We relied on business colleagues and friends to supply us with real-world cases, recast them for class use, and then tested them in university and industry PC labs and training programs. Since then we began publishing new cases in a new edition every November. This way Fall semester students will have different problems than Spring semester students.

From working with business recruiters and interviewing corporate human resources personnel, we have learned that industry wants students to possess not only certain computer skills, but to be adept at solving some common, even classic, business problems. Problems like inventory management, accounts receivable and payable, payroll, financial analysis, sensitivity analysis, human resource tracking, and even some small applications development. *Solve it!* continues to reflect these concerns.

New Features and Web Exercises: *Solve it! 3.1*

Solve it! 3.1 is designed to support Microsoft Office XP. Version 3.1 reflects the growing business use of the World Wide Web and the Internet by including a chapter containing an introduction to the Web, exercises, and case studies. This edition can also be used to support Microsoft Office 2000 and instructions for this edition of Office are inserted in the text where they differ from Office XP instructions.

Other new features of *Solve it! 3.1* include the more frequent use of screen shots to guide students through the software. In addition to expanding the software base, we have added a number of unstructured exercises that usually require a written response, or enhancement to an existing data set. The Tutorial instructions have been expanded and refined considerably to assist learning, and more screen shots have been added.

Using Excel and Access

Solve it! is fully compatible with virtually all Windows-based software tools. The Student Data Files are delivered in industry standard formats for spreadsheets (.XLS) and Access databases (.MDB). These files can all be imported into each of the software tools described in *Solve it!* as well as to other packages like Lotus 1-2-3, Foxbase, dBase Windows, and Quattro. Access database files are availabe at the Web site (see below) in Office 2000 and Office XP formats.

Macintosh Compatibility

The files for both spreadsheet cases and database cases can be used on Macintosh machines. For instance, Microsoft Excel on the Mac reads the .XLS files distributed on our Web site (see below). And products like Foxbase MAC will also read the *Solve it!* database files.

You can download the Student Data Files from the Solve it! Website using any Macintosh compatible browser.

We sincerely hope you find the new Solve it! both challenging and rewarding.

Download Student Data Files From www.MySolveIT.com/Student/

In order to complete the cases in this book you must download the Student Data Files from the *Solve it! Web site* **www.MySolveIT.com/Student/**. See the last page of the book for instructions and for your personal access code printed in this book. If this book contains no student access code or last page with this information, return it at once to the bookstore for a new product.

If you have questions about Solve it!, visit the Web site first for answers. If you need additional information or have suggestions for improving *Solve it!*, email us at support@www.mysolveit.com. The authors would very much like to hear from students and instructors in order to make this a more useful product.

Ken Laudon
Jane Laudon
Ken Rosenblatt
2003

1

Introduction to Solve it! 3.1

Welcome to the challenge of *Solve it!*

    Solve it! For Windows 3.1 is a new learning system that teaches management problem solving skills through the use of PC spreadsheet and database software. *Solve it!* is designed for use by university students in schools of business and management.

    The management cases in this *Solve it!* package will help you learn how to solve management problems using contemporary spreadsheet and database software on micro computers. The cases are all derived from actual business applications.

    When you successfully complete these cases, you will have mastered the basics of the software and learned how to apply it in realistic settings.

Learn Through Discovery

    Solve it! uses real world case studies to present students with problems and challenges. The cases range from small businesses on Main Street, to banks and brokerage firms on Wall Street, to government agencies. It's up to you to discover the answer.

    For each case there is a corresponding data file on the diskette. You will be asked to enter data, formulas, data fields, and programs in response to problems posed in the cases.

    In general, we have sought to reduce the amount of elementary data entry to a bare minimum and to emphasize conceptual tasks. The cases do not require advanced financial analysis or accounting skills. Explanations are provided for all formulas and analytic tasks.

Industry Standard

    Solve it! is widely used in Fortune 1000 training programs. It is designed to bring students and working professionals up to a common intermediate level of proficiency in Microsoft Windows, Excel, and Access. From this level, industry training programs and seminars are advised for more advanced training.

Many universities and businesses use one of several powerful alternatives to Excel and Access. *Solve it!* works well with Access workalikes such as Foxbase+ and Paradox, and spreadsheet alternatives like Lotus 1-2-3 and Quattro Pro.

You may also use the data files included with *Solve it!* on Macintosh computers using software such as Microsoft Excel and Foxbase+/Mac. You can use the *Solve it!* data diskette with any Macintosh software that can read .XLS, .DBF, and/or ASCII files. Ask your instructor for more information.

You may wish to keep both the book and the completed, graded exercises to show potential employers precisely what skills you have learned. You should also place this information on your resume.

Classic Business Problems

Solve it! uses cases that illustrate classic business problems typically encountered in the real world.

Problems like net present value analysis, payroll accounting, inventory management, break-even analysis, accounts receivable aging reports, pro forma financial statements, quality assurance, production planning, marketing database management, sales management systems, and personnel tracking.

When you complete the cases in *Solve it!,* you will be well prepared to work effectively in a contemporary business environment.

Web Exercises and Cases

Solve it! now contains a new chapter of exercises and case studies that explore the use of the World Wide Web in business problem solving. While the Web is still evolving, it has already proved itself a valuable research tool for business. On the Web you can discover industry trends, statistics, growth patterns, markets, and resources. In short, all the ingredients needed to make a well-informed business plan. The Web cases in Chapter 6 will show you how to use the Web to build a business plan, plus help you explore other features of the Web.

Documentation Included

Solve it! contains all the documentation you will need on how to use spreadsheet software like Excel and database software like Access. The documentation is provided in the form of hands-on tutorials, which show you how to use the software skills required by each of the cases.

The cases and documentation were written using Microsoft Excel and Access for Windows. You will find the data files in *Solve it!* are compatible with all versions of the software. In general, the documentation instructions work equally well for clone software with only minor changes.

Students may wish to consult the original documentation for the software being used, or any one of several large reference manuals. These are generally available in your PC Lab, corporate or college library.

Solve it! assumes the student has a basic familiarity with the Windows operating system. If this is not the case, you should read through an introductory text on Windows or the Windows Users Guide.

The Skills Matrix

In order to select and develop cases, we created a Skills Matrix to identify both the PC software and management skills we sought to teach.

The Skills Matrix for spreadsheet software is shown on the following page (see Figure 1-1). A similar matrix is used for database problems.

The management skills are to organize, plan, coordinate, decide, and control. The PC software skills are basic (set-up and editing), intermediate (data analysis and organization), and advanced (database management, programming and interfaces).

Each *Solve it!* package contains a mix of skill levels and skill areas. About one-third of the problems involve basic PC skills and elementary management skills of organization and planning. The remaining cases develop intermediate and advanced PC skills along with more advanced management skills.

As you proceed from beginning to more advanced cases, the problems become less structured and more analytic. More advanced cases require a written summary.

Each *Solve it!* case identifies in the beginning the specific skills involved in the case. In addition, the approximate completion times for persons at different skill levels are also included. These expected times are based on our experience in university classrooms and industry settings.

Figure 1-1

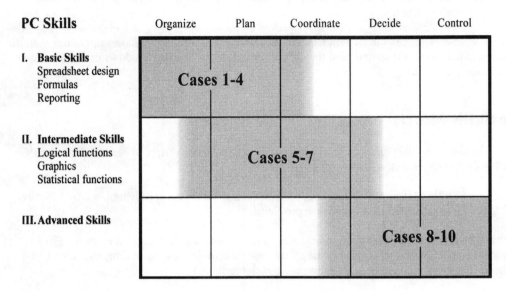

PC Skills

	Organize	Plan	Coordinate	Decide	Control
I. Basic Skills Spreadsheet design Formulas Reporting	Cases 1-4				
II. Intermediate Skills Logical functions Graphics Statistical functions		Cases 5-7			
III. Advanced Skills				Cases 8-10	

How to Use Solve it!

There are ten spreadsheet, ten database, and three World Wide Web cases in each *Solve it!* package. The cases are graduated in difficulty, both in terms of software skills and management skills. The cases are short enough to be answered in one computer session lasting no more than 2-3 hours for a novice.

Each case has an estimated completion time. Students are strongly advised not to skip early problems. If you skip early problems you will not learn the software skills required in later cases. This will, in turn, lengthen the time required to answer later cases by several hours.

A Tutorial Documentation section that carefully describes the software skills needed to solve each case follows the case. The software skills are demonstrated using sample spreadsheets and database files.

You should first read the case to understand the nature of the problem. Then you should study the Tutorial carefully to be sure you understand how the software works. Last, you should begin work on the case itself.

How to Cope With Ambiguity in Cases

Because *Solve it!* cases derive from real world events and circumstances, they often contain ambiguities--just like the real world. In advanced cases you will typically find more than one way to solve a problem, and you will find that certain assumptions and value judgments must be made in order to arrive at any solution.

You should first identify clearly the nature of the ambiguity. Then consider the alternative solutions. Choose the solution you prefer and clearly state the assumptions and value judgments you are making. Be prepared to defend these assumptions, as well as to learn from others who made different assumptions.

System Requirements

Solve it! assumes that you have some knowledge of IBM or IBM compatible computers, including the operating system. *Solve it!* provides specific instructions on how to start up the software in special **Getting Started** sections of Chapters 2 and 4.

Solve it! assumes you are using an IBM or IBM compatible PC computer with at least 32 megabytes of RAM and sufficient hard disk capacity to run the application software. You will also require a printer with graphics capabilities.

General Instructions for Working With Student Data Files

1. Download the Solve it! Student Data Files. Go to http://www.mysolveit.com/student/ and enter the **access code found on the last page of this book**. Follow the directions on the Web site for downloading and storing the files on your hard drive.

   You will have personal access to the student files for a period of 4 months. You can access the Student Data Files from any computer for a period of 4 months from the date of initial issue. Student Data files contain the case data needed for the exercises in this book.

2. Read the appropriate case study in the case book quickly to identify the specific data file used in the case. This will also provide an overview of the basic issues of the case.

3. Start Excel (or Access) and then open the case study data file required by the case.

You are now ready to begin. Chapter 2 introduces you to spreadsheet software in general, and specifically guides you through the basics of Microsoft Excel. This is followed by ten spreadsheet business cases in Chapter 3. Chapter 4 introduces you to database concepts, and Microsoft Access. This is followed by Chapter 5, which contains ten database business cases. Chapter 6 describes the World Wide Web and provides several exercises and cases for you to solve.

2

Introduction to Spreadsheet

Software

An *electronic spreadsheet* is the computerized version of traditional financial modeling tools—the accountant's columnar pad, pencil and calculator. It is organized into a grid of rows and columns. The power of the electronic spreadsheet is that when you change a value or values, all other related values on the spreadsheet will be recomputed automatically.

Spreadsheets are especially well suited to business applications that involve numerous calculations with pieces of data that are interrelated with each other. The power of electronic spreadsheet software is the ease with which modeling and "what if" analysis can be performed: after a set of mathematical relationships has been constructed, the spreadsheet can be recalculated immediately using a different set of assumptions. As models become more complex, this capability for instant "what-if" analysis becomes even more valuable.

The term *spreadsheet* should be distinguished from the term *worksheet*. A spreadsheet is a set of program instructions (such as Excel), whereas a worksheet is a model or representation for a specific application that is created using the spreadsheet software package. (Excel uses the term workbooks. Individual worksheets are considered part of workbooks similar to the pages in a spiral notebook.)

We will now teach you how to use Excel, the leading spreadsheet software package. Each spreadsheet case is followed by tutorials showing you the Excel software skills you will need to solve the case.

Introduction to Microsoft Excel

An Excel spreadsheet is divided into rows and columns, with each row and each column uniquely labeled. A sample spreadsheet is illustrated in Figure 2-1.

Rows are identified numerically, with values ranging from 1 to a maximum of 65536 in the latest version of Excel. Columns are identified alphabetically, with letters ranging from A to Z and then from AA to AZ, BA to BZ and so on to IV. Excel can accommodate a maximum of 256 columns.

Cells

The intersection of every column and row is called a *cell*. Each cell represents a unique location on the spreadsheet for storing a piece of data. Cells are identified by their column and row coordinates. For example, the cell located at the intersection of column B and row 8 is called B8. The maximum number of cells on the spreadsheet is equal to the number of rows times the number of columns. In recent versions of Excel, this amounts to nearly 17,000,000 cells.

Ranges

A rectangular block of cells is termed a *range*. A *range* can be a single cell, a row, a column, or several rows and columns. Many Excel commands are based on ranges. Ranges are identified by naming the cells that bound their diagonally opposite corners, usually those on the upper left and lower right cells. Thus the range occupied by the cells containing NAME, QUIZ, MIDTERM, and FINAL in the following illustration could be identified as either A1:D1 or as D1:A1. Range naming conventions require that you separate the cell addresses that specify the boundaries of the range by a colon or by two periods (e.g., A1:C4 or A1..C4). Ranges may also consist of nonadjacent cells and groups of nonadjacent blocks of cells.

Another way to specify a range is to use a *range name*. Naming ranges can be easier than the other ways of specifying a range if you need to select the same range frequently for different tasks or if the range is very large. For instance, we could name the range D2..D5, which contains the final grades, FINAL. You will learn how to name ranges later on in this book.

When you work with your spreadsheet your cursor will always be positioned on one of its cells. The cell where the cursor is presently located is termed the *current cell*. The cell pointer, a rectangular highlight that appears on the cell, identifies the current cell. You can move the cell pointer from one cell to another by clicking the mouse pointer on the other cell; or you can press the arrow keys on your PC keyboard and other keys defined for movement by your spreadsheet software. Pressing the *<CTRL-Home>* keys together will move the cell pointer to the upper left most corner of the spreadsheet, cell A1.

The Excel Screen

At the top of the Excel screen there is a title bar followed by the main menu bar, one or two toolbars (which contain many useful "shortcut" buttons), and a formula bar (or the edit line, which contains the address and contents of the active cell). At the bottom of the screen is the status bar, which displays error and status messages or indicators.

The title bar of the Excel window is the line that has the program name ("Microsoft Excel"), the active file name, the maximize/minimize window buttons and the file name on it. The main menu bar contains the commands that you use with Excel in the current context. These include commands relating to file handling, editing, formatting, using specialized tools, and using help.

Below the main menu bar are sets of buttons that are shortcuts for many Excel tasks. For example, you can make an entry bold by clicking a button here instead of choosing the **Format-Cells-Font** command and selecting the bold option in the dialog box. These buttons (or icons) can be moved, hidden or customized. When you point to one of the buttons on the toolbars, a ScreenTip appears to explain the function of the button. Familiarize yourself with the Undo and Redo buttons, which undo (or redo) your last action. (For example, if you deleted a range of cells by mistake and you want to undo your action you could click on the Undo button).

The first item in the formula line is the selection indicator, which displays the name or address of the current selection. The last item on the formula bar is the contents box. When you enter data, such as formulas, numbers, labels and functions, Excel displays the data in the contents box.

Figure 2-1 shows an Excel worksheet screen for a course roster with data entered in range A1..D5.

Figure 2-1

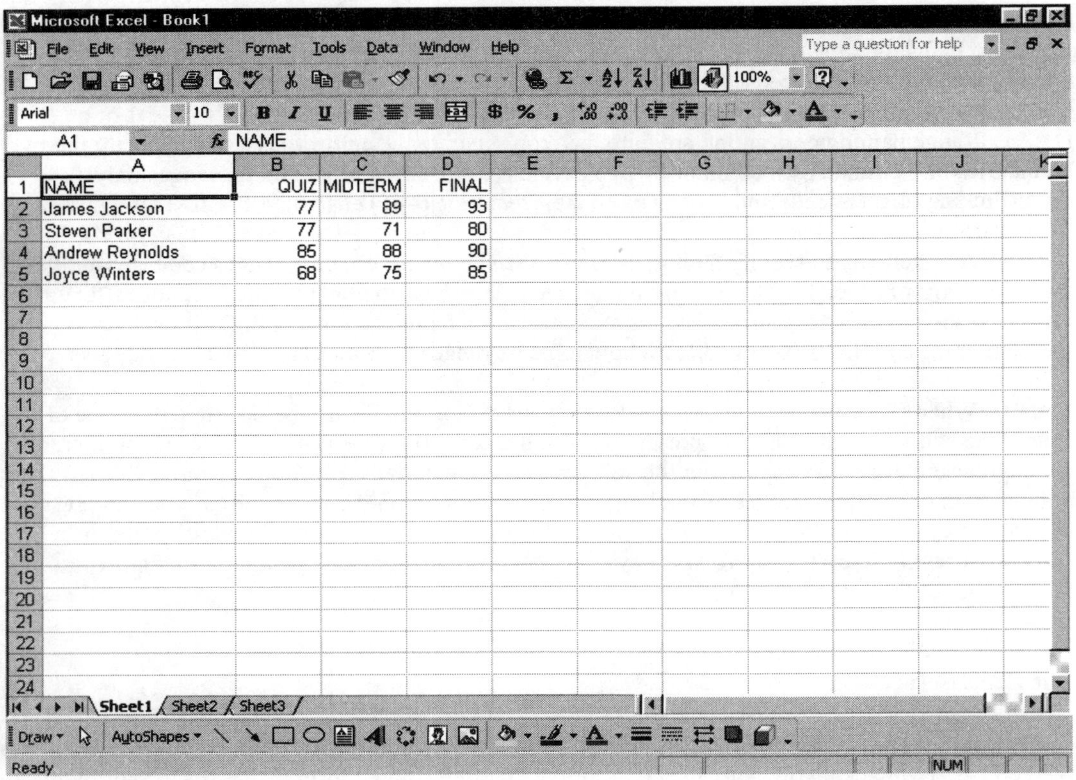

The status bar is located at the very bottom of your Excel window. This gives you information about the current selection and tells you what Excel is doing in addition to allowing you to perform certain simple tasks with the mouse.

Also, just before the status bar is the "sheet-tabs" line where you can see small icons for the different worksheets within the file. An Excel 2000 or Excel 2002 file opens with 3 worksheets, and allows you to include many more worksheets per workbook (the number of worksheets permitted is limited only by your computer's available memory). Multiple worksheets allow you great flexibility when working with large amounts of data.

The status bar displays the status and mode indicators that contain useful information on the current context in which you are operating the spreadsheet. The mode indicator at the lower left portion of your screen indicates the state or condition under which the spreadsheet software is currently operating. Some important mode indicators are READY, indicating Excel is in ready mode, and EDIT, indicating that a cell's contents are being edited.

The status indicator, at the lower right portion of the screen, describes a particular program or key condition. Some important status indicators in Excel are: NUM, indicating the Num Lock is on, SCRL, indicating the Scroll lock is on, and END, indicating that the End key has been pressed and is active.

Moving Around the Spreadsheet

Usually spreadsheets are too large to be viewed on the screen at once. To view other parts of the spreadsheet you must *scroll* the cell pointer up and down the worksheet or across it using the mouse, the arrow keys and other cursor movement keys. When the cell pointer reaches the edge of the current screen, the screen will shift to follow the cell pointer in the direction it is moving.

Clicking the mouse pointer on any cell makes that the current active cell. At the right and at the bottom of the Excel worksheet window are the vertical scroll bar and the horizontal scroll bar. Clicking on the arrow buttons on these scroll bars moves your window one line up/down or one tab right/left. You can also click on any point inside these scroll bars to scroll faster. For instance, clicking in the middle of the vertical bar (and holding the mouse button down) will move you to the middle of your file.

You can also use the keyboard to navigate around the spreadsheet. When Excel is in READY mode, various keys will behave as follows:

Excel Keyboard Pointer-Movement Keys

Key	Function
LEFT ARROW	Moves left 1 cell
RIGHT ARROW	Moves right 1 cell
UP ARROW	Moves up 1 cell
DOWN ARROW	Moves down 1 cell
SHIFT-TAB	Moves left 1 cell
TAB	Moves right 1 cell
PAGE UP	Moves up 1 screen
PAGE DOWN	Moves down 1 screen
CTRL-HOME	Moves to upper left corner
END HOME	Moves to lower right corner of the active area

Using the Mouse

You can use the mouse, like the keyboard, to choose commands, highlight ranges, resize windows and perform many other tasks. There are some actions that you can do only with a mouse such as using the "shortcut buttons" on the toolbars. Whenever a selection is to be made with the mouse, use the left mouse button (unless you specified left-handed use of the mouse in the Windows Control Panel).

Spreadsheet Commands

Commands are tools provided by spreadsheet software to manipulate the spreadsheet in various ways. For example, there are commands for copying data, formatting your worksheet, or printing your worksheet. Some commands affect the entire worksheet, but others only affect certain cells or groups of cells.

Commands appear on the menus that you access from the main menu bar, directly below the title bar. You choose commands from the menu to perform actions in Excel. The commands in the main menu change depending on your current selection. When you open a worksheet the initial commands that appear in the main menu are:

File Edit View Insert Format Tools Data Window Help

When you choose a command in the main menu a pull-down menu appears listing additional commands you can choose. For example, if you choose "File" from the menu, you see the File pull-down menu from which you can choose "New" to open a new file.

You can choose a command from the menu by clicking with the mouse on the command or by using the arrow keys to select the command and pressing Enter. You can also hit ALT-F to bring up the File pull-down menu. Every command in the menu has a character that is underlined. For example the Format command has "o" underlined. Pressing ALT-O would open the Format pull-down menu.

When you choose a command not followed by an "..." (ellipsis) or an arrowhead, Excel performs that command immediately. For example, if you choose "New" under the File pull-down menu, Excel opens a new worksheet. However, when you choose "Save As..." under the File pull-down menu , the command is not performed immediately since you need to specify the new file name in the dialog box that comes up. A command followed by an ellipsis generally leads to a dialog box.

Pressing ESC at any time you are working with menu commands will return you to the previous command. Pressing ESC as often as necessary will return you to whatever point you wish in the command menus and even bring you out of MENU mode altogether.

Setting Up a Worksheet

Consult with your technical support specialist about how to install and configure Excel for your particular computer system and whether you are allowed to make a backup copy of the program.

To illustrate how spreadsheet software works, we will be developing a simple spreadsheet with which you are very familiar. Let us start by creating a course roster with information on student names and grades for a quiz, midterm, and final exam. The final product will look like Figure 2-1.

Assuming Excel has been properly installed, you can start using it by guiding the mouse pointer over the Start button, clicking on Start, and moving the pointer up the Start menu to Programs. Highlight Programs and then highlight Microsoft Excel on the Programs menu. Click once to open the application. (If Excel is not on the Programs menu, try looking under Microsoft Office.) Excel will open up with a blank worksheet. You can now start entering data into your worksheet.

How to Enter Data into a Worksheet

The student roster illustrated in Figure 2-1 is a very simple list. You need only enter data about the student's names and grades. No calculations are required. You can start at cell A1 and enter your column headings. Enter NAME in cell A1, QUIZ in B1, MIDTERM in C1, and FINAL in D1.

You enter data into a cell by moving the cell pointer to the cell, typing the entry, and pressing ENTER. The entry appears in the cell as you type.

Each character you type appears in the contents box of the edit line (below the main menu). The insertion point indicates where the next character you type will appear. In addition to pressing ENTER, you can complete a cell entry by clicking on another cell or by pressing one of the pointer-movement keys. This will complete the entry and move the cell pointer to another cell as directed by the mouse or the pointer movement key. If you click the Enter button on the formula bar, the cell entry will be confirmed but the cell pointer will remain in the current cell.

You can complete your roster by entering the student names in cells A2 through A5, the quiz grades in cells B2 through B5, the midterm grades in cells C2 through C5, and the final grades in cells D2 through D5.

How to Change Column Widths

You will notice that after you enter the quiz grades in Column B, the student names in Column A become truncated. This occurs because the column widths are at the default width of 8.43 characters, and the names on our list are longer. Since the cells in Column B contain the quiz grades, Excel cuts off the entries in Column A at the right edge of the cells. (However, if the cells to the right of Column A were empty, the entries in Column A would extend into the blank cells in Column B.)

Sometimes pound signs (########) will appear in a cell containing a numeric value. This happens when the column width is too narrow to accommodate the number of places in the numeric value plus additional punctuation for decimal points, commas, dollar signs, and so forth.

You can make column widths smaller or larger by using the **Format - Column** and then **Width** command. Let us reset the column for student names in our example to 20 positions.

First, select the range for which we would like to adjust the column width. You can select a range by first clicking at the center of the cell, and then holding the mouse button down while dragging the mouse pointer to the opposite corner of the range. To select more than one range at a time keep the Control key pressed while selecting the next range. In our example we need to select an entire column, which can be done in an easier manner. Every column in the worksheet has column headings just above the first row of the worksheet (the column headings range from A to IV. Clicking on a column heading marks (selects) the entire column. Click on Column A and you will find the whole column highlighted.

Then choose **Format** in the main menu by clicking on it and the Format pull-down menu will appear. Point to **Column** and a sub menu will appear. You have five choices here. You could adjust the column width for the selected range to a certain number of characters. To do this, click Width and then enter the desired width in the **Width** box. You could also select the **Auto Fit Selection** option to adjust the column width so that the widest entry in the column fits exactly. You could hide or unhide the column. You could also change the default width of all the columns in the worksheet. In our example set the width of Column A to 20 characters and click on OK.

Values and Labels

Excel has two types of cell entries: *values* and *labels*. Values are numbers, functions or formulae. Labels are used for text entries within your spreadsheet. Labels can't be used in calculations.

As long as there is a letter in the cell Excel will consider the entry as a label, even if the entry begins with a numerical character. The entry will always be treated as a value if the beginning character is one of the following:

= + - $

Position the cell pointer on the student name Steven Parker. Then position it on the column heading NAME. You will notice that the contents box in the edit line displays Steven Parker or NAME. Any cell containing a letter is considered a label. The entries could be aligned left, right or center, but labels are left-aligned by default.

Aligning Labels

You can right-align the labels above the grades by selecting them and clicking the align right button or center them by clicking the center button. Alternatively, you can use the **Format - Cells** command to align a selected range of labels. In the dialog box that appears you can specify the alignment and the range.

Numbers in Excel

In Excel a number can contain a maximum of 240 characters, cannot contain spaces and is limited to only one decimal point. (You can change the cell formats for displaying a number, which will be discussed later.) A number can be entered in scientific notation, or can end with %

to indicate percentage. When a number ends with a percent sign, Excel will divide the number that precedes the sign by 100.

Let us review the student roster you've entered. At this point, the labels will all be right-aligned except for NAME and the numbers will be right-aligned as well. The width of column A will be 20 characters and that of the rest of the columns will remain at the default value of 8.43 characters. The worksheet will look like Figure 2-1.

How to Edit Data

You can edit a cell entry in either of two ways:

1. You can enter data into a cell that already contains information using the same procedure for entering data into an empty cell. This will cause the new data to replace the earlier entry.

2. You can also use the F2 (Edit) key to edit data in a cell. Position the cell pointer on the cell you wish to edit and press the F2 key. This will switch Excel into EDIT mode. The easier way to switch into the EDIT mode is to click the mouse button inside the Contents Box on the edit line (where the contents of an active cell appear). You may also double-click a cell to edit its contents.

Erasing Worksheet Data

To delete data, use the **Edit-Clear-Contents** command. You may also right-click a cell and then select Clear Contents from the shortcut menu.

If you want to delete an entire range of cells you would first have to mark (or select) the range that you want to delete. If the range you want to delete is A1..B2 (4 cells), click inside A1, hold the mouse button down and drag the mouse pointer to B2. This procedure highlights the range selected. Once the range is selected you can press the Delete key or use the Clear command.

Moving Data

It is a good idea to document each worksheet you create. Figure 2-2 illustrates how the worksheet we just created could be documented. Cell A1 explains the purpose of the worksheet. Cell A2 provides the name and location of the worksheet file. Cell A3 identifies the author of the worksheet and the date it was created.

Figure 2-2

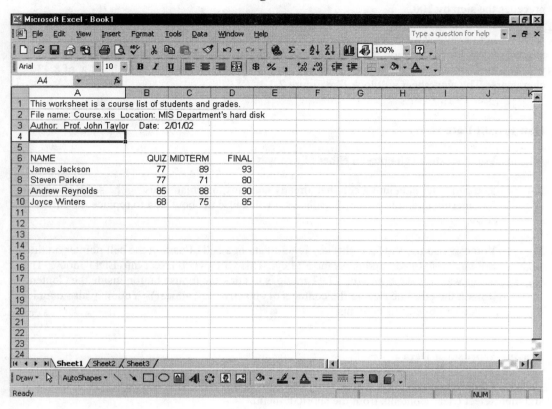

We need to make room for this documentation at the top of the worksheet by moving the worksheet down five rows. To do this, first highlight the range A1..D5 using the mouse. Choose **Edit-Cut** from the main menu. This will send the data in the selected range to the Clipboard so that it can be pasted elsewhere using the Paste command. Then click in cell A6 (which is where you want the upper-left corner of your selected range to be) and choose **Edit-Paste**.

You could equivalently use the shortcut buttons to make the task simpler. After highlighting the range A1..D5 click on the "Cut" button. Then click inside the cell A6 and click on the "Paste" button.

Another method of inserting rows is to use the main menu. First highlight the number of rows you would like to insert and then from the menu bar choose **Insert - Rows**. For instance, if you want to insert three rows at the beginning of your worksheet you could select the first three rows using the mouse and choose **Insert -Rows**. Similarly if columns needed to be inserted, the same procedure could be repeated using the **Columns** command from the **Insert** menu.

Once you have moved the worksheet down, you can enter the documentation in cells A1..A3 so that your worksheet looks like Figure 2-2. Note that the contents of these cells seem to extend into the blank cells in Columns B through F because the cells to the right of A1..A3 are empty.

How to Save Files

You will learn more about formatting and organizing the worksheet in the case problems. Let's save the practice worksheet for future use. To save a file, you must use the **File-Save** command. This command will make an exact copy of your worksheet on disk, including any special formats and settings you have specified.

First, click on **File** on the main menu bar. On the pull-down menu that appears, click on **Save**. If this is the first time that you are working on this file and saving it, Excel will provide a default filename (book1.xls) in the **File name** box. You can click inside this box, delete the default name and type in a name (such as "Course") that you choose for the worksheet. The "Save in" box indicates the drive and folder in which Excel will store the file. (The drive and folder are established during configuration but they can be changed.) You can change the folder in which you want to save the file by clicking the "Save in" list arrow.

Enter the name you have assigned to your worksheet file in the **File name** box and click on **Save**. Let's call the worksheet Course. Windows supports file names of up to 255 characters. The file name can contain uppercase or lowercase letters, numbers, and most symbols. When you save a file, Excel will automatically assign a three character extension, depending on the type of file. (Recent versions of Excel use the extension .xls for an Excel workbook.) You could choose to save the file in other formats (including Web page format) using the **File - Save As - Save as type** commands.

Be sure to save Course.xls after you use it for a tutorial. You can save it under the same name after each tutorial session. Most of the changes you make to your worksheet during a tutorial will be required by subsequent sessions. Follow tutorial instructions to determine what changes to your worksheet must be saved or erased.

Ending Your Excel Session

To exit Excel, choose **FILE-EXIT** from the main menu bar. It is a good practice to save all your files and close them before quitting. If you have not saved a file, Excel brings up a dialog box that asks you whether you want to save the file before the program closes. Click on **YES** to save the file or on **NO** to lose the changes and exit. Clicking on **CANCEL** takes you back into Excel in the READY mode.

Spreadsheet Design Principles

Like any helpful tool, Excel worksheets can be abused and misused, especially if worksheets are carelessly built, poorly documented, and based on false assumptions. These problems can be minimized by following a few basic principles of spreadsheet design that have emerged over the last decade.

A vertical five-section structure can produce more accurate and more easily understood spreadsheets. The five sections are: documentation, assumptions, input, calculations, and macros. These sections are illustrated in Figure 2-3.

The first section contains *documentation*--a complete description of the name, author, and purpose of the worksheet. In general, you should try to keep the description simple, and to the point. The first line of documentation section shows the purpose of the worksheet: to display three-year sales projections for Form Factor Fitness Centers.

The second line of the documentation section shows the worksheet file name and identifies where the worksheet is located in the firm's computer systems. Generally, spreadsheets will either be stored on a network or the hard disk of a specific machine.

The third line of documentation identifies the author of the worksheet and the date the worksheet was created.

The fourth line of the documentation shows where any table of range (block) names and any strings of commands called "macros" are located. A macro is a set of instructions for automating spreadsheet tasks. The documentation shows that the upper left corner of the macro area for this worksheet starts in cell A28.

The second section in a spreadsheet is reserved for *assumptions*. Assumptions are variable factors that may change in a worksheet. It is important the basic assumptions used to create the output are clearly identified. In Figure 2-3, we are assuming an annual sales growth figure of 10%. This could of course change and assumptions are frequently changed in spreadsheets to test various "what-if" conditions. For instance, the results of this worksheet will be different if we change the assumption for annual sales growth to 5% or to 15%. By isolating the assumptions in a specific section, it is very easy to change the spreadsheet as conditions change.

Figure 2-3

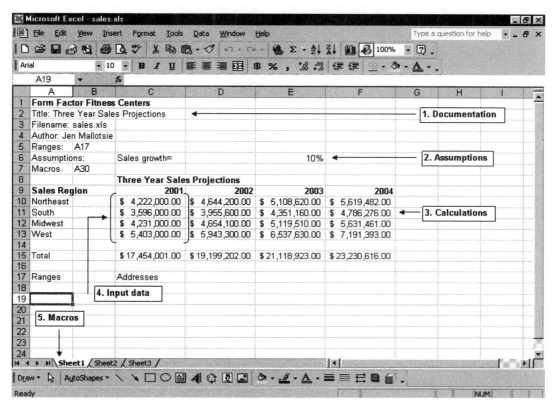

The third section is the *input* section. The input data are the raw data that must be supplied to the worksheet so that they can be manipulated to produce the required results. In the spreadsheet illustrated here, the data consist of the names of the sales regions and actual sales figures for 2001.

The fourth section is the *calculations* section. The calculations section presents the final output of the spreadsheet, the result of calculations performed on the raw input data. The calculations are the projected sales for 2002-2004 and the total sales for each year. Calculations are usually placed to the right of or below the input data.

The fifth section is the *macro* section. The macro section is the area of the worksheet for storing macros and their documentation. Macros should be located below and to the left of the current worksheet in a portion of the worksheet that will not be affected by changes made to the rest to the worksheet. Usually Macros are placed on the left margin of the spreadsheet. That way, macros are unlikely to be affected by having data copied or moved or by having columns inserted or deleted. The macros in the worksheet illustrated here print and save the worksheet automatically.

The Student Data File worksheets are designed to encourage you to use these spreadsheet design principles. The first four lines of each worksheet file are reserved for documentation. The *Solve it!* worksheet files provide much of the data for the input section of the worksheet. You will then complete the input and calculation sections of the worksheet to develop the solution for the spreadsheet case. If required by the problem, you can add an assumptions section by inserting rows above the input section or by moving the input section down several rows. Spreadsheet Case 10 will teach you how to add macros to your worksheet.

3

Spreadsheet Management Software Cases

Spreadsheet Case 1

The Office House, Inc.

Problem:	Develop a sales prospect tracking system
Management skills:	Organization Controlling
PC skills:	Data input Worksheet formatting Printing

File: OFFICE_Q.XLS   [For download instructions see last page of book]

Lyle Howard is a sales representative with The Office House, Inc., an office supply firm located in San Francisco, CA. His boss has instructed him to increase sales by ten percent by attracting new customers. Lyle locates the names of small business by using telephone directories, mailing lists, and the Internet. He makes a list of these sales prospects, noting the company name, telephone number, and the owner's name, if available. Then he starts telephoning them to describe The Office House's product offerings.

If Lyle's prospects are interested but not ready to purchase, he makes a follow-up call two weeks later. Sometimes, Lyle forgets whether he has called a prospect and calls that person again, or he forgets to make a follow-up call. Therefore, Lyle needs a way to keep track of prospects and phone calls that he can easily refer to and update.

From your diskette load the worksheet file OFFICE_Q.XLS. This worksheet contains a list of some of Lyle's sales prospects and their telephone numbers. Use your spreadsheet software to create a prospect tracking system that Lyle can refer to on screen or print out.

The worksheet should list each prospect's name, telephone number, and date of last telephone call. The worksheet also should include a column for Follow Up in which Lyle can enter a Yes or No to indicate whether a follow-up call is required. In order to locate names more easily, organize the prospect list in alphabetical order by last name.

The look and shape of spreadsheets are extremely important if you want to use the information they contain effectively. Professional-looking spreadsheets are formatted in special ways so that you can locate and digest their information quickly. The format should allow for easy changes and updating. This problem shows you how to develop professional looking, maintainable spreadsheets.

Tasks

There are 6 tasks to this problem:

1.   Create appropriate column headings to capture the required information. There should be column headings for Last Name, First Name, Telephone, Company, Date Called, and Follow Up. The column headings for Last Name, First Name, and Telephone already appear on the worksheet and can be used as models.

2.   Create appropriate widths for each column and decide whether to left justify, right justify or center the column labels. Some of the worksheet columns have already been widened for you.

3.   Complete the schedule by entering the required information suggested above. The following table will be helpful:

Last Name	Company	Date Called
Anderson	Western Supply, Inc.	6/28/02
Evans	A & L Hardware	7/11/02
Flaherty	Belltown Transport	7/16/02
Kim	Arts & Crafts Shop	7/1/02
Sternberg	Industrial Leasing	6/27/02
Suzuki	Talent Services, Inc.	7/9/02

4.   Be sure to enter the dates as labels, not as data. Lyle needs to make follow-up calls to Carla Anderson and Kathleen Flaherty.

5.   Charles has just found two more prospects. They are Sally Lundgren and Donald Bartholdi, both of whom need follow-up calls. Lundgren heads Lundgren Drugs & Cards and was first contacted on 7/22/02. Her phone number is 415-555-5504. Bartholdi works for Zynn Transportation and was first contacted on 7/3/02. His phone number is 415-555-4922. Add information about these prospects to the prospect list by inserting new rows at the appropriate places in the worksheet to make sure last names remain in alphabetical order.

6.   Improve the appearance of the log by underlining column labels. Print a report of the log. You should be able to print this worksheet on one 8-1/2 x 11-inch page.

Time Estimates

Expert: 30 minutes
Intermediate: 45 minutes
Novice: 1.5 hours

Excel Tutorial for Spreadsheet Case 1

This case draws upon the data entry skills you have already acquired in developing Course.xls and upon new skills for formatting and printing spreadsheets. You will need to use Course.xls again for this tutorial.

How to Retrieve a Data File

Begin by opening Excel again. When the spreadsheet screen appears, your first step will be to load the data file Course.xls. Do this either by clicking the Open button on the Standard toolbar or by accessing the Open command under the pull-down File menu. The Open dialog box will appear.

The settings within the dialog box may need to be amended in order to load the file. The four items that have to be set are the File Name, the File Type, the Folder, and the Disk Drive. A list of files of the type specified for the Disk Drive and Folder appears in the File List window. To change the settings to retrieve Course.xls, first ensure **Microsoft Excel Files** or **All Files** appears as the File Type. If it does not immediately, it can be changed by clicking the downward pointing arrow next to the File Type list box, revealing a list of File Types Excel can open. To move up and down the list, click the arrows on the scroll bars next to the list. Select the required File Type with the mouse pointer.

Use the **Look in** list arrow to select the Folder and Disk Drive where Course.xls is stored and display it in the File Name list. The files are listed alphabetically so if the desired file is not visible, you can move down the list using the scroll bar. Double-click the Course.xls file to open it. Alternatively, you can simply type Course.xls (or just Course) in the File Name box. Typing the three letter extension to specify your file is optional. When the settings are correct, click the OPEN button or press the ENTER key.

How to Insert or Delete Columns and Rows

Suppose you wanted to add lines under the column headings in your student roster. You can insert columns and rows in a worksheet in either of two ways in Excel: (a) through the menu command **Insert/Rows** and (b) using the shortcut menu displayed by clicking the right mouse button, and selecting **Insert,** which presents four options:

Shift Cells Right
Shift Cells Down
Entire Row
Entire Column

Selecting **Entire Row** from the options presented and clicking OK inserts a blank row.

A third method is to select an entire row and then select **Insert** from the shortcut menu, or by selecting **Insert/Cells** or **Insert/Rows** from the menu. To select an entire row, move the mouse pointer over the row number at the left of the worksheet and press the left mouse button. To select multiple rows, keep the left button depressed and drag up or down.

Now you will insert the blank line in your student roster. To do so, move the worksheet current cell to the row below the column headings—that is, move to row 7; it doesn't matter to which column. Now select **Insert/Rows** from the menu and you will notice a blank row is inserted in row 7 and the data previously in rows 7 through 10 will be moved to rows 8 through 11. Your worksheet screen now looks like Figure 3-1. The Insert Options button ⌫ that appears in Excel 2002 may be used to select formatting options for the new row. You may ignore the button.

You can delete one or multiple rows and columns using the same principles used in inserting rows and columns. There are two ways of accessing the **Delete** command in Excel: (a) through the pull-down menus, located at **Edit/Delete** and (b) through the shortcut menu activated by the right-hand mouse button. If entire rows or columns are selected when these commands are selected, the effects will be immediate: the row(s) or column(s) will disappear at once.

To make the worksheet documentation section conform to the spreadsheet design principles introduced in Chapter 2, let's add a fourth line to the documentation section. In cell A4 enter "Ranges: none Macros: none". (We will add macros and range names in later tutorials.) Then insert a row so that there are two rows between the documentation section and the course list itself.

Moving and Copying the Contents of Cells

After using the **Insert/Rows** command again, you will have a blank Row 8. You can now add separator lines in this row to further set off the column headings from the data on the list.

This is a convenient time to explain some extremely commonly used and useful operations: Moving and Copying. A Move is referred to as a Cut in Excel and is simply relocating the contents of one or more cells. A Copy reproduces the contents of the cells. Both Cuts and Copies have to be accompanied by a Paste operation. The Cut or Copy designates *from where* the cells are cut or copied while the Paste designates *to where* they are being placed.

Figure 3-1

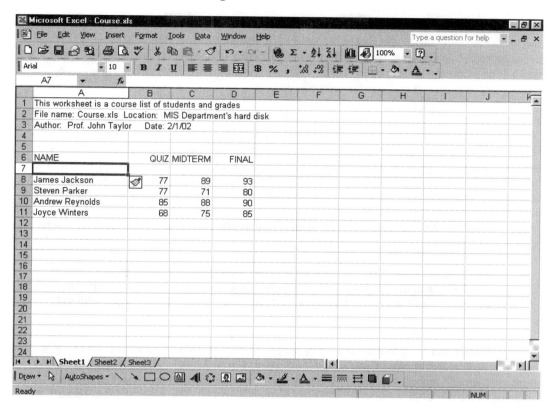

As with most operations in Excel, there are several ways to cut and copy:

1. Using the **Cut, Copy** and **Paste** functions from the **Edit** menu
2. Using the **Cut, Copy** and **Paste** functions from the **Shortcut** menu
3. Using the buttons on the Toolbar for **Cut** ✂, **Copy** 📋 and **Paste** 📋
4. Using the keystrokes for **Cut** (Ctrl-X), **Copy** (Ctrl-C) and **Paste** (Ctrl-V)
5. Using the mouse pointer to drag and copy

Each of these is worth exploring at least once, and you can decide which you find the most convenient. Generally speaking, most users use two of the methods listed. For example, some users cut and copy within a small area in a spreadsheet using the mouse to drag and copy, and cut and copy between larger areas and between spreadsheets using one of the other techniques. Once you become familiar with each method, you will see they are very similar, and they all require you to specify a source range of cells, an operation (cut or copy), a destination or target range, and the paste function.

It is worth explaining the mouse method of cutting and copying since it is extremely useful. This method applies to a single cell or a multiple selection. When you move your mouse pointer to the border of a selection on the worksheet, it transforms from a white cross to an arrow. This is the signal that you can now perform the drag or copy.

To drag (or cut) the contents of the selection, depress the left mouse button and move the mouse, keeping the button down. As you move the mouse across the worksheet, a shadow of the selection will also be moved until the mouse button is released to designate the destination of the drag. This operation may require some practice but will become second nature very quickly and an important editing function.

To perform the mouse copy, the actions are nearly identical to the drag (cut). The mouse pointer is moved to the border of the selection and the cross will turn into an arrow. At this time, press the Control key and keep it down. A small tell-tale cross will appear next to the arrow, indicating that we are performing a copy rather than a move. Now drag the selection as we did for the move; when the mouse button is released, you will see the copy operation has worked.

After practice you will realize that each of the different cut and copy methods results in identical results.

Returning to Course.xls, we now want to insert some decorative separators in the cells in Row 8 to distinguish the headings from the body of the table. To do this, we will enter "=" (without the quotes) and select the **Alignment Fill** command to fill the cell width with this symbol.

First, press "=" and click the Enter button ☑ on the Formula bar to enter "=" in cell A8. Now select **Format/Cells** for the Formatting box to appear. This box has six formatting tabs: Number, Alignment, Font, Border, Patterns, Protection. Select **Alignment** by clicking on the tab label at the top of the box. In the Horizontal Alignment section, select Fill and then click the OK Button or press ENTER. The cell will be filled with the "=" symbol.

Once you have set up the first cell, you can replicate it in all the cells in Row 8 below column heads. Do this by using the **Edit/Copy** command. First, select the **Copy** command from the **Edit** menu. Notice the moving border around cell A8, indicating a copy or cut source. Next, select cells B8, C8 and D8, referred to as range B8:D8. Do this by moving the mouse pointer to cell B8, depressing the left mouse button, and dragging to the right until the desired range is selected. Now select the **Paste** command from the **Edit** menu. This will copy the formatting and contents of cell A8 to the range selected. Your worksheet should look similar to Figure 3-2. In Excel 2002, the Paste Options button permits you to set formatting options for the data you have just pasted. Since you do not need to consider additional formatting, you may disregard the button.

Printing Your Worksheet

For printing a simple worksheet such as your student roster, which is one page or less, you need only know the basic printing commands. Select the **Print** command under the **File** menu to display the Print dialog box. The various options in this dialog box can be explored later. However, for our purposes, simply accept the default settings and click the OK Button.

Figure 3-2

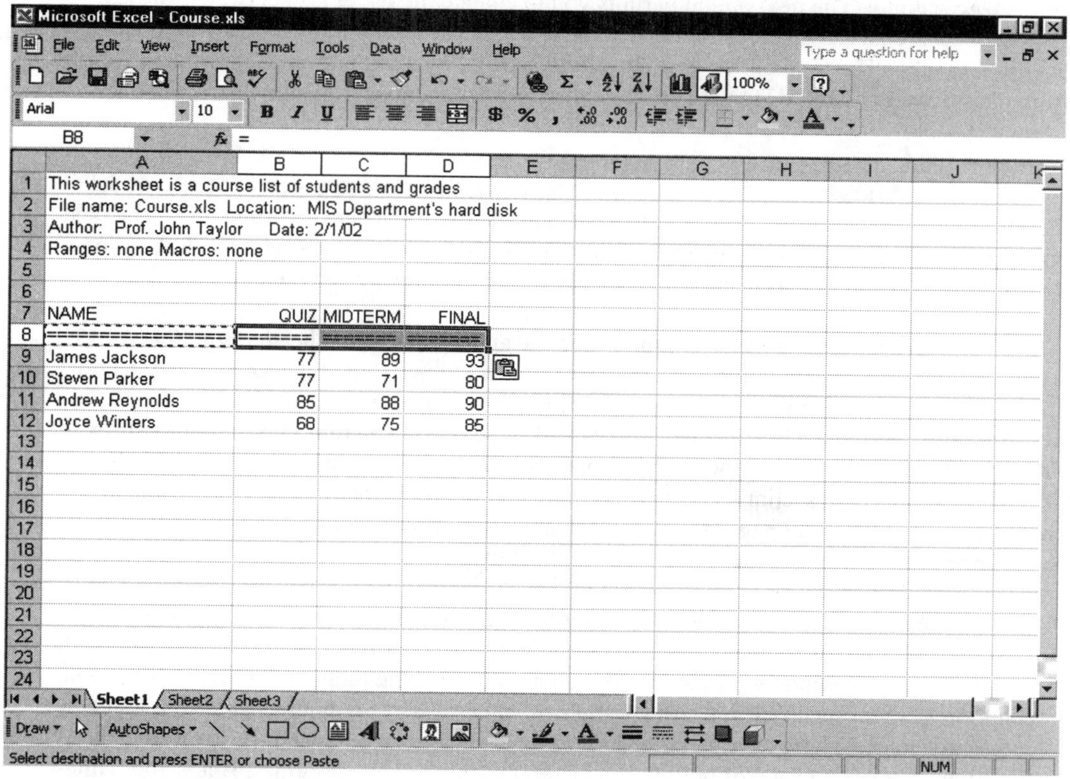

In this case, Excel will just print the page containing the student roster. Features can be adjusted, including paper size, page orientation, scaling, margin sizes, alignment, and header and footer contents and options, print titles, page print sequence, and print area. You find these features in the Page Setup dialog box under the **Page Setup** command on the **File** menu (see below). Before printing, the appearance of your page can be observed under **Print Preview** under the **File** menu so paper need not be wasted.

As Excel is printing your page, a small message box appears stating which page is currently being printed. This box contains a Cancel button, which you can choose if you want to stop the printing.

Changing Excel's Printer Options

The printing options in Excel can be changed under **File/Page Setup**. Four formatting tabs will appear in the Page Setup dialog box: Page, Margins, Header/Footer, Sheet.

Under **Page** you can decide on features pertaining to individual pages being printed. The first option is Orientation—that is, to decide whether the page should be printed in landscape (horizontal wide, vertical narrow) or portrait (horizontal narrow, vertical wide) mode. The second option permits you to scale the size of the print up or down a specific percentage, or scale to fit a certain number of pages where the computer determines the percentage scaling. The next option permits you to change the paper size between various standard sizes (e.g., Letter, Legal, Executive, A4, etc.). The next option allows you to change the print quality. The final option permits you to specify the starting page of printing. To print from the start, enter 1 or AUTO; otherwise enter the page number from which you wish to begin.

Under **Margins** you can change the margins that border the pages. The size of the margins on each page edge can be specified in particular units (inches, centimeters). The next option is the distance between the edge of the page and the header or footer. The last options are whether to center the print subject horizontally and/or vertically on the page.

Under **Header/Footer** you can change the appearance of the headers and footers of the printed pages. The operation and options of headers (appearing at the top of every page) and footers (appearing at the top of every page) are the same. Each includes a number of default sample headers, a list to which you can add. Selecting **Custom Header** or **Custom Footer** permits you to change the header/footer. Each is split into thirds: left, center and right. In each or any of these sections you can enter any text or enter any of the options offered: current page number, total pages in print, Current Date, Current Time, and Sheet Name. You can change the fonts of any text using an available button.

Under **Sheet** you can change the print features pertaining to the worksheet. First, you can specify precisely the range on the worksheet you want to print. This is done by placing the mouse pointer in the window provided and then highlighting the range on the worksheet. The next option lets you specify Print Titles, which are either rows or columns that are to appear on every printed page. These are useful for lists or tables that extend beyond the confines of a single page. The Next group of options are general purpose ones: Gridlines, Black and white, Draft quality, and Row and column headings, Comments, and Cell errors. The final option is the Page Order—that is, whether to print down and across or across and down.

Save Course.xls with the changes you made during this tutorial session. You will need it for the next Spreadsheet Case.

Spreadsheet Case 2

The Confidential Executive Payroll

Problem: Develop a payroll register

Management skills: Organization

PC skills: Formulas
                                                    Absolute and relative addressing

File: SUTER_Q.XLS

Suter Brothers, Inc. is a leading producer of machine tools with 10,000 employees and an operating budget of $950,000,000. All employees except the ten members of the corporation's executive steering committee are on the firm's automated payroll system. The executive steering committee consists of the ten top managers of the firm, including the CEO. It has a separate confidential payroll, which is processed manually because it contains highly sensitive information such as senior management salaries and bonuses. The executive committee, like other salaried employees, is paid monthly.

Hayley Darsch, executive secretary to the CEO, is in charge of preparing the confidential executive payroll. She must make all of the calculations for salary changes, deductions, and net pay using a hand-held calculator. Then she types the results onto a Payroll Register sheet. A Payroll Register is a report prepared for each payroll period that lists the names, gross pay, deductions, and net pay of all employees and the total gross pay, deductions, and net pay for that payroll period. Hayley writes out the checks by hand.

This is a very time-consuming process, which prevents Hayley from fulfilling other responsibilities. Her boss, the CEO, would like to use her time more productively for scheduling meetings and filtering correspondence. Also, there is a danger of miscalculations, which would invoke the wrath of senior managers. Hayley and the CEO would like to automate the process as much as possible while maintaining strict confidentiality.

Hayley feels there are so few checks to write that this part of the process could remain manual. However, many hours could be saved if all of the payroll calculations and the preparation of the Payroll Register report could be automated.

From your data diskette load SUTER_Q.XLS, which shows the names of the executive steering committee members, social security numbers, and annual salaries. You should develop a worksheet that creates a Payroll Register report for the executive steering committee. The worksheet should automatically calculate monthly gross pay, net pay, and all deductions. It should also provide totals for each of these categories for the pay period.

Monthly gross pay can be computed by dividing annual salary by 12. Federal withholding tax should be set to 25% of gross pay. State withholding tax should be set to 7% of gross pay. For the tax year 2002, FICA (the employee Social Security deduction) is 6.2% of the first $84,900 earned during the year. The Medicare deduction is 1.45% of gross pay for all wages earned during the tax year. Since this is the first pay period of 2002, FICA and Medicare deductions must be taken for all members of the executive committee for this payroll. Group health insurance is $100 per month. All executive steering committee members have elected a stock option plan, which deducts 5% of gross pay each month to purchase shares of the corporation's stock at a discount.

Tasks

There are 5 tasks to this problem:

1. Complete the column labels to include gross pay, all deductions and net pay.

2. Make all appropriate format changes for numbers and percentages. Columns containing numbers should be formatted to show two decimal places to the right of the decimal point.

3. Create an assumptions section for all deductions and other variables in the upper-left corner of the worksheet and label it "Assumptions." This way, you easily can make changes in deductions and formulas using the addressing function of spreadsheet software. By keeping all assumptions in a clearly defined assumptions section, you can make changes rapidly in the worksheet to respond to changing tax laws or other regulations. Listing variables also allows all assumptions to be visible and clearly reported.

4. Use formulas to calculate monthly gross pay, all deductions, and net pay. Be sure these formulas reference the appropriate cells in the assumptions section of your worksheet (e.g., A56) rather than actual values (e.g., 20%). Provide totals for gross pay, net pay, and each deduction category so that Hayley can track the company's expenses for the pay period. Widen columns if necessary.

5. Print the spreadsheet. This sheet should fit on a single page. If not, try changing the page orientation to landscape and fitting the worksheet to 1 page by 1 page (Page Setup).

Additional Problems

1. The company has decided to implement a before-tax savings plan. Employees can deduct 5% of their gross pay before taxes to put into this savings plan. Modify the Payroll Register Worksheet to implement this plan.

2. The company feels it should be withholding 33% of gross pay for federal tax. Modify your worksheet to change the federal withholding tax deduction and print it out again.

Time Estimates

Expert: 30 minutes
Intermediate: 1 hour
Novice: 1.5 hours

Excel Tutorial for Spreadsheet Case 2

This case draws upon all of the skills acquired in Spreadsheet Case 1 plus new skills for using formulas, formatting and absolute and relative addressing. You will need to use Course.xls again for this tutorial.

Suppose you want to expand your worksheet by including each student's final grade. You will need to add an extra column and label for FINAL GRADE and you will need to calculate the final grade for each student. The final exam counts for 50% of the final grade; the midterm for 35% and the quiz for 15%.

Formulas

To compute the final grade you would need to use a formula: A formula tells Excel what manipulations to perform on specific cell contents. The cells are specified using their cell references (e.g. A11, C3). Mathematical operators specify arithmetic operations. They are:

^	Exponentiation
*, /	Multiplication, Division
+,-	Addition, Subtraction
%	Percent (i.e. 75% represents 0.75)

Operations are always performed left to right within a formula in their order of precedence. The order of precedence in Excel corresponds to the order of the above list. Exponentiation will always be performed first, followed by multiplication and division, then addition and subtraction. Percent amounts are evaluated when they are encountered.

Parentheses can be used to override the order of precedence. Operations inside parentheses will be performed before those outside the parentheses. The order of operations remains the same within the parentheses, however. When multiple sets of parentheses are employed, the operations within the innermost set of parentheses will be performed before those within the next set.

Thus, the formula for James Jackson's final grade would be:

=B9*.15+C9*.35+D9*.50

or alternatively

=B9*15%+C9*35%+D9*50%

Enter this formula in cell E9. This cell will display Jackson's final grade. Note that the first cell in the formula is preceded by a = sign. In order to be treated as a formula, rather than a label, a formula must begin with an equals (=) symbol.

Thus a formula to add the contents of cells A6 and B6 must be expressed as =A6+B6. If you try to type this formula as A6+B6, it will be treated as a label.

Formula Errors

If you try to enter a formula with a logical or mathematical error, Excel will show a message box stating what error has occurred. To proceed you must click the OK Button. If you want further information on the error you can select the Help Button, which will provide a broader explanation of the error. You need only correct the problem to continue.

Another common problem is the circular reference, which is a formula that directly or indirectly refers back to the same cell it resides in. For example, if you tried to enter in cell B12 the formula =A12+B12, an error box will appear stating a circular reference has occurred. This is because cell B12 is an operand in the operation, as well as the cell that holds the result of the calculation.

Absolute and Relative Addressing

Suppose that we want to make our worksheet more flexible for future changes. The professor may decide that the quiz should only contribute 10% toward the final grade and the midterm 40%. In that case, the formula for the final grade would have to be adjusted to change the percentage weight applied to the midterm and quiz.

You could, of course, re-enter the new formulas. But an easier way to keep track of the percentage weight assigned to each grade would be to list the percentages assigned to each grade in an unused portion of the spreadsheet. Formulas would reference the cell addresses where these percentages reside rather than the percentages themselves.

Set up an Assumptions section in the upper left-hand corner of your worksheet. Move the course list down so that the column labels are in row 14. Enter the label "Assumptions" in cell A7 and enter underlining in cell A8. Below that, in cells A9 through A11 enter the labels "Quiz," "Midterm," and "Final Exam." In cells B9 through B11 you would enter the percentage weights for each of these grades.

You could then develop a formula to reference the cells where these percentages resided rather than using the percentages themselves. The formula for James Jackson's grade (which should be entered in cell E16 since the worksheet was moved down) would then be:

$$=B16*\$B\$9+C16*\$B\$10+D16*\$B\$11$$

The \$ designates an *absolute address*. An absolute address is one that will not change when that address is copied. Excel's default is to treat an address as a *relative address*, meaning that when you copy or move a formula, the addresses of the cells in the formula will be adjusted automatically to fit the new location. A relative address has no \$ symbols. Any formula with multiple cell references can have absolute, relative and mixed addresses (see the next section) all in the one formula.

In other words, if you copied the formula in cell E16 for James Jackson's grade to cell E17 for Paul Parker, the formula in E17 would automatically adjust to add the proper cell addresses for Parker's grade. The formula bar would show the formula in E17 to be =B17*\$B\$9+C17*\$B\$10+D17\$B\$11.

Mixed Addressing

There will be certain situations where you will want to combine relative and absolute addressing; that is, create a cell reference that is part relative and part absolute. Either the column letter or the row number remains constant.

For example, an address of \$B21 means that absolute addressing will be used on the column portion of the address, but relative addressing will be used on the row portion. Conversely, an address of B\$21 means that absolute addressing will be used on the row portion of the address and relative addressing on the column portion. You will need to use relative, absolute, and mixed addressing throughout your *Solve it!* Spreadsheet Cases.

Formatting

Suppose you want to express the percentages in your Assumptions section as 50% rather than .5. You can change the format in which numeric information appears by using Excel **Format/Cells** commands.

First, select the cells you want to change by selecting the range B9:B11.

The **Format/Cells** command activates the Format Cells dialog box, as explained in the tutorial for Spreadsheet Case 1. This box has six formatting tabs: Number, Alignment, Font, Border, Patterns, Protection. To change the format of numbers select Number. Do this by clicking on the tab label at the top of the box. The Format Category list is divided into the different types of numerical appearance. Select Percentage with zero decimal places and press the OK Button.

You should see the effects of this formatting on the three figures in the Assumptions area of the worksheet. They will be displayed as percentage figures: 15%, 35% and 50%. Excel often provides shortcuts to frequently used commands and operations by allocating buttons on Toolbars. In this case, Excel has placed a Percent Style Button on the Formatting Toolbar. To format the current cell(s) in a Percent Style simply click the Percent Style Button: $\boxed{\%}$

The different Number categories are:

General format is the default format for all new worksheets. With the General format the values are displayed in their natural state. No suppression or compression of formatting is permitted. Scientific notation will be used to display numbers that are too large or too small to be displayed normally. The General format displays up to 11 digits.

Number formats display a fixed number of decimal places, negative values in red, negative values in brackets, and combinations of these characteristics.

Accounting format displays four accounting formats keeping the dollar sign to the left of the cell, showing negative values in brackets and show zero values as hyphens.

Date and **Time** formats can represent dates and times in a number of formats where they can be used by Excel date and time functions in mathematical calculations. Default date formats include:

d/mm/yy	(Example 2/02/80)
d-mmm-yy	(Example 2-Feb-80)
d-mmm	(Example 2-Feb)
mmm-yy	(Example Feb-80)
d/mm/yy h:mm	(Example 2/02/80 15:15)

In order to use date and time formats, you must use one of the Excel date and time functions (such as =DATE, =DATEVALUE, =TIME, =TIMEVALUE, or =NOW) to enter dates and times onto your worksheet. Excel date functions will be treated in more detail in Spreadsheet Case 8. A date can also be entered as a label if it is not involved in any calculations.

Percentage format displays numbers as percentages. The number of decimal places in the default formats are zero and two.

Fraction format displays numbers as fractions, separating whole numbers and the fractional parts.

Scientific format displays data in exponential scientific notation.

Text format displays the values as labels rather than values.

Currency format places a dollar sign before each number and uses commas to separate hundreds from thousands, etc. There are options for zero or two decimal places and for red or black negative values.

Custom format can be used to create custom formats for numbers such as product codes.

After you have finished formatting, calculating final grades, and adding a column heading for FINAL GRADE your worksheet should look like Figure 3-3.

Totalling the Values in a Range

This case requires totals of gross pay, net pay and all deductions for the payroll register so that the employer can determine the total amount paid out for each of these categories during a particular pay period. The =SUM function of your spreadsheet software can help you do this. The =SUM function calculates the sum of all of the values in a specified range. The form of the =SUM function is:

=SUM(range)

Solve it!

For example, if you wanted to total the percentages in the Assumptions section of your sample worksheet to make sure they added up to 100 percent, you could use the =SUM function instead of the formula =B9+B10+B11. The values in range B9:B11 could be totalled much more easily by entering in cell B12:

=SUM(B9:B11)

Excel provides a shortcut for this formula: the Sum Button $\boxed{\Sigma}$.

This button appears on the Standard Toolbar and if pressed, the =SUM formula will be placed in the current cell and a sample range will be assumed, typically above or to the left of the current cell. All you have to do is press ENTER to complete the operation. Try the button as well as entering the formula yourself. When entering the formula, select the range B9:B11 using the cursor keys or the mouse, rather than typing the range. This tends to be easier and more accurate; typing is more prone to error.

Figure 3-3

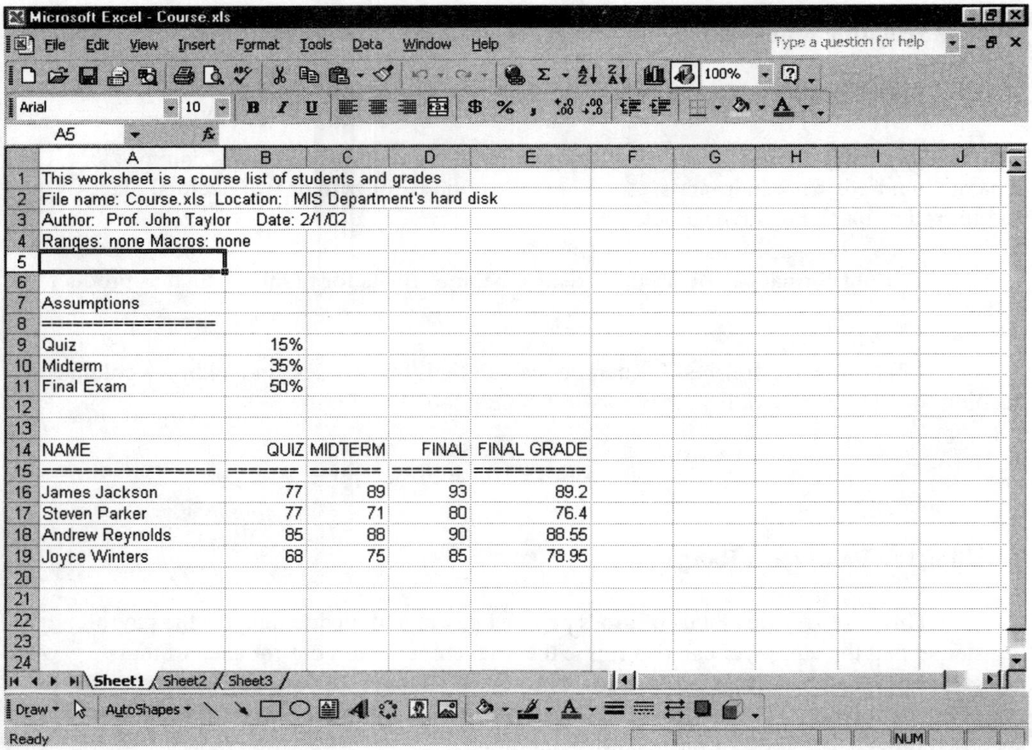

Save Course.xls with the changes you made during this tutorial session. You will need it for subsequent Spreadsheet Cases.

Spreadsheet Case 3

Camby Investment Advisers

Problem:	Analyze financial ratios
Management skills:	Deciding
PC skills:	Formulas
	Spreadsheet control
	Reporting

File: CAMBY_Q.XLS

Camby Investment Advisers (CIA) is a small-investment advising firm that has just opened in Pittsburgh, PA. It is trying to take market share from large brokerage houses by offering custom advice to clients on long-term investing, rather than recommending the stock-of-the-week strategy touted by its competitors.

Clients may call or visit to seek expert advice about particular stocks they are interested in. Paul Morgan, a prospering attorney, has expressed an interest in two firms in the do-it-yourself, home-improvement sector, and he wants to know if either one will make good investments. These firms are Home Depot and Lowe's, both of which are listed on the New York Stock Exchange.

Home Depot is the world's largest home-improvement retailer and is among the top ten retailers in the entire United States. As of late December 1999, the company operated over 900 stores and employed roughly 200,000 employees in the U.S., Canada, Puerto Rico, and Chile. Fortune Magazine voted Home Depot as "America's Most Admired Specialty Retailer" for over five years. The company advertises itself as offering the lowest prices in home improvement with "the highest levels of customer service."

Lowe's is one of the United States' largest retailers. Operating in 30 to 40 states, the company operates between 500 and 600 stores and has annual sales over $10 billion. Like Home Depot, Lowe's focuses on the do-it-yourself market as well as contractors and other commercial customers. Lowe's stocks roughly 40,000 home-improvement items—from tools to lumber to appliances to home-décor items. Like Home Depot, Lowe's also offers a huge ordering program. Both companies offer common stock.

To make sound recommendations, CIA's analysts must carefully examine a company's financial statements. The purpose of financial statements is to identify the major sources, uses, and flows of funds within an organization. The three principal financial statements used in business are income statements, balance sheets, and cash flow statements.

Income statements (also called operating statements) summarize the income, expenses, and profits of businesses for a specified period. The purpose of income statements is to show the profitability or unprofitability of firms during a specified period, usually a year, quarter, or month.

Balance sheets identify the assets, liabilities, and owner's (or shareholders') equity of a firm at a particular point in time. The difference between assets and liabilities is net worth or equity (literally what the organization is worth net of all other factors). Cash flow statements provide detailed information on total receipts and disbursements of cash. Cash flow statements are like checking account registers for individuals. You will use the 2001 income statements and balance sheets of Home Depot and of Lowe's for this case.

Certain financial ratios based on figures from financial statements have been traditionally used to assess a company's financial health and performance. There are five kinds of financial ratios that you can apply to assess the financial position of a firm.

1. Liquidity Ratios

Various liquidity ratios measure a firm's liquidity, its ability to draw on cash and other current assets to pay its financial obligations. Two commonly used liquidity ratios are the *current ratio* and the *quick ratio*, or *acid test*.

(a) Current Ratio =   Current Assets
                                 Current Liabilities

(b) Quick Ratio, or Acid Test = Current assets - Inventory
                                 Current liabilities

The current ratio is the most commonplace measure of short-term solvency. If current liabilities are rising faster than current assets, this may be a harbinger of financial difficulty. The quick ratio measures the firm's ability to pay off short-term obligations without relying on the sale of inventory, which is the least liquid of the firm's current assets.

2. Asset Management Ratios

Another group of ratios measures how effectively a firm is managing its assets. One of these is the *total assets utilization ratio*, which measures the utilization or turnover of all of the firm's assets.

(c) Total assets utilization=   Sales
                                         Total assets

3. Debt Management Ratios

These ratios determine the extent to which a firm uses debt financing. If equity, or owner-supplied funds, accounts for only a small portion of a firm's total financing, the risks of the firm are borne mainly by creditors. On the other hand, by raising funds through debt, owners can control the firm with a smaller investment of their own. If the firm returns more on the borrowed funds that it pays in interest, the return on the owner's capital is magnified, or leveraged. An important ratio is the *debt ratio*, which measures the percentage of a firm's total funds provided by creditors.

(d) Debt ratio =   Total liabilities
                                 Total assets

Creditors prefer low debt ratios, whereas it may be advantageous for owners to seek higher debt to leverage their money and earnings. However, a debt ratio that is too high signals trouble repaying loans and too much reliance on borrowed money to pay for the firm's operations.

4. Profitability ratios

Profitability ratios illustrate the combined effects of liquidity, asset management, and debt management on profits. Important profitability ratios measure the *return on total assets (ROA)*, the *return on common equity (ROE)*, or return on stockholders' investments, and the *profit margin on sales*.

(e) Return on Total Assets (ROA) = $\dfrac{\text{Net profit after taxes}}{\text{Total assets}}$

(f) Return on Equity (ROE) = $\dfrac{\text{Net profit after taxes}}{\text{Net worth (equity)}}$

(g) Profit Margin = $\dfrac{\text{Net profit after taxes}}{\text{Sales}}$

5. Market Value ratios

These ratios help indicate what investors think of the company's past performance and future prospects. The market value ratios (and stock price) will be high if a firm has strong liquidity, asset management, debt management, and profitability ratios. The most widely used market value ratio is the *price/earnings ratio*.

(h) Price/Earnings Ratio = $\dfrac{\text{Price per share}}{\text{Earnings per share}}$

To evaluate a firm's financial ratios properly, you must compare the ratios to ratios for comparable businesses. You can find financial ratio data on comparable businesses in publications like Dun and Bradstreet's *Industry Norms & Key Business Ratios* and Robert Morris's *Annual Statement Studies*. Both publications group businesses by standard industry classification codes and provide financial ratio data by standard industry classification code.

Tasks

There are five tasks to this case:

1. Examine the 2001 income statements and balance sheets of Home Depot and Lowe's, which can be found by loading the file **CAMBY.XLS** from your data diskette. All data are based on the publicly available 2001 annual reports of these firms.

2. Print out the financial statements so you have a hard copy to work with. Look at them very closely.

3. Assign range names to the income statement data, the balance sheet data, and the area of the worksheet containing the financial ratios. Create a table of range names below the worksheet. Format the ranges with the income statement and balance sheet data to display a comma with zero decimal places. Format the ranges with the financial ratios, earnings per share, and stock price to display two decimal places.

4. Calculate the eight financial ratios outlined above for each company at the end of the financial statements. Print out the ratios for both companies.

5. In a single paragraph write an analysis of both companies. If possible, find statistics on financial ratios for comparable businesses using either the Dun and Bradstreet or Robert Morris publication. Based on the information provided in this case, is each firm financially sound? Which would make the better investment? Review the financial statements of both companies for any items that might help explain their financial position.

Additional Problems

1. Obtain the current stock price for each of these companies and recalculate the Price/Earnings ratio.

2. Use the Web to search the EDGAR database [www.sec.gov/edgar.shtml] maintained by the Securities and Exchange Commission. This database contains companies' quarterly and annual financial reports and other documents filed with the SEC. Use this information to recalculate the financial ratios for both companies. Would that make a difference in your decision?

Time Estimates

Expert: 45 minutes
Intermediate: 1 hour
Novice: 1.5 hours

Excel Tutorial for Spreadsheet Case 3

You do not need to use range names for the solution to this case, but they can be used if you wish when you use different formats for different ranges in your worksheet.

In Course.xls, name the range with the student grade data as GRADES. Name the range with the percentages used in the Assumptions section as PERCENT.

Naming Ranges

You can name a range the with the **Insert/Name/Define** command. To name the range with the percentages PERCENT, you would do the following: highlight the three cells B9:B11, select **Name** from the **Insert** menu, and then select **Define** from the sub-menu. A Define Name dialog box will appear, already containing the percentage range reference. Type the name PERCENT and click the OK Button.

You can alternatively select **Insert/Name/Define**, then select the range once within the dialog box and type the name. Use either procedure to name the range B16:E19 as GRADES.

Creating a Table of Range Names

You can document your range names in a table in your worksheet using the **Insert/Name/Paste** command. Place the table in an unused portion of the worksheet where it will not overlay any data. The spreadsheet design principles introduced in Chapter 2 suggest placing the range name table below the leftmost portion of the worksheet.

To create the range name table, move to the cell where you want the table to appear and select the **Insert/Name/Paste** command. A dialog box appears, listing the named ranges. The purpose of this dialog box is to paste a selected Name in the formula bar. However, we are using the alternative purpose of the dialog box: pasting a list of range names and their references onto the worksheet. To do this, click the Paste List button. This will result in a worksheet resembling that in Figure 3-4.

Figure 3-4

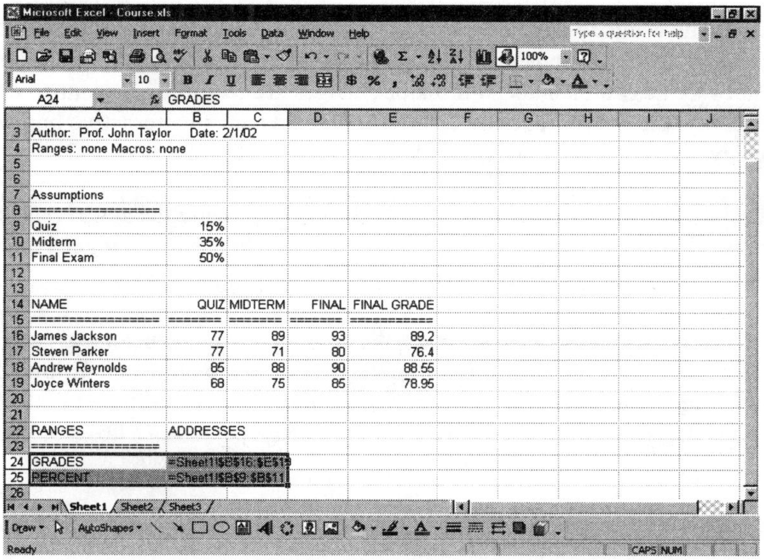

Spreadsheet Case 4

The Village of Peconic

Problem:	Prepare a budget for a small municipality
Management skills:	Planning
	Deciding
PC skills:	Formulas
	Spreadsheet control
	Reporting

File: PECON_Q.XLS

The Village of Peconic has a population of 8700 and is located in Suffolk County, New York. Each October, Harvey Williams, the village manager, works with the village Mayor and Board of Trustees to develop the village's budget for the forthcoming year. The Village's main source of revenue is the local property tax, but it also receives some aid from the state government and some revenue from miscellaneous licenses and fees.

The village leaders want to hold to their campaign promises of not raising taxes. Their community has become very environmentally-conscious and they do not want to encourage new businesses that would add to the traffic congestion or pollute the air. They fear revenues may be going down because New York State is facing severe financial problems and wants to cut the state aid it provides to local governments.

Harvey Williams wants to develop a budget that can be supported by anticipated revenues. Anticipating continued cutbacks in state aid, Harvey would like to develop preliminary budgets for the next two years. That way he can plan ahead if major changes are required. If planned expenditures exceed revenues, Harvey, the Mayor, and the Trustees must develop an alternative budget that does balance. Can they develop a balanced budget without raising local property taxes?

From your data diskette load the file PECON_Q.XLS, showing the actual receipts and disbursements for the Village of Peconic in 2002. Harvey wants to use this budget as the basis for projecting the Village budget for the next two years.

One way to analyze a budget is to estimate the amount of each category of cash receipts and disbursements. The projected outflow of funds is subtracted from the projected inflow. If the amount of outflow is greater than the amount of inflow, the village must secure additional funds to pay for its expenditures or reduce its expenditures. For instance, the village could raise taxes or borrow money to meet its costs or it could reduce some of its expenses.

In projecting the next two years' budgets, the village manager wants to use the following assumptions. He expects the state will reduce its aid to the village by 20% each year. Historically, expenditures for employee benefits have been rising 10% annually. He expects all other expenditures to rise at a rate of 3% annually and miscellaneous receipts to rise 5% annually. The village's expenditure for debt service to pay off previous loans will remain constant. Can the village balance its budget if it keeps its promise not to raise taxes or go further into debt?

Tasks

There are 5 tasks in this case:

1. Print out and review PECON_Q.XLS.

2. Create an assumptions section of the worksheet to identify factors in your calculations of receipts and disbursements. Make sure formulas reference cells in the assumptions section wherever possible.

3. Calculate the receipts and disbursements for each of the categories on the worksheet for 2003 and 2004. Calculate total receipts and total disbursements. The case has been simplified so that all revenue is collected in the year it is due.

4. Complete the worksheet by subtracting total receipts from total disbursements in 2002, 2003, and 2004. Print the results.

5. Write a brief analysis of the projected 2003 and 2004 budgets for the village of Peconic. If these budgets don't balance, what steps would you recommend that the village take? Revise your worksheet to incorporate your recommendations, save it under another name, and print it out again. Keep revising the worksheet until you have developed a balanced budget. Is there some way for the village to come up with a balanced budget without raising taxes?

Additional Problem

1. What if state aid is not reduced but remains constant for the next two years? What impact would this have on the budget? Revise your worksheet and save it under a different name. Print out and analyze the results.

Time Estimates

Expert: 30 minutes
Intermediate: 1 hour
Novice: 1.5 hours

There is no tutorial for this case because it uses skills introduced in earlier chapters.

Spreadsheet Case 5

Low-Fat Pastries, Inc.

Problem:	Develop a breakeven analysis model for a start-up venture
Management skills:	Planning Deciding
PC skills:	Graphics Worksheet organization

File: FAT_Q.XLS

Low-Fat Pastries, Inc. is a newly formed, one-person company located in Phoenicia, New York that produces low-fat and fat-free baked goods for the health conscious. By substituting egg whites and applesauce for whole eggs and fat, Low-Fat Pastries can make such products. Its founder, Marie Latella, has arranged to sell a new line of fat-free baked muffins in a network of organic food stores, supermarkets, and department stores. Marie believes that a huge demand for fat-free muffins among aging baby boomers makes this a promising business opportunity.

Before Marie invests heavily in advertising, baking equipment, warehouse, and office space, she must know if there is a future in this type of business and at what point it will produce a profit. Marie has not done any formal market research, but she would like to sell each six-pack of muffins to her retailers for a wholesale price of $2.90

This is a classic problem for all businesses: determining what objectives they must meet to produce a profit or to minimize losses. What Marie must do is utilize the managerial accounting concept of Breakeven Analysis. Breakeven Analysis establishes the *breakeven point*, which is the number of units that Marie must sell to yield no profit and incur no loss. Any units sold beyond the breakeven point will represent profit, and a sales volume below the breakeven point will put the firm at a loss.

To perform Breakeven Analysis, a company must examine its operating costs. Some of these costs are fixed and do not change over the range of the operations activity, no matter how many units of an item the company produces or sells. Variable costs, on the other hand, increase with increasing production and decrease as production decreases.

In the case of Low-Fat Pastries, Inc., fixed costs are Marie's rent for a large office-storage-baking area ($6000 per year), the cost of a commercial oven ($2000), the cost of baking equipment, such as bowls, pans, and muffin tins ($800), and the cost of an initial advertising campaign ($4000). Marie's variable costs are the cost of baking supplies, packaging, and shipping. Marie has calculated that the cost of baking and packaging each six-pack of muffins is $1.80 and the cost of shipping each package is $.35. Marie has decided not to pay herself a salary right away. Until the business starts producing a profit, Marie is planning to live off her savings, which amount to $15,000.

Once a product's costs have been determined, the contribution margin per unit must be calculated. The contribution margin per unit is the difference between the selling price per unit and the variable costs per unit. (The contribution margin per unit = average selling price per unit - variable costs per unit.) Once the contribution margin per unit has been determined, one can then calculate the breakeven point. In a company such as Low-Fat Pastries, Inc., which produces only a few products, the formula for the breakeven point would be calculated by dividing the total fixed costs by the contribution margin per unit.

Often the best way to display the results of breakeven analysis is in graphic form. It is also useful to use breakeven analysis to generate pro forma income statements that convert unit data to dollars and display projected sales revenue.

Tasks

There are four tasks in this case:

1. Load the data file Fat_q.xls from your data diskette. Create a worksheet that displays the total fixed cost, variable cost per unit, and average sale price for one package of muffins from Low-Fat Pastries, Inc. and that calculates the contribution margin per unit and the breakeven point. Include an Assumptions section that identifies variable factors used in calculations.

2. Use your results to generate pro forma income statements using the framework supplied on the data file. Include two projections of sales and income below the breakeven point and two above it. Include a projection of sales and income right at the breakeven point. The income data below the breakeven point should reflect zero sales and sales at half of the breakeven units. The income data at the breakeven point should reflect sales at 1.0 times the breakeven units. The income data above the breakeven point should reflect sales at 1.5 and 2.0 times the breakeven units.

3. Create a line chart (graph) to display the most important data from the pro forma income statements and the breakeven point. The X-axis of the chart should display the range, indicating units sold in your pro forma income statements. The first data series should display fixed cost (which will be constant). The second data series should display total cost figures. The third data series should display revenue figures. Give your chart (graph) a title and supply titles for the X and Y axes. Supply legends for all of the data series. The point on the chart where the data lines for total cost and revenue intersect is the breakeven point.

4. Be sure to name and save your chart as well as your worksheet. Print both the chart and the worksheet. Examine your output. Write a one-paragraph statement analyzing the results of the breakeven analysis. Is Low-Fat Pastries, Inc. a worthwhile business venture for Marie?

Additional Problem

1.   Marie has been told that packaging material costs will rise 7% in a few weeks.
     Packaging material costs account for approximately 5% of the baking and packaging cost
     for each package of muffins. What impact will this have on Marie's breakeven analysis?

Time Estimates

Expert: 45 minutes
Intermediate: 1 hour
Novice: 2 hours

Excel Tutorial for Spreadsheet Case 5

This case draws upon all of the skills acquired in previous Spreadsheet Cases plus new
skills for creating and printing graphs, or Charts as they are known in Excel. You will need to
use Course.xls again for this tutorial.

Creating Charts with Excel

Excel provides an excellent facility for generating charts to display data graphically on
your worksheets. The facility is known as the ChartWizard. The idea behind Wizards is that
the program helps you through a complicated process by splitting it into easy steps with clear
instructions. The ChartWizard helps you through the process of creating a Chart in Excel in
four easy steps.

Charts in Excel can be stored in separate chartsheets or be Embedded in worksheets.
With the Chart embedded in the worksheet, you can instantly observe the effects of changes of
the data in the worksheet, and create attractive documents with the chart accompanying the
original data. The steps to achieve each of these graphs are identical.

The ChartWizard can be invoked in two ways: by selecting **Insert/Chart** from the
menu bar or by clicking the ChartWizard Button on the Standard Toolbar.

We will create a separate chartsheet for our chart. The information we want to graph
is the grades of each assessment task for every student. It is easier to select the range
containing the data before selecting the ChartWizard. However, currently the data headings are
separated from the values in the worksheet by a row containing the "=" symbol, in Row 15.
Since we want to include the headings as Labels in the chart, it would be easier if we deleted
Row 15 and had an undivided range. Select Row 15 and select the **Edit/Delete** command to
delete Row 15.

Select the range A14:E18. This range contains the values representing the Students'
Grades and also the Students' Names and the Assessment Tasks. Now, select **Insert/Chart**
from the menu bar.

You should now be faced with the ChartWizard's first dialog box. This dialog box, titled "ChartWizard-Step 1 of 4-Chart Type" is asking for the chart type you want to display the data. The most important chart types are:

Major Excel Chart Types

The **Area Chart** shows each data series as a shaded area, each added onto the previous area.

The **Bar Chart** shows the values as solid horizontal bars of differing lengths. This type is ideally suited to categorized data.

The **Column Chart** is similar to the Bar Chart except the bars are vertically aligned. Again, this type is ideally suited to categorized data.

The **Line Chart** show trends and values, typically over a time horizon at even intervals, representing each series as points connected by a line.

The **Pie Chart** shows values as a proportion of a whole or total. The values are represented as a slice of a circular pie. This is used when there is only a single data series.

The **Doughnut Chart** shows values as a proportion of a whole or total, similar to the Pie Chart, except more than a single data series can be represented. Each data series is shown as a concentric circle.

The **XY (Scatter) Chart** shows the degree of a relationship between the numeric values on both the X and Y axes, for several data series. This chart type is useful since it represents data with uneven intervals on the axes.

Choose the Line type of chart in the Chart type list by selecting it with the mouse or with the arrow keys. You can also select a specific format for your line chart from the samples in the Chart Sub-type section of the dialog box. When you have selected Line type and the format for your Line chart, click the "Next >" Button or press the ENTER key.

The second dialog box appears. It asks for the range containing the data for graphing. Since we have already selected the range, it appears in this dialog box. This stage permits you to redefine the range if you wish. (This dialog box also asks you to specify whether the individual data series are in the rows or in the columns. The data series we want to graph should be specified as in rows.) When you are satisfied with the specified range, click the "Next >" Button or press ENTER.

The third dialog box deals with Chart Options. They include Titles, Axes, Gridlines, Legend, Data Labels, and Data Table. Make sure the Titles tab is selected so that you can add a Chart Title and Axis Titles. Enter the Chart Title "Student Grades", the X-Axis Title "Assessment Types" and the Y-Axis Title "Grade". As you enter these titles, the sample chart will incorporate them. After you have specified these titles, click the "Next" Button or press ENTER.

The fourth and final dialog box asks for the Chart Location. Here, you can specify how you want to store your chart—"As object in" and "As new sheet." "As object in" means that you want to store the chart as an embedded object on the current sheet. "As new sheet" means that you want to store the chart on a separate sheet. Since we want the chart on a separate sheet, select the "As new sheet" option. When you have finished, click the "Finish" Button.

The ChartWizard has now finished. Notice the Chart1 tab at the bottom of the screen. This is where the newly created chart is stored. To move between the chartsheet and the worksheet, simply click the respective tab at the bottom of the screen.

Graph Formatting

Excel provides extensive features for formatting of objects within charts. Although the ChartWizard has produced an attractive chart, further enhancements can be made to improve certain aspects of it. You can select virtually any object in an Excel chart and adjust its features. You can select objects in a chart using the arrow keys to step through each of the objects that can be changed, or simply select the object with the mouse.

Objects that can be selected are: Axis (X and Y), Axis Title, Chart Title, Chart Area, Plot Area, Data Series, Data Point, Legend, Legend Key, Legend Entry and <Chart Type> Group.

Once the object is selected you can choose **Format/Selected <Object>** from the menu or double-click on the object. This will produce the **Format <Object>** dialog box containing different tabs for adjusting different aspects of the object.

For example, if you selected the Y-Axis by clicking on it (a black square will appear at each end of the axis when it is selected) and then selected **Format/Selected Axis ...** from the menu, you will be presented with a dialog box with tabs for Patterns, Scale, Font, Number and Alignment. These tabs can also be applied to other objects in the chart but in this context they refer to the Y-Axis. For example, the Patterns tab contains settings for the axis thickness, style, colour, tick type, tick location and a sample. The Patterns tab for other objects would have different settings. Other tabs, such as Scale, refer to this type of object alone.

Select the Scale tab. The settings here permit you to change the minimum value, the maximum value, the major interval value, and the minor interval value of the Axis. Other settings also let you specify where the X-Axis crosses, whether the scale is logarithmic, whether the values appear in reverse order and whether the X-Axis crosses at the maximum value.

Currently the graph has all the data points congregating at the top of the chart. It would be preferable for the data to be spread more evenly up the chart. In order to do this we would adjust the minimum value of the Y-Axis to 60. If you have not already done so, select the Y-Axis and choose **Format/Selected Axis ...** from the menu. Now select the Scale tab. To change the minimum value, first click the Auto Check box next to Minimum so a check does not appear in the box. This permits manual entry of values. Now enter 60 in the Minimum value box and click the OK Button. Your chart should now resemble that in Figure 3-5.

Figure 3-5

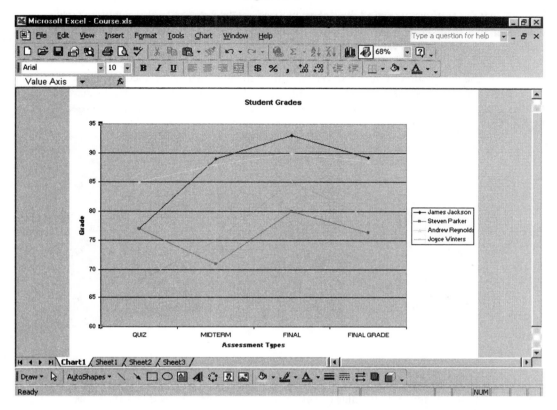

The other tabs under various objects are:

Font - Changing the appearance of text (size, font, style etc.)
Number - Changing the presentation of values
Alignment - Changing the arrangement and orientation of objects
Placement - Changing the location of the Legend (Bottom, Corner, Top, Right, Left)
Y Error Bars - Lets you arrange error bars on data points
Axis - Lets you distinguish between primary and secondary axes
Data Labels - Lets you attach labels to data points
Names and Values - Lets you redefine the worksheet cells that contain the names and values of the current data series
X Values - Lets you redefine the worksheet cells that contain the X values
Subtype - Lets you define cumulative and percentage cumulative charts
Series Order - Lets you change the order of the data series
Options - Further options for the current object, not included in other tabs

You can change most Excel chart objects merely by selecting the object and double-clicking to bring up object settings. You can change Title text simply by selecting the object and placing the mouse pointer where you want to insert or replace text.

Embedding a Chart in a Worksheet

All the features discussed for a chart in a separate chartsheet apply equally to a chart embedded in a worksheet. You could embed a chart by selecting "As object in" for your Chart Location when using ChartWizard dialog boxes.

At the completion of the ChartWizard, you will have the chart embedded in the worksheet. You can identify a selected embedded chart by a thin border with black squares, known as handles, which permit you to resize the chart size. A selected chart can be seen in Figure 3-6.

Figure 3-6

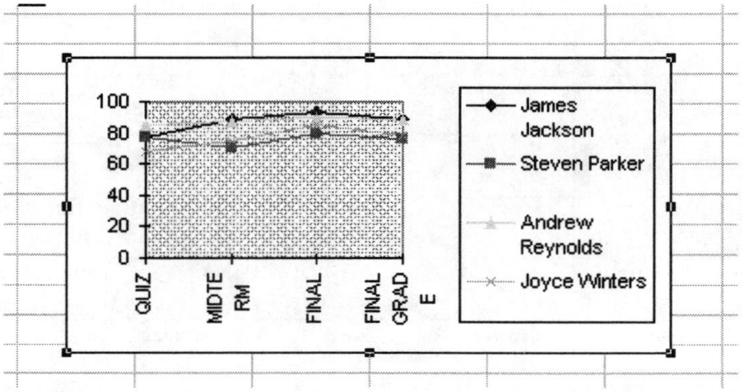

To select an embedded chart, simply click it once with the mouse pointer. To resize the chart, grab one of the eight handles (on either the selected or activated chart) and drag it in the desired direction. To move the chart, grab the selected chart anywhere inside the border and drag to the new location. To delete the selected chart, simply press the DEL or DELETE key.

Printing and Saving a Chart

Excel chartsheets can be printed in exactly the same way as Excel worksheets can, as described in the Tutorial for Spreadsheet Case 1. The **File/Print Preview** and **File/Page Setup** operations apply in the same way as for a worksheet also.

A chartsheet will be saved when the workbook it resides in is saved. Similarly, an embedded chart will be saved when the worksheet containing it is saved, as described in the Tutorial for Spreadsheet Case 1.

Spreadsheet Case 6

Helton Office Supply

Problem:	Develop an inventory control system
Management skills:	Organizing Controlling
PC skills:	Spreadsheet control Logical functions

File: HELTON_Q.XLS

Helton Office Supply in Grand Rapids, MI, manufactures paper office supplies like forms, envelopes, folders, fax paper, computer printer paper, and labels. Helton sells the supplies to retail office-supply stores and mail order houses that in turn sell them under their own brands. The office supply business is highly competitive. Helton has acquired a long list of clients by producing attractive office supplies within the budgetary limits specified by clients.

Because the company is new, Carolyn Ahmed, the production manager, has been tracking the supplies kept in inventory by hand using a ledger sheet. This process is time consuming and errors sometimes have resulted in missed production deadlines due to inadequate inventory. In response, Ahmed has increased the level of safety stock in order to avoid running out in the future. However, this increase raises operating costs, and Helton Office Supply needs to keep these down in order to remain competitive. Ahmed has decided to implement her own inventory control system using a PC and spreadsheet software.

To ensure efficient use of funds, a good inventory control system will maintain an inventory level that is neither overstocked nor understocked. It will match existing inventory levels against desired levels so that understocked items can be reordered.

There are two basic models for accomplishing this. The first is to use a *reorder level system*, which merely makes sure that required items are ordered with sufficient lead time to arrive when needed in the production process. The second is to use a system that determines the least expensive quantity to order, or most economic quantity. This approach, based on the *economic order quantity model*, strikes a balance between carrying costs (e.g., taxes and insurance) and procurement costs (e.g., ordering, shipping, and receiving costs).

Ordering in large quantities reduces procurement costs but raises carrying costs. The *economic order quantity* represents the number of units where procurement costs equal carrying costs. The exact size of the economic order quantity depends upon the estimated amount of the product needed each year, its unit cost, the fixed cost of placing and receiving an order for the item, and the carrying cost for the item in inventory, expressed as a percentage of inventory value. The formula for calculating an item's economic order quantity is:

$$EOQ \ = \ \sqrt{\frac{2FU}{CP}}$$

$$\sqrt{\frac{2(\$3.17)(F18)}{(\$B\$8)(E18)}}$$

where

- EOQ = the item's economic order quantity
- F = the fixed cost of ordering the item
- U = the amount of the product needed each year
- C = the item's carrying cost, expressed as a percentage of inventory value
- P = the item's unit cost

The calculation of the economic order quantity often results in a fractional amount that you must round to the next whole number to determine the economic order quantity.

Load the data file Helton_q.xls from your data diskette. This file contains a list of office supplies that Helton Office Supply keeps in its warehouses, balance on hand, balance on order, unit cost per item, estimated annual usage per item, and the order point. The order point is the number of units of an item in inventory that triggers the decision to order more items. There is usually a lead time period (say, of two weeks) between the time an order is placed and when it is actually fulfilled. Having some inventory while reordering reduces the possibility of an out-of-stock situation.

Assume that order cost is a fixed cost of $100.00 for all items in this problem. Also assume that inventory carrying cost is 20% of inventory value for all items in this problem.

Tasks

There are four tasks in this case:

1.   Below row 7, add rows to hold Assumptions for carrying costs and for order costs.

2.   Add the following columns to the worksheet to track:
  a.   "Balance Available" that can be calculated by adding balance on hand + balance on order.
  b.   "Order Quantity" for those items in need of reordering. If the balance available is less than the order point, then calculate the economic order quantity. If the balance available is greater than the order point, then put a zero in the column for order quantity. Format the Order Quantity column to comma format with zero decimal places. (Hint: Use absolute cell references when referring to the cells containing your Assumptions data.)

3.   Develop a method to identify any stock items that need reordering on the worksheet. (Hint: One way is to add a column containing an formula to print an asterisk next to needed stock items.)

4.   Write a short paragraph suggesting some enhancements to this application to make it a better management tool.

Time Estimates

Expert: 1 hour
Intermediate: 1.5 hours
Novice: 2 hours

Excel Tutorial for Spreadsheet Case 6

This case draws upon all of the skills acquired in previous Spreadsheet Cases and new skills for using the logical functions of your spreadsheet software and the =SQRT function. You will need to use Course.xls again for this tutorial.

Excel includes a set of logical functions that enable the software to perform conditional tests and evaluate a condition in your worksheet. Depending on whether the condition is true or false, different values will be returned to cells.

The most important conditional function in Excel is =IF. The =IF function enables you to test one or more conditions in your worksheet and perform different tasks, depending on the outcome of the test. The form for the =IF function is:

=IF(condition, action if true, action if false)

This formula tests the "condition" to determine if specific results or cell contents are true or false. The "action if true" portion contains specific instructions to execute if the result of the test is true. The "action if false" portion contains another set of instructions to execute if the result is false. The instructions to be executed can return cell contents that are labels as well as values.

To perform conditional tests, the =IF function and other conditional functions require logical operators. These operators help establish the relationship between two numbers, strings, or cell references.

Logical Operators

Operator	Meaning
=	Equal
<	Less than
>	Greater than
<=	Less than or equal to
>=	Greater than or equal to
<>	Not equal

To establish relationships between two or more conditional tests, Excel provides Logical Functions.

Logical Functions	Description
AND(*logical1, logical2, ...*)	Returns TRUE if each *logical* condition is true; returns FALSE otherwise
OR(*logical1, logical2, ...*)	Returns TRUE if any *logical* condition is true; returns FALSE otherwise
NOT(*logical*)	Returns TRUE if *logical* is FALSE; returns FALSE otherwise
TRUE()	Returns TRUE always
FALSE()	Returns FALSE always

The logical functions NOT, AND, and OR contain conditional tests to result in a single TRUE or FALSE. The following are examples of logical statements using =IF, using the logical operators, and using the logical functions:

=IF(A5>20,B5,0) means that if the value in cell A5 is greater than 20, then use the value in cell B5. Otherwise, assign the number zero.

=IF(AND(B11<>0,G11=1),10,0) means that if the value in cell B11 is not equal to zero and the value in cell G11 equals 1, then assign the number 10. Otherwise, assign the number 0.

=IF(OR(E13="Profit",F15>=G15),"Surplus","Deficit") means that if either cell E13 contains the label "Profit" or the contents of cell F15 are greater or equal to the contents of cell G15, then assign the label "Surplus". Otherwise, assign the label "Deficit".

The second and third examples just above show that logical functions can have more than a single condition as the =IF conditional test.

For your student roster, you can develop a conditional test to print an asterisk (*) after the name of any student whose final grade is less than 80. In cell F15, add a formula that will examine the student's final grade. If the grade is less than 80, an asterisk will appear in the cell next to the final grade. If the grade is greater than or equal to 80, a character string consisting of a blank space will be placed in the cell. The formula for this would be as follows:
=IF($E15<80,"*"," ")

Copy this formula into range F16:F18. Observe on your screen and in Figure 3-7 that the final grades for students Parker and Winters will be followed by an asterisk. The final grades for the other students will be left blank.

Figure 3-7

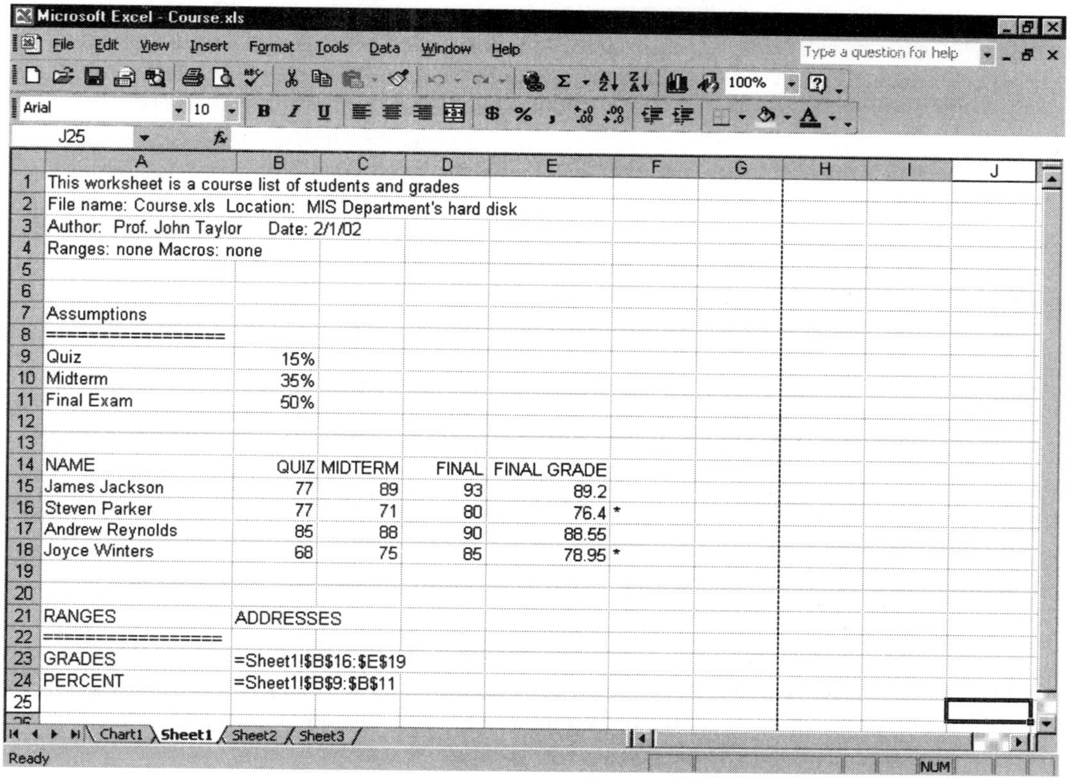

The =SQRT Function

The =SQRT function is one of a series of functions that perform mathematical, statistical, and trigonometric operations. The =SQRT function calculates the square root of a positive number. The form of this function is:

=SQRT(number or cell reference)

For example the square root of the average of James Jackson's quiz and midterm grades would be =SQRT((B15+C15)/2)

You do not need to save Course.xls with the modifications you made during this tutorial session.

Inserting Functions

Excel provides a facility to make retrieving and entering functions easier. You can activate it by selecting **Insert/Function** from the menu, or by selecting the Insert Function button f_* , located between the Name box and the Formula bar.

Press the Insert Function button now, which will display the Insert Function dialog box. Select the function that you want to use. In the "Search for a function" text box, you can enter a question describing what you want to do. Otherwise, you can use the "Or select a category" list box to select a major category of formulas (e.g., Financial, Statistical, Logical, etc.). For example, if you wanted the IF function, select "Logical" from the "Or select a category" list box, then scroll down the list in the Select a function list box until IF appears.

Select IF, then press the "OK" Button to open the Function Arguments dialog box. In this second and final dialog box, type your logical test in the top box, your desired output for a true result in the middle box, and your desired output for a false result in the bottom box. When you have completed the Function Arguments dialog box, click the "OK" button to close the dialog box and to enter the desired formula in the selected cell.

"Nested" functions use a function as one of the arguments within another function. ("Arguments" are the values that functions use to perform operations or calculations.) To create a nested function, follow the same general procedure as described above for creating a formula with the IF function. First, click in the cell where you want to place a formula. Second, open the Insert Function dialog box and select your desired function. Third, enter the arguments required for the nested function, and then click "OK" to close the dialog box.

When entering arguments for nested functions, you can type the desired cell references into the relevant text boxes in the Function Arguments dialog box. However, to avoid typographic errors, click the Collapse Dialog button at the right end of an argument's text box to collapse the large dialog box to a small rectangular one and do the following: (a) Select the worksheet cell(s) needed to create the first part of your formula. (b) Click the Expand Dialog button at the right end of the small dialog box to return to the Function Arguments dialog box. (c) Tab to the second argument box, collapse the dialog box, select the desired cells for that part of the formula, and re-expand the dialog box. (d) When you have filled all required argument boxes in the Function Arguments dialog box, click "OK" to close it.

Spreadsheet Case 7

Exact Cartridges

Problem:	Determine a relationship between defects and production volume
Management skills:	Controlling Planning
PC skills:	Regression analysis Graphics
File:	EXACT_Q.XLS

Exact Cartridges in San Jose, CA is a small manufacturer of cartridges for computer laser printers. Exact has been able to take advantage of a growing market and its business has expanded dramatically. Since opening twelve years ago, the company has doubled its workforce and more than tripled production.

Exact's customers are computer supply companies who sell the cartridges to owners of laser printers. Many defective cartridges go undetected until people try to use their printers. Exact's customers feel that any incidence of defects threatens their reputation and credibility.

A zero defect rate is an impossibility, but a rate below one per thousand is acceptable. Unfortunately, Exact Cartridges's defect rate has been steadily rising. Jorge Freeman, Exact's quality control supervisor, wonders if the rise in defects grows from the company's growth and increased production volume.

To meet production demand, Exact Cartridges had to double its labor force. Its recent recruits tend to be fresh from high school and largely untrained. Exact's internal training programs have been minimal because many of its positions, such as wrappers and loaders, do not involve high technology or special skills. Freeman feels these younger workers do not pay as close attention to quality control procedures, nor do they operate equipment as carefully as veteran workers do. There also are many more workers and work groups to supervise.

Senior management has ordered Freeman to "do something" to curb the rise in cartridge defects. Exact Cartridges's targets are to produce 1,200,000 cartridges by 2002 and 1,300,000 by 2003. Freeman wants to institute a stronger training program and quality controls but needs some data to convince senior management that, if unchecked, the frequency of defects will worsen. In addition to predicting future defect levels, Freeman also wants to use this data as a base line to gauge the success of his quality control problems.

Load the data file Exact_q.xls from your data diskette. It shows Exact's production volume and defects per 1000 cartridges from 1992 to 2001. Freeman will use this data to determine the historical relationship between frequency of defects and production volume so he can predict the level of defects in the future.

You can predict the level by performing a regression analysis, a statistical method for measuring the relationship between two or more variables. If the relationship is between only two variables, the method is called simple regression. If the relationship is between more than two variables, the method is called multiple regression. We have simplified this case for instructional purposes so that only two variables—incidence of defects and production volume—will be analyzed.

A regression analysis results in an equation that describes the behavior of one dependent variable in terms of other variables, called independent variables. In this case, there is only one independent variable, production volume, and one dependent variable, incidence of defects. The regression analysis also produces statistics that measure the strength of the relationship between the independent and dependent variables. You can visualize regression analysis as a way of drawing the "best line" through a series of data points.

You then can use the regression equation to forecast future incidence of defects given projected production volumes. Some popular business applications for regression analysis are determining the relationship between a product's price and cost of production, or determining the level of sales to be generated by an advertising campaign.

Tasks

There are four tasks in this case:

1.   Carefully examine the template for the data file, Exact_q.xls, which you have just loaded. Use the regression analysis commands of your spreadsheet software to perform a simple regression analysis. For the dependent variable (Input Y Range), select the level of defects range. For the independent variable (Input X Range), select the production volume range. For your Output Range text box, select cell I1, so the regression analysis will not overwrite any existing cell contents.

2.   In Cell D8, enter the label *Regression Line*. In cell D9, calculate the Regression Line as follows: (a) Multiply the value of the X Variable 1 Coefficient by each value of the independent variable (Pieces Produced). (b) Add the value of the constant (i.e., Intercept of Coefficients). (c) Be sure to apply absolute cell referencing to the X Variable 1 Coefficient and Intercept of Coefficients. (d) Use the fill handle to copy the formula into the remaining rows (i.e., down to year 2001). Print out the worksheet and the Regression Output.

3.   Construct an XY (Scatter) type chart showing the independent variable (Pieces Produced) on the X-axis, the dependent variable (Percent Defective) on the Y-axis, and the Regression Line. Entitle the graph as "Production Volume vs. Defects, 1992-2001." If needed, add an explanatory legend. Print out this graph.

4.   Extend the independent variable range with values of 1,200,000 for 2002 and 1,300,000 for 2003. Then extend the regression line to predict future levels of defects. Revise your graph to incorporate this data and print again. Entitle this graph "Production Volume vs. Defects, 1992-2003."

Time Estimates

Expert: 45 minutes
Intermediate: 1.5 hours
Novice: 2.5 hours

Excel Tutorial for Spreadsheet Case 7

This case expands on graphics and other spreadsheet skills that you used previously and introduces the use of an Excel command for regression analysis.

You can use your sample student roster (Course.xls) if you expand it to include a column for the students' ages. (If you saved Course.xls with the formula to place asterisks in column F, erase range F15:F18, then enter student age data in this column. Also, erase the range name table.)

The professor and school administration want to see if there is any correlation between student age and academic performance. In cell F14, enter the column heading AGE. Assign the age of 25 to James Jackson, 23 to Steven Parker, 22 to Andrew Reynolds, and 19 to Joyce Winters. Place ages in corresponding cells in range F15:F18. If needed, widen column E. If needed, reduce the widths of columns B, D, and F so you can display columns A through H on your screen.

The number of students on this worksheet is too small a sample to be statistically valid in actual life. Nevertheless, the worksheet will illustrate the concept of regression analysis and the Excel **Regression** Analysis Tool. Excel provides a variety of Analysis Tools that can be accessed through **Tools/Data Analysis**.

> If **Data Analysis** does not appear in the **Tools** menu, the Analysis ToolPak add-in has not been loaded. (An "add-in" is a file that provides additional functions, commands, and menus.) Select **Tools/Add-Ins**. In the Add-Ins dialog box, choose Analysis ToolPak. Click the OK Button. Select **Tools/Data Analysis**. Follow the on-screen instructions that appear to complete the installation. (Note Well: To install the Data Analysis add-in file on a stand-alone computer, you will need the Office XP or Excel 2002 CD-ROM. In a networked environment, the file already may exist on the network. Consult your instructor if you have difficulty installing the file.)

In the Data Analysis dialog box, scroll down the list as needed, click "Regression," and press the OK button. To determine the relationship between students' ages and final grades, make age the independent variable and final grade the dependent variable.

The Regression dialog box (see Figure 3-8) requires that you specify the ranges that hold the dependent values and the independent values.

At the **Input Y Range** setting, specify your dependent variable. In the window provided, enter the range E14:E18 (the range for final grades). This dialog box permits you to select ranges on the worksheet. Select the Final Grades range using your mouse, or type the range E14:E18.

At the **Input X Range** setting, specify one or more independent variables. In the window provided, enter the range F14:F18 (the range for students' ages). As with the Y-range, ranges on the worksheet can be selected with the mouse. Select the Students' Ages range or type the range F14:F18.

Check the **Labels** check box to indicate that the selected ranges include the Labels in the first row. (Another input setting available is the **Constant is zero** check box, which lets the user force the Y intercept to zero. We will not use this setting for this problem.) If you wanted to apply confidence intervals to the regression in addition to the default 95% levels, you would click the Confidence Level check box. Leave this box unselected.

The Output options section of the dialog box contains several option buttons and check boxes. Three Output Options option buttons are available: (1) The **Output Range** deposits the output on the same sheet and asks for the upper-left cell reference of the output range. (2) The **New Worksheet Ply** creates a new worksheet in the same workbook and (optionally) asks you to name the new worksheet. (3) The **New Workbook** creates an entirely new workbook and places the output in cell A1 of its first worksheet. Select the **Output Range** option button and place the cell reference H1 in the available window. (Generally, you should allocate a blank worksheet area.)

Excel provides four check boxes for residual values: **Residuals, Standardized Residuals, Residual Plots,** and **Line Fit Plots**. "Residuals" are the differences between the actual values and predicted values using the regression coefficients for the same dependent values. The plots will be embedded charts in the worksheet where the output tables will appear. Choose the Line Fit Plots setting to compare the actual values and the predicted values.

The final check box is for **Normal Probability Plots**. You would add a check mark here to create a chart to plot normal probability. Leave this check box unselected. Click the OK Button to start the regression calculations and to place their upper left cell in column I, row 1, of your worksheet.

Figure 3-8

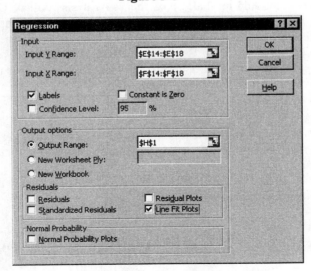

Once the Regression table and related chart appear, double-click the right edge of each table column to autofit the contents of the columns. Also, hold down [Alt], click and drag the bottom edge of the chart to the bottom of row 13, then release [Alt] and deselect the chart.

The output tables (see Figure 3-9) contain Regression Statistics, ANalysis Of VAriance (ANOVA) table, and Regression Coefficients. If selected, Residual Tables also are delivered. The Regression Coefficients are the values enabling you to construct the Regression line. For example, the Y-intercept of the regression you created is 54.94, and the gradient is 1.273. If you placed the following formula in cell G15, you would receive the predicted Student Grade for the age in cell F15:

=B42+F15*B43

You then could produce a set of values to construct a line plot of the predicted values. You could create the chart in a way described in the Tutorial for Spreadsheet Case 5. Excel's Regression Tool creates such a chart for you. If you selected the Line Fit Plots check box in the Regression dialog box, you would have a chart resembling the one in Figure 3-10.

You may save your worksheet, but you will not use the changes you made to Course.xls for the regression analysis in later cases.

Figure 3-9

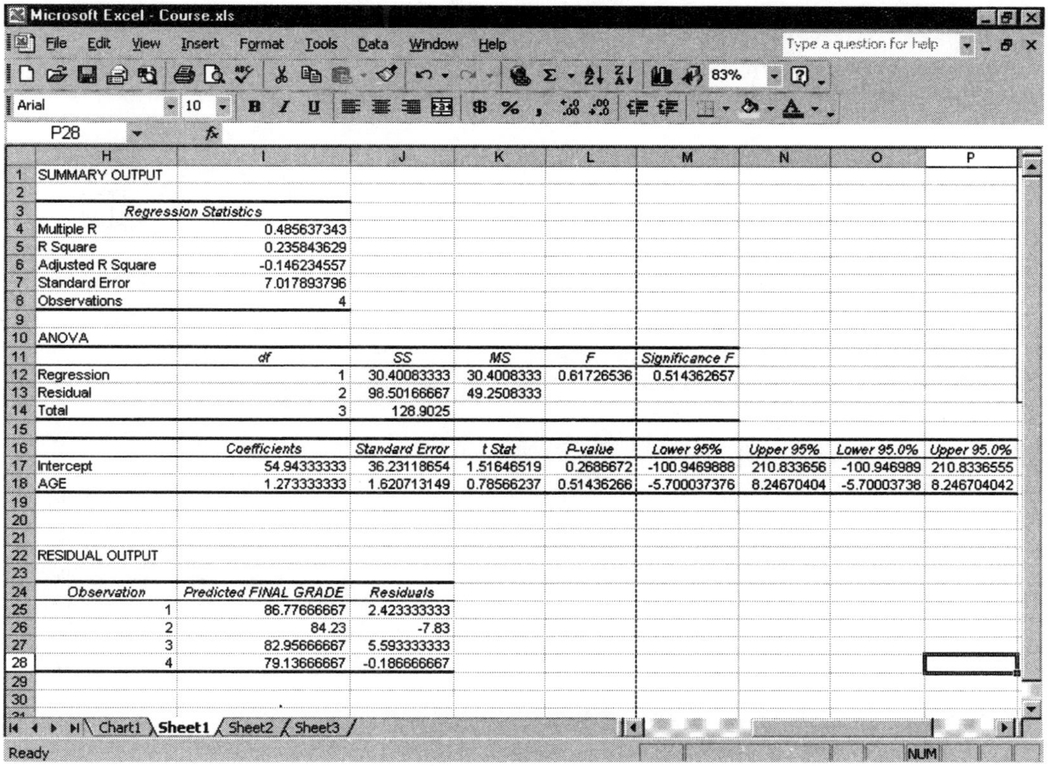

	H	I	J	K	L	M	N	O	P
1	SUMMARY OUTPUT								
2									
3	*Regression Statistics*								
4	Multiple R	0.485637343							
5	R Square	0.235843629							
6	Adjusted R Square	-0.146234557							
7	Standard Error	7.017893796							
8	Observations	4							
9									
10	ANOVA								
11		*df*	*SS*	*MS*	*F*	*Significance F*			
12	Regression	1	30.40083333	30.4008333	0.61726536	0.514362657			
13	Residual	2	98.50166667	49.2508333					
14	Total	3	128.9025						
15									
16		*Coefficients*	*Standard Error*	*t Stat*	*P-value*	*Lower 95%*	*Upper 95%*	*Lower 95.0%*	*Upper 95.0%*
17	Intercept	54.94333333	36.23118654	1.51646519	0.2686672	-100.9469888	210.833656	-100.946989	210.8336555
18	AGE	1.273333333	1.620713149	0.78566237	0.51436266	-5.700037376	8.24670404	-5.70003738	8.246704042
19									
20									
21									
22	RESIDUAL OUTPUT								
23									
24	*Observation*	*Predicted FINAL GRADE*	*Residuals*						
25	1	86.77666667	2.423333333						
26	2	84.23	-7.83						
27	3	82.95666667	5.593333333						
28	4	79.13666667	-0.186666667						
29									
30									

Solve it!

Figure 3-10

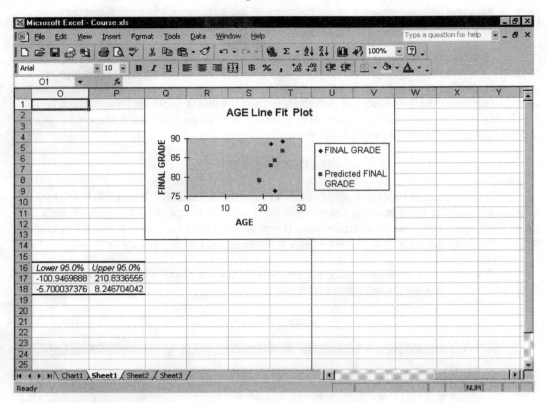

Spreadsheet Case 8

Martin Lumber Company

Problem:	Develop an accounts receivable system
Management skills:	Organize
	Control
PC skills:	Date functions
	Database querying
	Logical functions

File: MARTIN_Q.XLS

Martin Lumber Company has been a major wholesale and retail supplier of lumber and paneling for the Green Bay, WI, area since 1939. Its customers include contractors and local families. Martin employs 12 people, including an accountant, warehouse workers, and sales floor staff. Gross revenues total $8,000,000 annually.

Martin has remained essentially a family business. The original owners, Sam and Janet, have retired to The Oceans condominiums in East Palm Beach, FL. Their son, Michael, has taken over. Michael fears that the firm does not generate as much revenue as it should to pay his monthly salary and that of his staff. He suspects this is because too many bills are outstanding. His parents ran the business on a largely goodwill basis. They maintained some of their key accounting records manually, and they would remember who had not paid up. They shied away from calling late payers about their bills if they were "old timers."

In the past, Martin's suppliers were quite lenient about repayment. Now they are much more demanding of small firms, since their primary business is the large discount and home supply chains. The large manufacturers offer Michael a 2% discount for payment within 10 days. However, they have threatened to stop supplying him if he does not pay strictly within 30 days. Michael must collect his own bills faster to remain in a business dominated by giants.

Michael would like his accounts receivable organized and automated so he can easily locate late payers. Load the data file Martin_q.xls from your data diskette to see the outline of the accounts receivable file. It contains a sample of Martin's accounts receivable list as of April 1, 2002. Using the =DATE function, Michael would like to type in the date (today's date) whenever he accesses the file and then automatically calculate the days outstanding for each account. He also would like to produce an aging report that automatically classifies the records according to four aging categories of lateness: Current (30 days or less), 31-60 days, 61-90 days, and Over 90 days.

Michael would also like some reporting mechanism to identify late payers so that he can contact them and expedite reimbursement. He wants to sort the accounts receivable file first by largest number of days outstanding to smallest and then by highest invoice balance to lowest. He also would like to have a listing of customers more than 60 days late with outstanding balances.

Tasks

There are five tasks to this problem:

1. Calculate the number of days each invoice has been outstanding. This is the difference between the invoice date and today's date. Format the results with the General Category of numbers.

2. Classify the invoices using formulas into the four aging categories shown on the worksheet. (Hint: you can use logical functions to classify the invoices.) Design the formulas to display the invoice amounts, not the number of days outstanding, and to display a zero if no result belongs there. Display overall invoice totals in cell E36 and in the cell range G36:J36.

3. Sort the database in descending order using the number of days outstanding as the primary sort key and in descending order using the invoice amount as the secondary sort key. Print the sorted database (including the information you just provided on categories of lateness.)

4. Using the sorted database from Task 3, use the Filter command of your spreadsheet software to extract two reports. Output Range 1 should show the relevant information on customers who are more than 60 days late. Output Range 2 should show relevant information on customers more than 60 days late who also owe more than $400.

5. Print the two reports resulting from your Filter command task.

Note Well: For this problem you can use the =DATE function or the simplified date entry method, both of which are explained below. Whichever style you use, do so consistently throughout the problem; do not mix styles within your worksheets.

Time Estimates

Expert: 1 hour
Intermediate: 2 hours
Novice: 3 hours

Excel Tutorial for Spreadsheet Case 8

This case requires new skills utilizing Excel data management capabilities and date functions. You will need an earlier version of Course.xls for this tutorial. If you saved the file with the regression analysis data or the range name table, you should erase these parts of the worksheet.

Excel Date Functions

To determine how many days an account is overdue, you must be able to calculate the difference between today's date and the date of a customer's invoice. You can calculate the difference by using the =DATE function of Excel and by formatting the ranges involved in date calculations in **Date** format.

The =DATE function converts a date into a date number. Excel can represent any given date as a serial number equal to the number of days after December 31, 1899. For example, January 1, 1900 is serial number 1 because it is the first day after December 31, 1899. Likewise, January 1, 2000 is serial number 36526 because it is day 36,526 in the number sequence. (Excel supports two date systems: the "1900" and "1904" date systems. In Excel for Windows, the default date system is 1900. To change the default system, click **Tools/Options**, then click the Calculation tab in the Options dialog box. Select or clear the "1904 date system" check box as desired, then click OK to close the dialog box.) With the =DATE function, you can use dates and times in calculations like any other number in Excel.

The format of the =DATE function is:

=DATE(year number, month number, day number)

For practice purposes you will modify your sample spreadsheet to include data about due dates for students' library books. You then will calculate the number of days overdue by subtracting the date due for each student's books from today's date.

Create a new range for book due dates in F14:F18. The first row (F14) should contain the column label DUE DATE, and F15:F18 will contain date information for each student as follows:

James Jackson:	2/2/02
Steven Parker:	3/3/02
Andrew Reynolds:	4/11/02
Joyce Winters:	5/5/02

To enter this date for James Jackson using the =DATE function, enter in cell F15 the formula =DATE(02,2,2). F15 will display 2/2/02 since Excel automatically formats cells containing the DATE function. (The latest version of Excel also assumes that the digits "02" represent the year 2002, not 1902.)

Enter the due dates for the rest of the students using =DATE. In cell E20, enter the label REPORT DATE. In cell F20, enter the date of this student roster report (5/15/02) using =DATE. Using this date and the student book due dates, calculate the overdue days.

In range G15:G18, calculate the number of days each student's book is overdue. Enter a label for DAYS OVERDUE in G14. Perform the calculation by subtracting each student's due date from the report date. Since both dates are entered using the =DATE function, the formula for calculating DAYS OVERDUE for James Jackson is =F15-F20. Enter this formula into cell G15 and copy it to G16:G18. Be sure to format the cells in DAYS OVERDUE column with the General Category. Your worksheet should look like Figure 3-11.

Note Well: Excel also allows you to type in dates as if you were writing them out by hand. For example, you could enter James Jackson's date by typing "2/2/02" and then pressing [Enter]. This simplified entry method can be faster and easier than using the =DATE function. If you use this simplified method, use it consistently throughout your worksheet, especially in cells that you will calculate with other cells. In other words, do not mix the =DATE function with the simplified method. Also, remember to format any cells containing the simplified entry method by using the Date Category on the Number tab of the Format Cells dialog box. Using the =DATE function or the simplified entry method does not affect the design of your formulas.

Database Management with Excel

The student roster you have created in A14:G18 can be treated as a database, where data can be extracted, sorted, and analyzed. Consider each row with data about a student as one *record* in the database. Within each row, each cell represents a *field* of that record. The one-line headings at the top of each column, such as NAME or QUIZ, represent *field names*.

Figure 3-11

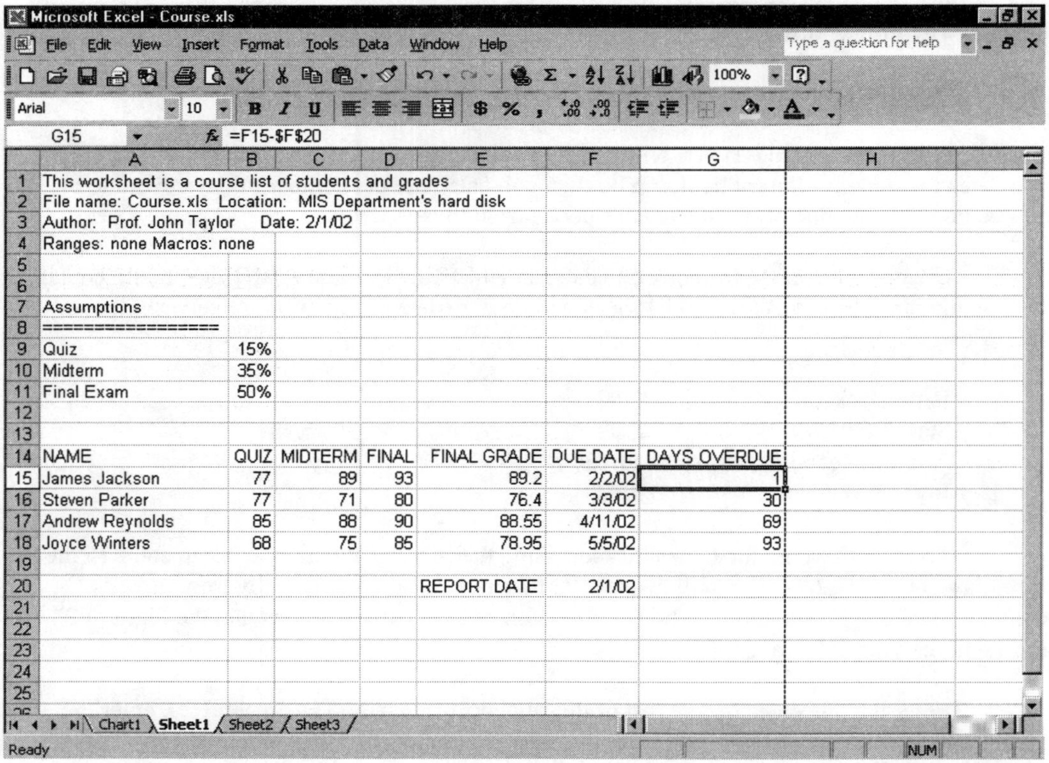

With Excel, you can treat any collection of data organized into records and fields as a database. Fields in an Excel database may contain either labels (such as the student names in our roster) or numeric data (such as the student grades).

You can use various data commands with an Excel database to sort its records in numeric or alphabetical order, or to find and list records that match criteria that you specify. Sort the student roster database and arrange it by number of days overdue in ascending order.

To sort, select the range A14:G18, which contains the data and the column headings. Click Data/Sort from the menu. The resulting dialog box shows three sort keys are available to rearrange the sequence of the database. These keys are known as the *primary, secondary*, and *tertiary* sort keys. The selected range now highlights the data only, excluding the headings. Excel has recognized that the selection has field names in the first row and has deselected the headings.

Each of the sort keys in the dialog box has a drop-down list of field names. By clicking the downward pointing arrow, the list will display. Select the DAYS OVERDUE field from the primary sort key at the top of dialog box, and then select Descending order for the sort. (We could select a secondary sort key to perform a second sort on records that have the same entries on the primary key. However, in our list of Students' Grades, there are no equal entries on DAYS OVERDUE.)

The setting at the bottom of the Sort dialog box asks whether the list includes or excludes a Header Row (containing field names). Specify that the selection (A14:G18) contains a Header Row. (If you specify that the list does not contain a header row, the heading row will be sorted with the data.)

To execute the sort, select the OK Button. Your course roster will then sort so that Joyce Winters, with 93 days overdue, will be first on the list and James Jackson, with 1 day overdue, will be last on the list. (See Figure 3-12).

Figure 3-12

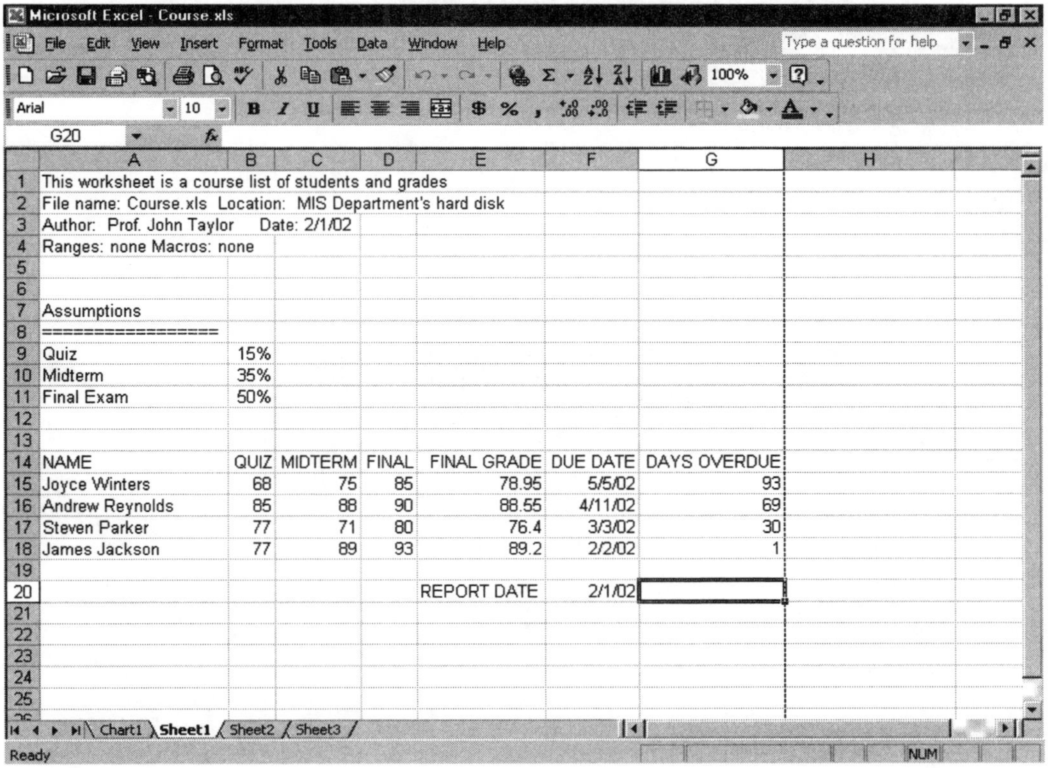

Filtering a Database

You can search a database for particular records, and copy or extract records from a database using the **Data/Filter/AutoFilter** or **Data/Filter/Advanced Filter** commands of Excel. For example, you can filter your student database to produce a list of all students whose books are more than 45 days overdue.

The **AutoFilter** and **Advanced Filter** do the same thing in different ways. An Excel Filter enables the user to dictate some criterion or criteria that will include some records and exclude others. **AutoFilter** performs the filter operation on the list at the same location. The **Advanced Filter** gives the user the option to filter on the same location as the list or to copy to a new location. The **Advanced Filter** also permits more complex criteria than the **AutoFilter**, although the **AutoFilter** satisfies most demands.

The **AutoFilter** is a simple but extremely effective tool to distil large amounts of data very quickly. To demonstrate its usefulness, highlight the database in the range A14:G18. Now select **Data/Filter/AutoFilter** from the menu. You will notice the AutoFilter drop-down arrow buttons next to each of the field names. These buttons are how the query is achieved. Press the drop-down arrow on the QUIZ field and your screen should look like Figure 3-13:

Figure 3-13

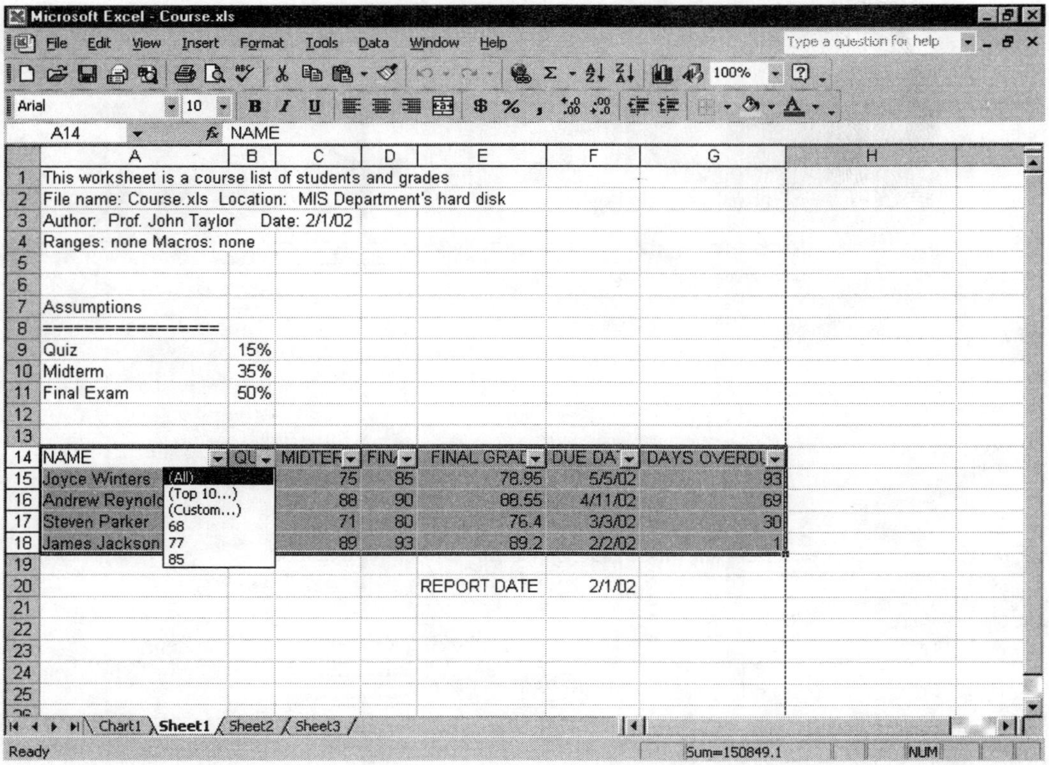

The **AutoFilter** drop-down menu contains items such as: (All), (Custom...), (Top 10), (Blanks), (NonBlanks), and an entry for each unique list entry:

- The **(All)** item displays all the records.
- The **(Custom...)** item lets you enter a criterion for the current field.
- The **(Top 10)** item displays all rows that fall between the upper and lower limits you specify.
- The **(Blanks)** item displays the blank records in this field only.
- The **(NonBlanks)** item displays all the records that are not blank.

These last two items appear in the AutoFilter menu only when the column you want to filter contains a blank cell. The remaining items are the entry items. Selecting one of these entries will display those records with that entry only. Select 77 from the QUIZ drop-down list and observe the effects. All entries other than those with 77 in the QUIZ field are hidden and the row numbers of the remaining entries are colored. Select (All) from the QUIZ drop-down menu to return to a full list.

Select the DAYS OVERDUE drop-down menu and select (Custom...) from the menu. The Custom AutoFilter dialog box permits one or two simple conditions connected with an OR or an AND. If the field being queried is text, the box for the first logical operator on the left should be an "equal to" or "=". For our purposes, select "is greater than or equal to" (">=") as the logical operator. Then type 45 in the value window to the right of this logical operator box to represent DAYS OVERDUE >= 45 (greater than or equal to) 45 days. Press the OK Button to execute the query. The list should have two records displayed now: Joyce Winters and Andrew Reynolds. If you wanted a separate permanent copy of the results of an AutoFilter query, you would have to copy them manually. To turn off the AutoFilter, select **Data/Filter/AutoFilter**.

The Advanced Filter permits more advanced criteria than the AutoFilter. It requires criteria in a separate location on the worksheet. This is best done by copying the field names from the original list so no typing error can creep in. Copy the headings to Row 23, directly below the list. Type >45 under the DAYS OVERDUE heading in the criteria. (You will have to erase or move further down the range name table you created in an earlier tutorial.)

Now select **Data/Filter/Advanced Filter**. In the Advanced Filter dialog box, select Copy to Another Location to provide a separate list for the result of the query. For this Action setting, the Copy to: window becomes active and requires a reference. Three references are required for this dialog box: the List Range, the Criteria Range and the Copy to Range. Select the ranges:

List Range	A14:G18
Criteria Range	A23:G24
Copy to Range	A27:G27

Now select the OK Button to execute the query. The resulting screen should look like Figure 3-14.

The **Criteria Range** setting in the Advanced Filter dialog box tells Excel which records to search for in the database. Your search criteria may include one or several fields in the database. The criteria range will have at least two rows: one for the heading and one for the selection criteria.

The first criteria row *must* be the field names of all of the fields that will be referred to in your search criteria. The second row of the criteria range is where the various selection criteria are entered. You must enter each criterion directly below the field name to which it applies. Criteria may be numbers, labels, or formulas. A criteria range can be two or more rows long.

Figure 3-14

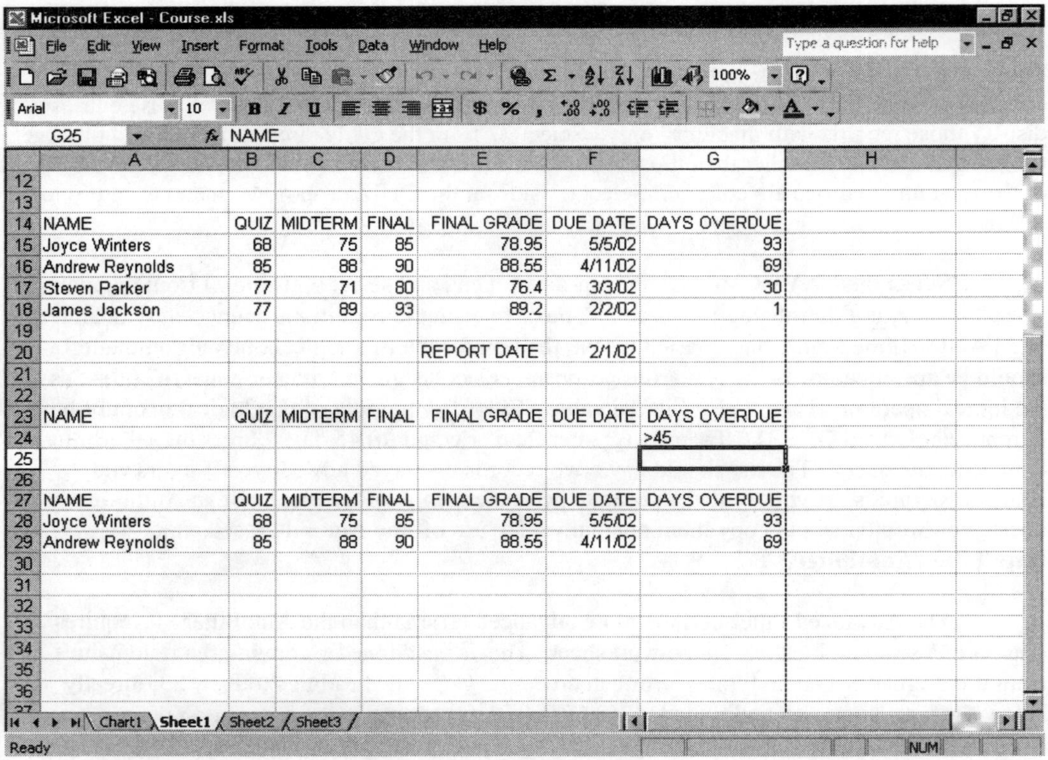

To search for exact matches of labels, enter the label used as a criterion exactly as it appears in the database. You can also search for similar, but not identical, label entries using special characters called *wildcards*. You can use wildcards in both Advanced Filter criteria and AutoFilter criteria:

- ? instructs Excel to accept any character in that specific position and can be used only for fields of the same length (for example, "b?t" matches "bit" or "bat" but not "beet").

- * instructs Excel to accept any and all characters that follow and can therefore be used for fields of unequal length (for example, "bat*" matches "batch" or "batter" but not "butter").

- The Copy to Range determines the destination of the extracted records and the field names are copied as well. This option is only active when the Copy To Another Location has been selected. The Copy to Range should be an unused area of the worksheet.

- Be sure to save Course.xls with the changes resulting from the Advanced Filter operation. You will need the revised file for the tutorial for Spreadsheet Case 10.

Spreadsheet Case 9

Western Industries

Problem: Develop a sensitivity analysis for capital budgeting

Management skills: Planning
                                      Deciding

PC skills: Data base creation
                                      Data table building
                                      Financial functions

File: WESTERN_Q.XLS

Western Industries of Tucson, AZ makes fasteners and metal parts for the automotive industry. To increase productivity and profits, the company has started investing in sophisticated machinery enabling it to design and make metal parts faster and with fewer defects. In keeping with the investment strategy, the company's production manager, John Esposito, wants to spend $550,000 for a new programmable machine tool. Esposito estimates that the new tool should increase the firm's after-tax income by $105,000 each year over five years by reducing production costs. At the end of five years, Esposito hopes to sell the tool for a total of $186,000. The sale price of the tool at the end of its useful life to the firm is the "salvage value."

Purchasing new, expensive equipment or upgrading plant facilities often requires substantial investment in order to produce future benefits. Such investments are "capital expenditures." The process of analyzing and selecting various proposals for capital expenditures is "capital budgeting." A capital expenditure is not worthwhile unless it produces at least the same rate of return on the investment as if the expenditure were invested at a certain rate of interest that the firm specifies. Businesses use several methods for evaluating the desirability of capital expenditures. One widely used method is the "net present value method."

You must compare the initial cost of the investment to the total cash flow from the investment. The total cash flow is the sum of the additional income produced by the investment plus the salvage value of the machine tool. You must discount the cash flow from the investment to account for the declining time value of money. A dollar earned ten years from now will not be worth one of today's dollars because you could invest today's dollar at a certain rate of interest. Ten years from now, you would have not only the dollar but also the interest income from the period. For instance, $1000 invested at a 7% interest rate, compounded monthly, would be worth $2010 at the end of 10 years.

To arrive at the return from the investment in today's dollars, first calculate the present value of the total cash flow from the new machine tool discounted at the prevailing interest rate for borrowing money. (This discount rate is the minimum return on the investment desired by the company.) Western wants a minimum return of 8% on its investment. Then subtract the initial purchase price of the tool in today's dollars from the present value of the total cash flow from the investment to arrive at the net present value of the investment. If the net present value for the investment is positive, it is a worthwhile investment. If it is negative, you should reject the investment.

Since investments vary greatly with changes in interest rates, Esposito wants to see whether the new machine tool makes a good investment under a wide range of situations. What if the interest rate and annual income from the new tool are lower (or higher) than original assumptions? He can perform a *sensitivity analysis* in a data table that shows how interest rate changes and annual income from the investment affect the net present value.

Tasks

There are five tasks in this case:

1.   Print out the data file Western_q.xls to see the assumptions for the problem and the basic outline of the template. In the table in rows 16 to 21, calculate the total additional income from the investment for the years 2003-2007.

2.   In cell B23, calculate the cumulative cash flow from the investment for 2003-2007. In cell B24, use the =NPV function to calculate the present value of this amount. (Hint: In the Function Arguments dialog box, the Rate equals the interest rate required by the firm. Value 1 equals cumulative cash flow from the investment. You do not need data in the Value 2 text box.) In cell B26, calculate the net present value of the investment by subtracting the cost of the investment from the present value.

3.   In cell B27, calculate the profitability index by dividing the present value of the cash flows by the cost of the investment. AutoFit the width of Column B to display all decimal places in the profitability index. The profitability index is another capital budgeting method that helps firms compare the profitability of different potential investments. (For instance, if the present value of the total cash flow from an investment was 24,000 and the initial cost of the investment was 22,500, the profitability index would be 1.066.) Using this method, firms can compare various capital investment projects and select those with the highest profitability indices. You should reject any investment with a profitability index of less than one.

4.   Develop a data table showing the impact of different interest rates and different annual additional incomes on the profitability index. In cell B29, type the formula =**B27**; copying and pasting the value of cell B27 (or typing in the decimal value by hand) will cause the data table to yield incorrect data. Second, enter the interest rates on the X axis (row 29). The interest rate should begin with a value of 6% and end with 12% in half percent increments. Third, enter the annual incomes from the investment on the Y axis (column B). The annual income should begin with $80,000 and end with $110,000 in $5000 increments. (Hint: Use the **Edit/ Fill/Series** command of your spreadsheet software to set up these values on the data table.) Finally, use the **Data/Table** command to open the Table dialog box, insert the appropriate values in the text boxes, then close the dialog box.

5.   Write a one-paragraph evaluation of the proposed investment. Should Esposito make the investment? Should he reject it at all costs? Are there are conditions under which it would be worthwhile? If so, what are they?

Additional Problem:

1.   What if annual income from the investment remained at $105,000, but the machine tool's salvage value varied in column B from $150,000 to $210,000 (in $10,000 increments)? How would this variation affect the net present value of the investment? To determine changes in net present value, create another data table using the same interest rate range used before, but the salvage value variations indicated above. (Hint: Be sure that the net present value placed just above the column B salvage values and just to the left of the interest rates equals cell B26; do not just type the dollar equivalent of B26 into that cell.)

Time Estimates

Expert: 45 minutes
Intermediate: 1.5 hours
Novice: 2 hours

Excel Tutorial for Spreadsheet Case 9

This case requires knowledge of the table-building features of spreadsheet software and the =NPV function of Excel. You do not need the Course.xls file for this tutorial.

Sensitivity analysis is the process of exploring various "what-if" situations in order to determine the impact of one or several variables on a model. Table-building automates the "what-if" process so that sensitivity analysis does not have to be performed manually. Instead of performing repeated "what-if" analyses, the Excel table-building function allows various values to be substituted for existing values in your worksheet. Excel then will generate a table to detail the results.

To demonstrate, create a new worksheet that calculates sales commissions. Save the worksheet as Case_9_Tutorial.xls. You want to see the impact on commissions on sales of $5000 when they are based on different percentage rates. In order to display fully the data table on your worksheet screen, we will not enter documentation into the first four rows.

Set up your worksheet so that the labels PERCENT, SALES, and COMMISSION appear right-justified in cells A1, B1 and C1, respectively, and the values for percent (5%) and sales ($5000) that we want to use in our calculation are in cells A2 and B2, respectively. In cell C2, place the formula, =A2*B2, for calculating the commission. In cell A5, type DATA TABLE 1. In cell A7, type Percent, and in cell B7, type Commission.

You could enter different percentages in the A column and then copy the formula for commission calculation to appropriate cells in the C column. However, you can also use the **Data/Table...** commands to perform this analysis automatically.

The Edit/Fill/Series Command

Before using these commands, you must enter the different percentage values in a column. Instead of entering each value individually, use the **Edit/Fill/Series** command. This command fills a range of cells with a series of numbers or dates that increase or decrease by a specified increment or decrement, or increase or decrease with a multiplicative growth factor.

First, in cell A9, type .05, but do not press [Enter] or [Tab]. Open the **Edit** menu, select the **Fill** item, and select **Series** in the submenu. In the Series dialog box, check the Series in Columns setting, and be sure that the Type is Linear. In the Step value text box, type .01. In the Stop value text box, type .10. Press [Enter] or click the OK button when finished.

Alternately, if you did not have a required Stop value but had a desired range for the series, you could select the range with the first cell containing the starting value and select **Edit/Fill/Series**. In the dialog box you would not specify a Stop value; instead, Excel would finish filling the series when it reached the end of the selection.

Data/Table Commands

After generating the column of interest rates in range A9:A14, you must enter either the formula for calculating commissions or the cell address from which to draw the formula. *This entry goes next to the column of percentages and one row above the first entry.* In cell B8, enter the formula =C2. (You could also have entered the formula for computing commission in cell B8.)

Select the range A8:B14, the range containing the percentage values, the formula, and the blank cell where the results will go. Next, select the **Table** item from the **Data** menu. The Table dialog box has two available settings: the Row input cell and the Column input cell. Since you are examining only the impact of changes in one variable—percentage—you will enter a cell reference in only one of these. The variable numbers you are examining are in a column, so you should enter the cell reference for the percentage variable. Enter the reference A2 in Column input cell and select the OK Button.

By entering only a single input cell reference in the dialog box, you are examining the impact of changes to one value in a formula. (If, instead, you had entered data in both the Row input cell and Column input cell, you would have shown the impact of changes to two values in a formula.) The results should look like Figure 3-15.

Now examine the impact on commissions if the sales amount, as well as the percentage, is variable. What happens when sales are $5000, $10,000, and $15,000? You would enter the values for our second variable (Sales) in the row just above the first entry of our first variable (Percentage). But, first, in cell D5, type DATA TABLE 2. In cell F7, type Sales. Then, in cell range E8:G8, enter the Sales values. In cell range D9:D14, copy and paste the Percentage values that appear in cell range A9:A14. *You also must enter the address of the formula (=C2) in the cell directly above the first entry of the first variable.* (In your tutorial file, this would be in D8.)

Figure 3-15

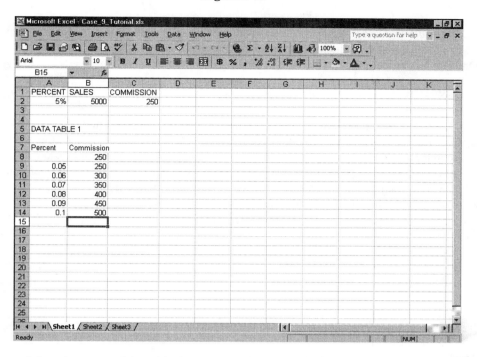

Select the range of the table (D8:G14) and then choose **Data/Table**. In the Table dialog box, choose cell reference B2 as the Row input cell and cell reference A2 as the Column input cell. Then select the OK Button. The two-dimensional data table should resemble Figure 3-16:

Figure 3-16

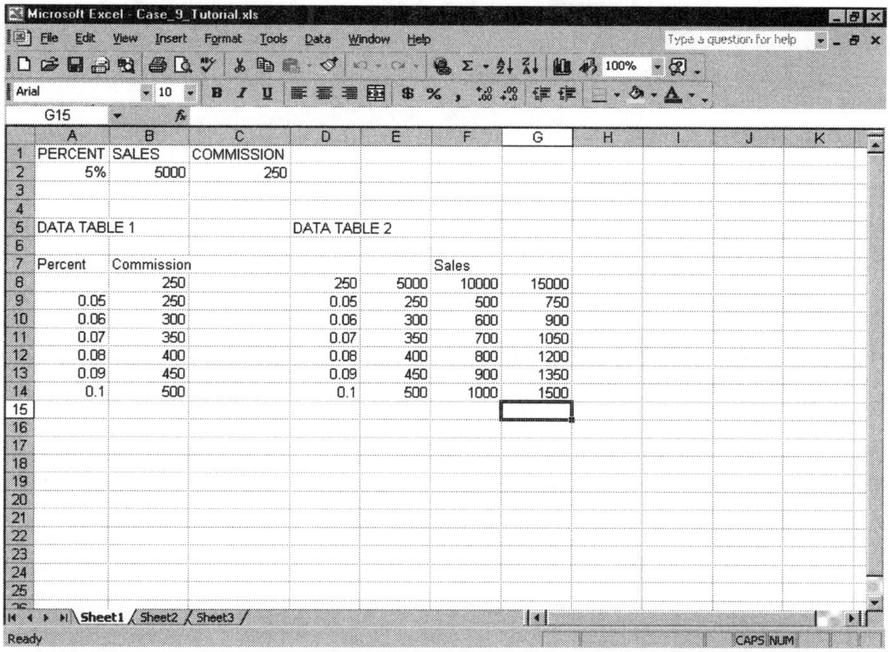

=NPV Function

Spreadsheet Case 9 requires that you compute the projected value of an investment in today's dollars. The **=NPV** function computes the present value of a stream of cash flows discounted at a fixed periodic interest rate. The form of this function is:

=NPV(*Discount Rate, Value1, Value2, ...*)

The discount rate is the interest rate, and the Values are the series of cash flows to be discounted. The interval between cash flows must be constant and must agree with the period of the discount rate. The Value parameters can be values in the formula, references to cells, and references to ranges of cells. Excel allows up to 29 Value parameters, although each can be several values in a range on the worksheet. Be aware that Excel takes the order of Value1, Value2, and so on, as the sequence of the cash flows.

Homework

Spreadsheet Case 10

Hellen Aerospace Products

Problem:	Develop a parts inventory scheduling system.
Management skills:	Controlling Deciding
PC skills:	Macro building Spreadsheet query and extract
File:	HELLEN_Q.XLS

Hellen Aerospace Products is a moderately sized aerospace company in the mid-Hudson River valley in New York. The company specializes in assembling small items into larger aircraft components and selling them to business airplane manufacturers. Marcus Hellen founded the company only 15 years ago.

Business grew steadily over the last few years, and scheduling both the supply and production sides of the business became more complex. Hellen's small amount of factory space limited the amount of inventory the company could keep on hand and restricted assembly operations to only one or two jobs at a time. Hellen had a hard time getting all of its vendors to ship items on a timely basis. Production job due dates also caused problems. For example, an order having a two-month deadline might take three months to complete.

With such uncertainty on both the supply and production sides, shipments in all areas of the aerospace industry sometimes go out late, with little or no penalty to the supplier. However, Hellen Aerospace knows that maintaining superior customer loyalty in such a competitive industry requires that the company minimize the number of late shipments.

Thankfully, the company has solved its basic problems on the production side of the business. Better worker training, more assembly space, and more efficient shipping services have enabled Hellen to deliver products at the quality level that its customers desire and on time. However, Hellen still has problems getting its vendors to deliver promptly and reliably the small items it needs. These delays make it hard to keep storage space needs and essential inventory as low as possible and have reduced profit margins.

Hellen's purchasing director, Althea Walker, recently started using spreadsheet software to track vendor inventory, inventory costs, and delivery performance. She laid out the worksheet, set up the fields and records that the company needs to track, and entered the main data about its vendors. However, Walker now needs you to complete the worksheet so that the company can identify the information related to the company's vendors.

Tasks

There are three tasks in this problem:

1.   Create a macro that sorts the entire spreadsheet in ascending order by Vendor Name, then in ascending order by Item No., and then in descending order by Cost per Order. Name the macro "VendorMacro". Design the macro with as few steps as possible to achieve the desired result. (Hint: Before creating any macros, delete row 1 containing the company name, then resave the file.)

2.   Create two additional macros. The first should sort the spreadsheet column "Days Overdue" in ascending order to indicate which shipments arrived quickest. Name the macro "FastMacro". The second should sort the same column in descending order to indicate the slowest shipments. Name the macro "SlowMacro". If instructed, include a secondary sort to organize Vendor Names alphabetically in ascending order in both macros.

3.   Write a one-paragraph summary that identifies the fastest supplier and slowest supplier. If instructed, also determine if your conclusion should change based on the additional factors of Item Cost and A/P (accounts payable) terms.

Time Estimates

Expert: 1 hour
Intermediate: 2 hours
Novice: 3 hours

Excel Tutorial for Spreadsheet Case 10

This case requires that you use Excel to build a *macro* to extract records from a spreadsheet to produce a report automatically, and to perform a sort on a list. A macro is, in essence, a collection of commands. The commands are contained in a module sheet that can be stored in a workbook. You can execute the macros through the **Tools/Macro** menu item or through a custom Toolbar button.

For this exercise you will need Course.xls with some of the changes you made during the Spreadsheet Case 8 tutorial session.

Current versions of Excel have an extensive macro language called Visual Basic. Several Microsoft applications can use this language. Excel allows macros to be recorded by transcribing a series of operations performed by users to the equivalent Visual Basic commands. The commands are stored in a module.

You can record a macro by accessing the command **Tools/Macro/Record New Macro** and naming the macro.

You can create a macro, for example, to automate the sorting of your student roster spreadsheet by number of days overdue in ascending order, the same task you performed during the tutorial for Spreadsheet Case 8.

To record an Excel macro, select the **Macro** command from the Tools menu. This opens a sub-menu with more choices. From this menu, select **Record New Macro** to open the Record Macro dialog box. The Macro name text-entry box is highlighted, with the default name "Macro" followed by a number. Type in the name "SortMacro" for the macro. The highlighted default name for the macro is automatically deleted and replaced with the new name you assigned. (Macro names cannot have any spaces or punctuation marks, and must begin with a letter. Otherwise, they can contain letters, numbers and underscores.)

Below the name box is a Description text box where you explain what your macro does. In this text box Excel automatically includes the recording date and the name of the spreadsheet's author. Type a period and a space after the descriptive information included there, then type a second sentence: "The SortMacro sorts the number of overdue days in ascending order." (See Figure 3-17.)

Figure 3-17

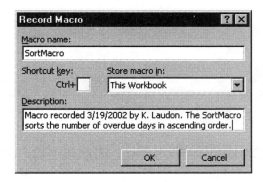

To start recording, click the OK button. (**Note Well**: At this point, be careful to include only those commands, keystrokes, and typing that are absolutely necessary to create the macro. Avoid mistakes, as Excel will include them in the macro if it is still recording.) To turn macro recording off, select **Tools/Macro/Stop Recording** from the menu. Excel will not record the Stop Recording command as part of the macro.

To automate the sorting of your student roster spreadsheet, record the following actions:

1) Select the range A14:G18.
2) Select **Data/Sort** from the menu.
3) Select the DAYS OVERDUE field as the primary sort key.
4) Select Ascending Order for the sort.
5) Makes sure that Header Row is selected.
6) Click the OK button to execute the sort.
7) To finish, select **Tools/Macro/Stop Recording**. (Notice that the macro has stopped recording.)

To test the macro, undo the changes you made while creating the macro. To run the macro, open the **Tools** menu, click on the **Macro** command and select **Macros** from the sub-menu. The Macro dialog box opens. Beneath the Macro/Name text box is a larger box listing all available macros. Click on your macro's name in this box. The name displays in the text box above, and the macro's description appears at the bottom of the dialog box. Then click the Run button.

If the macro runs correctly, the spreadsheet will sort in ascending order. For most purposes, recording a macro is the best way of creating macros and learning Visual Basic.

Viewing the Macro

You can view your macro commands by selecting **Tools/Macro/Macros**, then selecting the Edit option from the Macro dialog box. The Visual Basic module for the macro will appear and can be edited. The module for the macro to sort the student roster spreadsheet would look like Figure 3-18.

As you can see, modules have a non-tabular format, and lack the rows and columns typical of regular worksheets. Instead, data displays as lines of text against a white background.

Figure 3-18

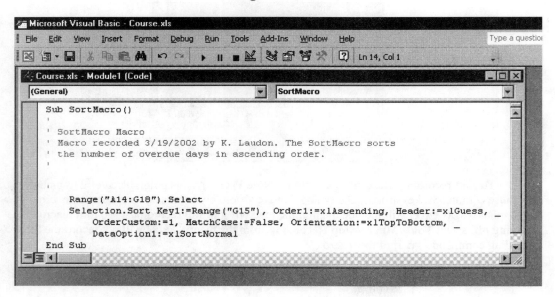

Managing Your Macros

To write and edit macros easily, you should become familiar with the Visual Basic Editor. By using this editor, you do not have to learn Visual Basic itself in order to make simple edits to your macros. The editor enables you to edit macros, copy macros, rename macros, and so on. Note also that recent versions of Excel have increased safeguards against computer viruses transmitted by macros. To set the level of security most appropriate for your spreadsheet activities, click **Tools/Macro/Security**, then choose the High, Medium, or Low option button as needed. Each option button includes a description of the level of security that the button provides.

To edit a macro, you first must set the security level to Medium or Low. To do the actual editing, click **Tools/Macro/Macros**. In the Macro name box, enter the name of the macro, then click Edit to display the editing window. In the editing window, make the desired changes, then click the Close button at the right end of the blue Title bar. To delete a macro, click **Tools/Macro/Macros**. In the Macros in list, click This Workbook. In the Macro name box, click the name of the macro to be deleted, then click Delete.

Troubleshooting Macros

When troubleshooting macros, you generally will come across one of three different problems. First, if you click the Refresh button, a message may display, telling you that your macro changes will be lost. (This message displays if you have edited a macro in the Visual Basic Editor and have changed the copy of your workbook in the Microsoft Script Editor.) In such cases, click No in the message box, switch to the Visual Basic Editor, and export any modules you have changed. Then, in your workbook in Microsoft Script Editor, click Refresh on the Refresh toolbar. Finally, click Yes, then import the desired modules to restore the changes to your macro.

Second, while recording a macro, you may accidentally record an undesired action. To delete that action, open the Visual Basic Editor, remove the unwanted steps, then click the Close button. Alternately, you can delete the defective macro, then re-record it with the correct steps.

Third, a recorded macro may display an error message in some situations, but not in others. (For example, a macro that looks for a certain column header will run properly if the column header is displayed, but malfunction if the header is not displayed, thereby displaying the error message.) In these inconsistent situations, write down the number of the error message. Then open Visual Basic Help, search for "error messages," and find information about the message number you received.

4

Introduction to Database Software

This edition of the *Solve it!* database cases was developed for Microsoft Access 2002.
Access 2000 users should consider using the previous version of *Solve it!*.

This chapter describes the elements of a computerized database and how to use database software. The name "database" sounds formidable, but all of us have used databases before.

Some examples of common manual databases we all use every day are a telephone book, an address book, and the catalog in a library.

In the business world some common manual databases are a list of customers and customer addresses, a list of suppliers, a list of products sold and their respective prices, a list of products in inventory, and a filing cabinet that contains invoices arranged in numerical or date order.

Figure 4-1

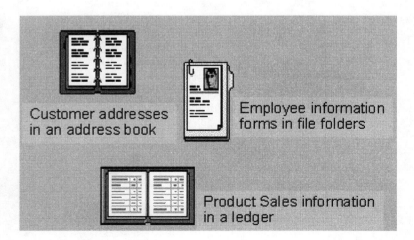

4.1   What is a Database?

These examples of common manual databases can help provide an initial definition of a database as any organized list or *file* of information pertaining to people, places, or things (see Figure 4-1).

For spreadsheet software the central metaphor is that of a matrix where quantitative information is organized in rows and columns, but in a database the central metaphor is that of a list or file where information is organized in rows (records) and columns.

Any problem in the real world that can be expressed as a problem of lists or files is potentially amenable to solution by a computerized database.

There are three basic types of databases: hierarchical, network, and relational. The student should consult a textbook for a detailed description of the various kinds of databases. Here we will describe only *relational databases*.

A simple example of a database file is a customer file:

Record #	Field 1 Last Name	Field 2 First Name	Field 3 Address
1			
2			
3			
...			

As you can see, in a database file all the information you have on an entry is called a *record*. Each record is composed of a number of *fields* that constitute the information stored on each entry. A collection of records is called a *file*. Below you will learn how to create a computerized database file. But modern database packages offer much more than just computerized files.

Two excellent Microsoft whitepapers on relational database basics and why businesses use databases can be downloaded from the World Wide Web at:

    ftp://www.mbs.unimelb.edu.au/pub/slides/solveit/dbback.ppt
    ftp:// www.mbs.unimelb.edu.au/pub/slides/solveit/whyuse.ppt

4.2   What is a Database Management System?

A database management system (DBMS) is a software package which, at a minimum, allows the user to create several different database files *and* relate information in one file to information in another file. Second, a modern DBMS provides a number of related tools needed to develop complete information systems.

One important advantage of *relational* database management systems over a manual filing cabinet is the ability to easily combine specific pieces of information *(fields)* from several different database files into a new file.

For instance, what if you wanted to determine a daily inventory which was calculated by deducting daily sales of all products from a beginning inventory?

Here, you would want to find out from the invoice file at the end of each day exactly which items were sold. You would then want to go to the inventory file and debit the existing inventory. In a truly sophisticated system you might want to go into a third file which contained the names and addresses of your suppliers and generate a purchase order and mailing label for those products where inventory was low.

In a manual record system stored in the traditional filing cabinet, a lengthy search process would be required to solve this problem. In a contemporary relational database management system, the job can be done in minutes.

A second feature of a relational DBMS is a set of powerful tools which can be used to develop a complete information management system. Included here are facilities to create and store memos and notes, data entry screens (forms in Access), reports, labels, and programs. These features are controlled through a powerful fourth generation language or menus which require little or no programming knowledge.

Briefly, a contemporary DBMS for the PC is a system development tool which permits the user to create complete management systems suitable for a small business or for an office within a large business organization.

4.3   Comparative Advantages of Database Packages

Once students learn a relational database package, they often find it more powerful and useful than spreadsheet packages. Yet the programs really have quite different strengths (and weaknesses).

Spreadsheet programs are very good at manipulating quantitative data, but they are poor at storing and manipulating lists or extracting parts of files from a larger data set. They generally are quite poor at combining information from several different files, and they typically have very limited macro or programming languages, although recent releases of popular spreadsheets defy this.

Database packages are very good at creating and manipulating lists of information, especially text information. Contemporary relational database packages all have very friendly, easy-to-learn, menu-driven command systems which permit the novice to accomplish many if not all of the program's functions.

In addition, relational database packages are accompanied by powerful fourth generation languages which are easy to learn and which permit intermediate users to build complete information systems suitable for a small business or an office within a larger business.

However, database software is comparatively weak at manipulating quantitative data. This gap is however rapidly closing with the advent of recent interactive Windows-based database products such as Microsoft Access.

To operate a contemporary business, both kinds of packages are needed. Data can be exchanged between the packages so that the most appropriate software is used.

4.4   Windows-based Databases

Database products developed for the graphical, Windows environment such as Borland's dBase for Windows, or Microsoft's Access for Windows utilize a user friendly, non-programming approach for many tasks which would have required programming in DOS-based (ie: non-Windows) database packages. For Access users, none of the cases in this edition of *Solve it!* will require explicit programming (although plenty of code will be generated in background).

4.5   Introducing Microsoft Access for Windows

An Access database is represented as a collection of objects. One .MDB file encloses all the tables, queries, forms, reports and other objects associated with a particular database. A brief description of these objects, the relationships between them within the database envelope, and the graphical buttons that identify them is shown in Figure 4-2

Figure 4-2

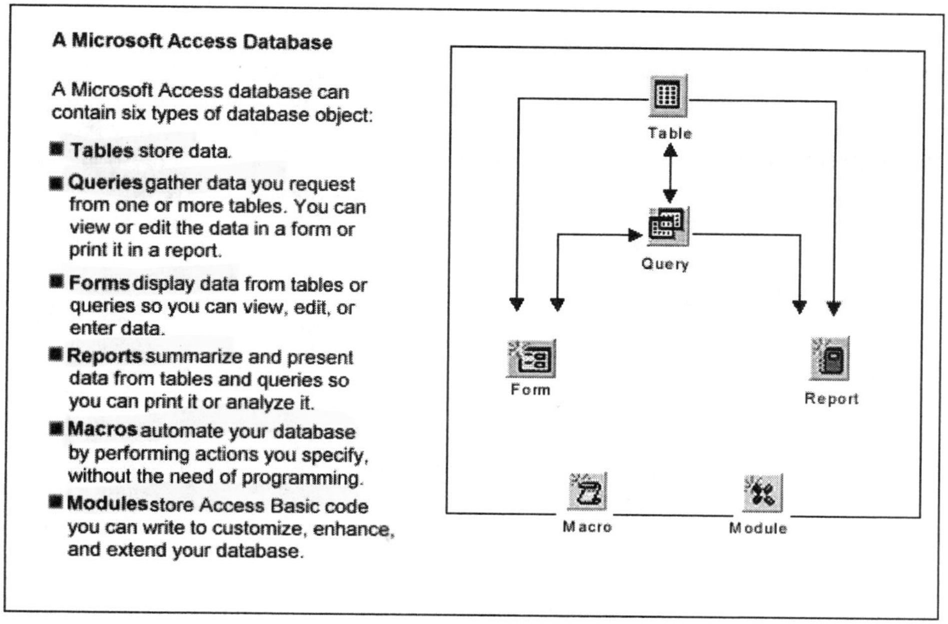

A Microsoft Access Database

A Microsoft Access database can contain six types of database object:

■ **Tables** store data.

■ **Queries** gather data you request from one or more tables. You can view or edit the data in a form or print it in a report.

■ **Forms** display data from tables or queries so you can view, edit, or enter data.

■ **Reports** summarize and present data from tables and queries so you can print it or analyze it.

■ **Macros** automate your database by performing actions you specify, without the need of programming.

■ **Modules** store Access Basic code you can write to customize, enhance, and extend your database.

Table

Query

Form

Report

Macro

Module

Access object names are not subject to DOS file-naming conventions which limit file names to 8 characters. Access object names (and field names in tables) can be up 64 characters in length, and can include spaces as well as a mixture of upper and lowercase letters. Access is also not case sensitive, and will find data within a field (as long as the spelling is correct!) regardless of the case used to originally enter it.

Toolbar Buttons

Access makes extensive use of Toolbar buttons. Each object view in Access has one or more toolbars associated with it by default. A segment of the Table object toolbar is shown above. The buttons on these toolbars provide shortcuts to menu commands, enabling the user to carry out frequently performed tasks at the click of a button. Another nice feature is that as the mouse pointer is positioned over a toolbar button, Access will display a short label describing the button's purpose.

Press the F1 function key and from the INDEX, type in the word *toolbar* for more information about using toolbars.

Get Help At Any Time!

The Office Assistant is a feature included with Access and other Office applications which provides tips, and attempts to interpret the help information you may need based on your current actions.

Access 2002 also includes two other interactive help tools: an extensive context sensitive help system (press the Shift + F1 key anywhere, at any time and click), and a series of Wizards that offer help in creating Access objects such as tables, queries, forms, reports and macros. Unlike the main help system, which you need to search or browse to find answers to questions, wizards ask you relevant questions and actually create a customised version of the object in question according to your responses. A summary of the wizards used in this edition of *Solve it!* is presented in Figure 4-3 below.

Figure 4-3

Table Wizard	walks the user through table setup and design. Users can choose from dozens of predefined sample tables, and hundreds of sample fields which can then be used to generate tables.
Query Wizard	helps users construct complex queries for common database management tasks such as the merging two tables or performing crosstabulations
Form Wizard	a tool for creating forms in a variety of predefined formats and presentation styles
Report Wizard	a tool for creating reports in a variety of predefined formats and presentation styles
Macro Wizard	a tool used for creating or editing a macro from within an event procedure in a form or report
Control Wizard	creates code behind command buttons, option groups, list and combo boxes used in forms or reports

Access Setup Requirements

To use Access 2002 you will need:

- a personal computer with Pentium 133-MHz or faster processor
- available hard-disk space usage will vary depending on configuration and operating system (245 MB recommended minimum for Office XP Professional)
- 64 MB of RAM
- a Microsoft mouse or compatible pointing device
  Operating Systems:
- Microsoft Windows NT (Server or Workstation) version 4.0 with Service Pack 6, Microsoft Windows 98, Microsoft Windows 98 Second Edition, Microsoft Windows 2000, Microsoft Windows Millennium Edition, Microsoft Windows XP

Terminology and Conventions Used in the Access Tutorials:

- *Double-click* means to press the left mouse button twice in rapid succession.
- *Click* means to press the left mouse button once only.
- *Right-click* means to click the right mouse button once.

- New terms, new filenames, key concepts and action words appear in *italics*.
- Menu choices and new object names are shown in capitals (eg: FILE/SAVE or FRIENDS.MDB).
- Toolbar buttons are shown next to or within the paragraph in which they are first described.

4.6   Getting Started - Access 2002 for Windows

To Start Access 2002

1.   From Windows , click on the *Start* button at bottom left of the screen, and then select the *Programs* option.

2.   Within Programs, select the *Microsoft Access* option. This last action will load the Access program.

Creating a Database in Access 2002

Practice: *Create a new Access database called CONTACTS.*

1.   Click *Blank Database* on the *New File* task pane. Access displays the New Database dialog box. (If the New File task pane is not visible, click the *New Database* toolbar button ⬜ or select FILE/NEW DATABASE from the menu to display it.)

2.   In the File Name box, type a name for your database (eg: CONTACTS) after selecting the appropriate path (eg: a:\CONTACTS). Click OK. Access creates a new database file, and opens the *Database Window* (see Figure 4-4).

Figure 4-4

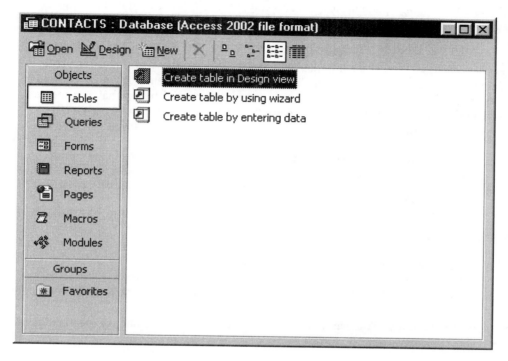

Building a Database Structure

Access allows you to create a structure for storing your data in three different ways:

- by *creating Tables*, and entering data into the table structure
- by *Importing Data* from another application or database file
- by *Linking Data* from an application other than Access

Access 2002 Data Sources

Access 2002 allows exporting, importing or linking from a number of different formats, as well as other Access databases (version 2.0, 7.0/95, 8.0/97, 9.0/2000, 10.0/2002). These include:

- fixed width text files
- a dBase III, III+, IV, and 5 files
- Microsoft Excel spreadsheet 3.0, 4.0, 5.0, 7.0/95, 8.0/97, and 9.0/2000
- Paradox and Paradox for Windows files
- Btrieve tables
- SQL tables, Microsoft Visual FoxPro, and data from other programs and databases that support the ODBC protocol
- Lotus 1-2-3 files

If you have data in dBase or Paradox databases, and you want to leave your data in its original format, choose the *Linking* option in Access. This way, files can still be used in their original application. If you plan to use your data only in Access from now on, you should choose the *Import Data* function.

Importing data creates a copy of the information in a new table in your Access database. The original source table or file is not altered in this process. *Linking data* enables you to read and in most cases update data in the external data source without importing. The external data source's format is not altered so that you can continue to use the file with the program that originally created it, but you can add, delete, or edit its data using Microsoft Access as well.

Access uses different icons to represent linked tables and tables that are stored in the current database. If you delete the icon for a linked table, you delete the link to the table, not the external table itself.

Creating Tables in Access

You can create tables in two different ways:

- via the *Table Wizard*. The Table Wizard is the easiest way and most common way of creating tables
- create one from scratch. You may want to do this if you plan to store unusual information in your table

---

Tip: To return directly to the Database Window at any time, click the [icon] button on the toolbar or press the F11 key.

To create a Table using a Wizard/Adding Records

1.   From an open Database Window, click the *Tables* button [Tables] in the Database Window.

2.   Double-click the *Create table by using wizard* option (you could also click the New button and then select *Table Wizard* in the *New Table* dialog box). The Table Wizard presents a listing of sample table templates which are already set up with fields. Toggle between the Business and Personal radio buttons to get a flavour of the type of tables the Table wizard can automatically create for you. The Table Wizard works as a series of dialog boxes. Follow the instructions to create a table to suit your purpose.

Practice: Create a simple table within the CONTACTS database using the Table Wizard. The scenario is as follows. You are a Phd student who has collected a number of business cards as a result of attending conferences and visiting organizations in the course of your research. On the back of each business card, you have made rough notes about where and when you met the person in question, and what you talked about. You would like to compile a simple database of professional contacts who you think may be useful people to know.

The fields you might need in your table could include:

First Name	State	Last Meeting Date
Last Name	Zip	Action Items
Organization Name	Work Phone	Notes
Address	Fax Number	

Create this table now. (Hint: use the Contacts table sample under the Business listing in the wizard. Call your new table Contacts). Add five new records to your new table by following the instructions provided in the Access Tutorial for database Case 1 in Chapter 5 of Solve it!

To Create a Table from Scratch/Adding Records

1. From the Database Window, click the *Table* button [🔲 Tables] .

2. Double-click the *Create table in Design view* option. Access will open the new table in table design view. Create fields for your table (refer Access Tutorial in database Case 1 for details on how to do this). Save your table by selecting FILE/SAVE from the menu, or clicking on the *Save* toolbar button. Add records to your new table following the instructions provided in the Access Tutorial for database Case 1.

Access Field Data Types

A data type defines the type and range of values you can enter in a field. For example, Access will not allow you to enter text in a field which is set to a Currency data type. Access 2002 includes the following data types:

Text	Use for text, or combinations of text and numbers, (such as an address), or for numbers you don't intend to perform calculations on (such as phone numbers or part numbers)
Memo	Use for longer text, such as notes and comments
Number	Use for data you might want to perform calculations on, unless it's money
Date/Time	Use for dates and times
Currency	Use for large numbers requiring rapid calculation, or for numbers that require highly accurate rounding, such as money
AutoNumber	Use to automatically assign consecutive or unique values, such as invoice

numbers

Yes/No   Use for true/false, yes/no, or on/off values

OLE Object   Use for graphical objects such as pictures and charts, and for Excel spreadsheets

Hyperlink   Use to store text or combinations of text and numbers as a hyperlink address. This is typically used for connection to data stored on the public World Wide Web or a firm's internal Intranet.

Lookup Wizard   Use to create a field that allows selection of a value from another Access table or from a list of values.

Note: If you change the data type of a field that contains data, you may lose some data. If you attach tables from an external application rather than importing them, Access will not allow you to change the data types.

To set or change the data type of a field:

1.   In Table design view, click the Data Type box
2.   Click the ▼ button to the right of the box
3.   From the drop down list that appears, select a data type

---

Tip: Access object (tables, queries, reports, forms, etc) names, are not restricted by the usual 8 character DOS file-naming rule. Names can be up to 64 characters long and can include spaces between words. After attaching or importing a table, you can rename your new Access table with a more expressive title.

Modify a Table Structure

After you create a Table with the Table Wizard or import or attach a file from an external application, you may want to change its structure by adding or deleting fields, setting primary keys, creating indexes to speed up data searches, or setting field or table properties to determine the types of data stored in the table and their method of storage.

Modifications of this nature are done in table design view. Click the *Table Design* button on the toolbar to change to this view. The Access tutorial for Case 1 contains instructions for working in Table design view. We will be looking at creating primary keys in the next section of this tutorial, and at other table structure modifications in later *Solve it!* tutorials.

Setting a Primary Key

Access uses a unique tag called a *primary key* to identify each record in a table. As a licence plate is unique to car, or a fingerprint is unique to an individual, the primary key uniquely identifies each record. Every table should have at least one primary key. Not all fields are good candidates for primary keys. For instance, if you chose a LastName field as a primary key, your table would not be able to contain two records with the LastName "Jones." Some number fields make good primary keys. For example, an Employee ID number would uniquely identify each record in an Employee table.

To set a Primary Key:

Figure 4-5

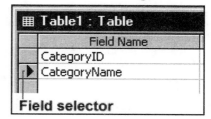

1.   In *Table Design* view ✎ click the *field selector* (refer Figure 4-5) for the intended primary key field. (If you need more than one primary key, select the wanted fields by holding down your Ctrl key as you click on the field selectors).

2.   Click the Primary Key button 🔑 on the toolbar. (A key symbol will appear on the field selector of every primary key field you highlight).

> **Note:** If you attempt to save a new table without creating a primary key, Access will prompt you to create one.

Creating Relationships Between Tables

Once you have created or attached or imported the tables that you want in your database, it's a good idea to establish relationships between them. You create relationships so you can view data from more than one table in the same report or form. (To create a relationship, you will need to have at least two tables in your database).

To Create Relationships:

1. From the Database Window, click the *Relationships* button ⊞ on the toolbar. Access displays the Relationships window. If you are creating relationships for the first time, Access will display the Show Table dialog box. If this does not occur, click the Show Table button on the toolbar. In the Table/Query box, double click on the table or query you want, and Access will add the table to the Relationships window. Click Close.

2. Click a field in the first table. This will usually be the primary key (always displayed in bold). Hold down the left mouse button, and drag the field to a field containing the same type of data in another table. Access displays the Relationships dialog box with the field names filled in. Click the Create button in the Edit Relationships dialog box, and Access draws a line to join the two related tables (see for example, Figure 4-6).

Figure 4-6

Related Tables

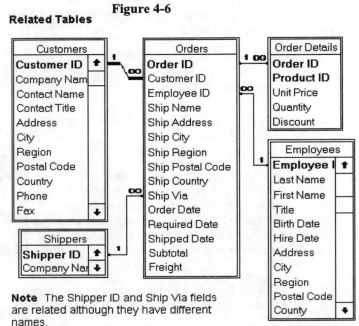

Note The Shipper ID and Ship Via fields are related although they have different names.

Note that relationships between tables can also be created at query design level. We will be doing this in a later tutorial.

Exiting Access

To exit Access, press the F11 key to return to the database window, and then select FILE/EXIT from the menu.

5

Database Management Software Cases

Database Case 1

Hanover Refinishing Supplies Inc.

Problem:	Create and modify a sales support system.
Management Skill:	Organize
Access Skill:	Data Table Setup Data Input and Editing Selecting Data Subsets Printing
Data Table:	HANOVER **[For download instructions see last page of book]**

Sullivan Blackburn had always been competitive. As long as she could remember there was always something to strive for: better grades, faster times in her long distance running and outdoing her two brothers. It therefore gave her great satisfaction to learn last week that she was "Salesperson of the Year". She had sold more abrasives, grinding wheels, and sandpaper last year than any of the other 120 sales staff at Hanover Refinishing Supplies.

Hanover Refinishing Supplies was founded in Wisconsin after the First World War. The founders recognized the growing need by metal and wood manufacturers for various abrasives and other finishing supplies to complete their products. The business had performed solidly between the World Wars and grew especially fast after the Second World War, particularly during the 1980's when capital equipment expenditures boomed. Although growth was curtailed by the economic downturn of the late 80's and early 90's, by the late 1990's Hanover was again experiencing growth as the economic situation eased.

Recent advances in computer controlled machinery, along with robotics and flexible manufacturing systems, provided a strong growth period for Hanover. The new machines required large quantities of high quality abrasives, particularly sandpaper belts. These expensive machine tools were used on a 24-hour basis. To minimize downtime and maintain high quality, sandpapers were changed frequently, often before wearing out.

Although very profitable, the abrasive supply industry had become very competitive. Hanover had many competitors who undercut them on particular items, but only 3M had as large a range of products. Hanover follows a high product quality and premium pricing strategy based on excellent customer service. Hanover's competitive advantage lies in three areas:

- a comprehensive product range
- a hard working and knowledgeable sales force
- guaranteed overnight delivery for stock items

Sullivan has been very successful in presenting Hanover to her customers as a provider of a full range of abrasive and refinishing supplies. Rather than approach new companies she has concentrated on increasing the average purchase of existing clients.

In the five years Sullivan Blackburn has been with Hanover, her rise to success has been rapid. It seemed only yesterday that she started out as a trainee sales representative with old Steven "the gentleman" Randolph. Steven preached that there were only two important things in sales: *"get close to the customer and know the products inside-out."*

Sullivan kept her client information in a large ledger stored alphabetically by the client's company name. She now had over 200 companies in her territory of Michigan, Indiana, Illinois, Wisconsin, and Minnesota.

Within each company, she called on an average of four different groups of people in purchasing, engineering, production and the workshop. So she had nearly 800 names, in addition to details on the products they ordered and all sorts of other useful information. Sullivan often asked about the client's wife or husband by name and always knew the pattern of the last few orders. If the orders were decreasing she asked why and found out if one of her competitors had met the client's needs more fully.

Sullivan's ledger was becoming too heavy to carry, and she was constantly trying to find information that was in the ledger but was not easily accessible. For example, last month a new low cost sandpaper belt for soft woods was introduced. Sullivan wanted to know which of her clients ordered the product it superseded. Then she could write or call on all those clients and demonstrate the new product. To find that information in her ledger would have taken a week of searching. So she relied on her memory, yet felt sure that she had overlooked some major users.

Sullivan had tried asking Hanover's overworked Information Systems department to get the information for her from past invoices, but the IS Manager replied *"we'd love to, but we can't even finish our own work and anyway I don't think it's possible. You'd be better off putting it on a Notebook computer and using a Windows-based database package like Access or Paradox. It will be much more flexible than our system, cheaper, and also portable."*

One of the perks of winning the "Salesperson of the Year" award was a new ideas budget of $25,000, which Sullivan has decided to devote to her new Sales Support System. Sullivan has purchased a Pentium-based notebook computer and a Windows-based database package. She wants you to prepare a prototype system.

Sullivan wants all of the important data to be entered into the database so she can look up information in many different ways, even while on the road. Then at night in her hotel room, she can update the database after visiting clients. Sullivan feels certain the new system will enable her to keep improving her performance and maybe even win her "Salesperson of the Year" again.

The important fields for the prototype system are:

Company Name	Client Name	Spouse Name
Address	Department	Order Pattern
City	Title	CompanyID
State	Last Order Date	
Zip	Product Group	

Hanover's products are classified into three major groups: grinding wheels (G), sandpaper (S), other Refinishing Supplies (O). Within each group are up to 99 subgroups, i.e. S01 to S99. Order patterns are coded as either: increasing (I), decreasing (D), or stable (S). Each client company is assigned an identification number that is five digits long.

A portion of Sullivan's database has been started for you in the table HANOVER in SOLVEIT.MDB. Create a new Access database and import this object now.

Tasks: There are seven tasks in this case:

1.   Complete the table structure to include the information desired by Sullivan.

2.   (a) Enter data for the new fields to complete the existing records. (b) Enter data for three new clients into the data table.

3.   Brian Pearson, the Production Manager for Rotary Wings in Green Bay, Wisconsin, has retired and has been replaced by Sam Jackson. Sam's wife's name is Gina, and he will now be known as the Engineering Director. Update the data in the table to reflect these changes.

4.   Print a listing of the entire table.

5.   Print all of the records in the table but only include the following fields: Company, City, Client, Last Order Date.

6.   Sullivan is traveling to Green Bay to meet Sam Jackson at Rotary Wings and wants to know her other clients in Green Bay. Create a query and then print a listing of all clients based in Green Bay. The list should only include the fields: Company, Client and Title.

*7.   After using the client database for three months, Sullivan reports tremendous savings in time and is able to do her job better. However, Sullivan has found the database does not handle customers that buy from more than one product group. For example, 3M purchases products from the G10, S20, S35, S40, S30, O50 and O70 product groups. Find a way to incorporate this extra information into the database.

Time Estimates (excluding unstructured * problem):

Expert:	30 minutes
Intermediate:	1 hour
Novice:	1.5 hours

Tutorial for Case 1 Using Access 2002

In order to learn the skills needed for this case and those following, you will need to use the practice database CONTACTS.MDB created in Chapter 4. If you did not create this database, use the sample database FRIENDS.MDB provided on your *Solve it!* disk, which has a similar structure. The FRIENDS.MDB database will be used for most of the Access tutorials in *Solve It!*

Remember that:
Double-click means to press the left mouse button twice in rapid succession.
Click means to press the left mouse button once only.

In order to complete the skills in this case and those following, you can also:

1. Create a new empty database named FRIENDS.MDB. The instructions on how to do this appear in Chapter 4.

2. Import the FRIENDS table object provided in the FRIENDS.MDB database on your *Solve it!* disk. The instructions on how to do this also appear in Chapter 4. The FRIENDS.MDB database will be used for most of the tutorials in Solve it! This tutorial and those following assumes this database has been created.

Remember that:
You can use the *Office Assistant* (click the [?] button on the Database toolbar) at any time to provide assistance with most Access procedures.

To start Access:

1. Enter the Windows environment and click START to open the Start menu. Point to PROGRAMS, then MICROSOFT ACCESS on the submenu. If you are having difficulties, ask your instructor for assistance.

2. Click to launch the Access program.

3. Click the Open button [icon] on the Database toolbar, or open the FILE menu and select the OPEN command to access the OPEN dialog box.

4. Use the **Look in** list box to locate the drive and folder containing the FRIENDS.MDB database. Select it and click [Open]. The FRIENDS database window will display as shown in Figure 5-1.

Figure 5-1:

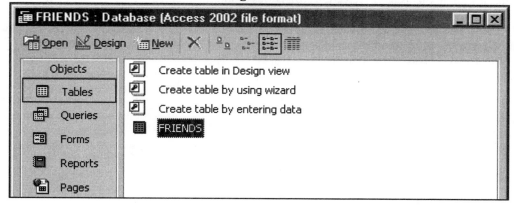

5.   Double-click the FRIENDS Table object highlighted in the Database window, to open the table and display the default Datasheet view. Refer to Figure 5-2.

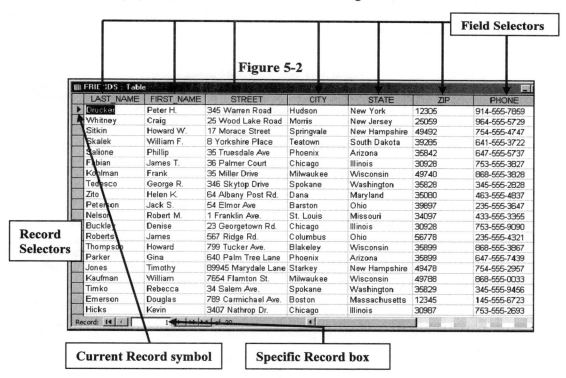

A short explanation for each of the object types shown in the Database window is provided in Chapter 4.

Access displays table data in columns and rows, similar to a spreadsheet. Each row in an Access table represents a *record*, and each column represents a *field*. For example, in Figure 5-2 there are 20 records in the FRIENDS table and the *Specific Record* box indicates that record 1 is currently selected. Above the rows of records are the *field selectors,* which contain the field names for each column. Fields describe various categories of information (e.g.: Last_Name, First_Name) that make up each record. To the left of each record are the *record selectors*, which are used to select a particular record and which contain symbols to indicate (a) the current record, (b) a record that is being edited, (c) a new record that you can enter data into, and (d) a record that you can't edit because it is locked by another user.

Tables can be displayed in two ways. Figure 5-2 shows the default Datasheet view, represented by the following toolbar button: Datasheets are used to display, edit, and delete records and to print tables. Later in this tutorial, we will also be using Table Design view, represented by the following toolbar button: Design view is used for adding, editing, and deleting fields and for defining field properties and indexes.

Navigating within a Datasheet

Use your *Tab* key or click with your mouse to move to a particular column within a record. Use the horizontal or vertical scroll bars to practice viewing records and fields in the datasheet. Use the Specific Record box and the navigation buttons shown in Figure 5-3 to move to a specific record in the datasheet.

Figure 5-3:

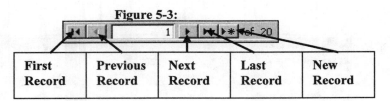

| First Record | Previous Record | Next Record | Last Record | New Record |

Resizing Columns and Rows in an Access Datasheet

To resize a column (field), position your mouse on the right edge of a column at the field selector level, (e.g.: LastName). When a horizontal resizing pointer displays as shown in Figure 5-4, drag until the column is the desired size. Double-click the right edge of any column heading to automatically resize the width to display all data in the column. You can also open the FORMAT menu and click the COLUMN WIDTH command to open the Column Width dialog box. Click BEST FIT to size the column so that all data in the column displays, or enter a specific width in the Column Width box.

Record rows can be resized by positioning the mouse pointer between any two record selectors at the left side of the datasheet. When a vertical resizing pointer displays as shown in Figure 5-4, drag either up or down until the rows are the desired size. *Warning: unlike column resizing, this will resize all of the rows.*

Figure 5-4

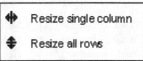

Resize single column

Resize all rows

Saving Datasheet Layout Changes

Open the FILE menu and click the SAVE command or click 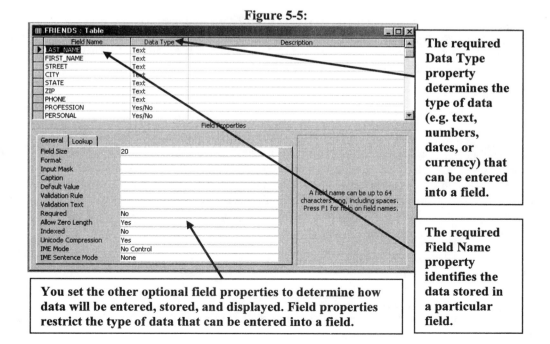 on the Table Datasheet toolbar.

Printing a Datasheet

With the table open in Datasheet view, open the FILE menu and choose the PRINT command. This action will open the Print dialog box. If you have selected only certain records for printing, click the *Selected Records* option button in the *Print Range* section of the dialog box and click OK. You can also choose the number of copies to print in the *Copies* section. To print the whole table, click the Print button on the Table Datasheet toolbar.

How to Change the Structure of an Access Table

Open the VIEW menu and click the DESIGN VIEW command, or click the Design View button to display the structure of the table. See Figure 5-5.

Table Design view is used for establishing and modifying the field structure of a table. As you move around this window, a help box on the right side of the Field Properties pane in the bottom half of the window describes the purpose for each of the properties. For example, the required Data Type property is used to determine the kinds of values that can be entered and stored in a field. Let's add a new field called TITLE to the table in order to store titles such as *Mrs., Ms., Mr.,* and *Dr.*

Figure 5-5:

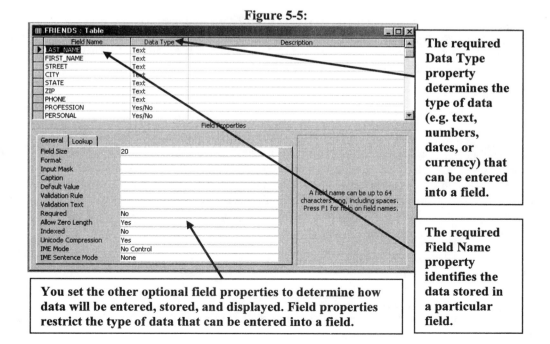

The required Data Type property determines the type of data (e.g. text, numbers, dates, or currency) that can be entered into a field.

The required Field Name property identifies the data stored in a particular field.

You set the other optional field properties to determine how data will be entered, stored, and displayed. Field properties restrict the type of data that can be entered into a field.

1. The Title field needs to be added before the Last_Name field. Position your mouse pointer on the *row selector* for the Last_Name field and click once to select the field and display the current field symbol (refer to Figure 5-5) Open the INSERT menu and choose the ROWS command or click the Insert Rows button ⊞ on the Table Design toolbar to insert a blank row above the LastName field.

2. Click in the blank FIELD NAME column and type: TITLE.

3. Click in the blank *Data Type* column to choose the kind of data the field will accept. In this case, the default *Text* data type is the one we need. Notice, however, the list arrow ▾ on the right end of the cell. Clicking the list arrow will open a list of the other available data types. Review the Access data types section in Chapter 4 for an explanation of each data type.

4. Click in the Field Size cell in the Field Properties pane. The default width for text fields is 50 characters. Since the field will contain only abbreviated terms, change the field size to 5 characters.

5. Select FILE/SAVE on the Menu bar, or click the Save button 🖫 on the Table Datasheet toolbar to save the changes.

6. Select VIEW/DATASHEET VIEW, or click the Datasheet View button ⊞ to return to Datasheet view.

How to Enter Records

Scroll down to the end of the record set as indicated by the New Record symbol in the record selector. Click inside the first empty field (e.g.: Title). Add one record to the FRIENDS table. Move between fields using the Tab key. Press Tab once more to move to the first field of the next record. Access will automatically save your data when you leave a record, either by moving to another record or by closing the table.

How to Edit Existing Records

In Datasheet view, move to the empty Title field and add appropriate titles for each of the records in the FRIENDS table. Click in the Title field for the first record (i.e. Peter Drucker), and enter the title *Dr*. Notice that the pencil symbol appears in the record selector, indicating that the record is being edited. Press the down arrow key to move to the Title field for the next record. Add a title and continue down the column to add titles for the remaining records. As you move down the column, the pencil symbol will appear in each record you are editing and Access will automatically save the changes.

Closing a Table

Select FILE/CLOSE, or double-click the Control Menu icon in the upper left corner of the table window. If you have unsaved changes to the layout of the table, Access will prompt you to save the changes. Choose the Yes button.

How to Display and Print Selected Fields: Building a Query 1:

A *query* is a question that you ask about certain data in a database, such as, "How many customers live in Melbourne?" or "What were our sales figures for last month?" Alternatively, you may just want to view selected fields of a database in a certain order. The Select Query window (see Figure 5-7) is a graphical query-by-example (QBE) tool. This means you can use the mouse to select and drag the fields you wish to view to the window. Then you can chose to view the data in a certain order or set criteria so that only records that meet those criteria will display (e.g. customers who live in Melbourne). In other words, you are defining an example of the records you wish to view.

Let's say that you want to display and print just three fields from the FRIENDS table: Last_Name, First_Name, and City. Here's how to create an Access query to do this:

1. On the Objects bar on the Database window (see Figure 5-6), select Queries. Then Click the *New* button on the Database Window toolbar. (If you still have the FRIENDS table open, press the [F11] function key to view the Database window.) The New Query dialog box opens. Select *Design View* and click OK so that a new Select Query window will open.

Figure 5-6:

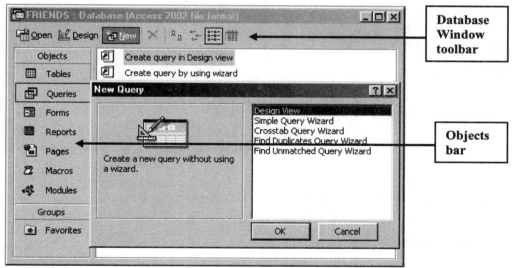

2. In the Show Table dialog box, the FRIENDS table is automatically selected. Click the *Add* button to add a field list for the FRIENDS table to the query window. Click the *Close* button to close the Show Table dialog box.

3. Select the Last_Name field in the FRIENDS field list. Hold down the *Ctrl* key and select First_Name and then City. (The [Ctrl] key is handy to use when selecting noncontiguous fields for a query.) Release the [Ctrl] key.

4. Use the mouse to drag the selection to the design grid. Release the mouse button when the selected fields symbol is in the first *Field* cell in the design grid. The three fields are added in order to the design grid, as shown in Figure 5-7.

5. Click the Run button 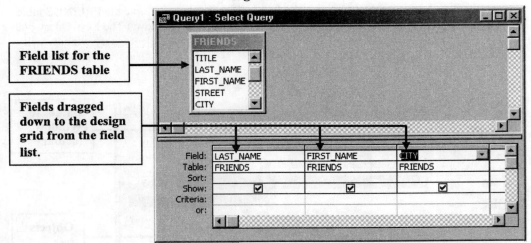 on the Query Design toolbar, or select QUERY/RUN to generate the query results set as shown in Figure 5-8.

6. Click the Print button , or select FILE/PRINT to open the Print dialog box and click OK to print the query.

7. Click the Design View button to return to the Query Design window.

8. Click the Save button , or select FILE/SAVE to save the query. Type a name (e.g. Tute1Query1) in the *Query Name* text box in the *Save as* dialog box and click OK.

Figure 5-7

Select VIEW/SQL VIEW to view the Structured Query Language code generated by Access for the query. You can also find the SQL View command by clicking the list arrow on the View button.

SELECT FRIENDS.LAST_NAME, FRIENDS.FIRST_NAME, FRIENDS.CITY
FROM FRIENDS;

This code can be cut and pasted into an event procedure within a macro or a module and used as part of a larger program. Access provides a number of useful programming shortcuts. We will be looking at some of these in later cases. Close the SQL View window.

How to Display Selected Records: Building a Query 2:

Now that you have constructed a simple query, let's go one step further and search the FRIENDS table for records that meet particular criteria. In this example let's extract only those records that contain *Mr.* in the Title field.

1. Open Tute1Query1 in Design view. Select the Title field in the FRIENDS field list. Drag the selected field to the design grid and release the mouse button over the Last_Name field. Access automatically moves the fields to the right and inserts the Title field as the first field in the query.

2. In the *Criteria* cell for the Title field, type: *Mr.* Click the *Run* button. The query result set is displayed in Figure 5-8.

3. Click  to return to Design view. Notice that Access has enclosed the criteria in quotation marks, indicating that this is a text criterion. Access is not case sensitive, so entering *Mr.* in lower case (or upper case) would produce the same search result.

Figure 5-8: The Query Results Sets

Original query showing all records

Query with selection criteria

4. To print the new query, click the **Print** button.

5. Press [F11] to view the Database window and the two query objects. Exit Access by selecting FILE/EXIT, or by clicking the Close button on the Microsoft Access Title bar.

Database Case 2

Martin and Schofield Attorneys-at-Law

Problem: Construct a Personnel Database

Management Skill: Coordinate

Access Skills: Table Setup
                         Data Input
                         Select Queries
                         Report Design
                         Printing

Data Table: M&S

Martin and Schofield is a large legal practice with offices in San Francisco, Los Angeles, Carson City, Salt Lake, and Phoenix that specialize in corporate law. The M&S Los Angeles office employs more than 300 freelance and contract personnel, including expert witnesses (EW) from a various fields and disciplines, private investigators (PI), process servers (PS), and legal researchers (LR). These people are hired on an as-needed basis to assist in the conduct of cases on behalf of the many client corporations the company represents.

M&S has 32 Principal attorneys who are also the main partners in the firm. Each Principal has a staff of assistant lawyers. In addition, each Principal keeps a separate list of contractors and freelancers with whom they have worked successfully in the past. Typically, these lists reside on 3" x 5" cards in a file cabinet in each partner's office. Whenever a client's case requires certain outside expertise, the partners reach for these cards and select their favorite people.

The partner's remuneration is based in part on their performance, thus the more successful cases they litigate, the more money they make. Moreover, the more experienced and competent freelancers they know, the more likely they are to successfully litigate and the more clients will seek them out for assistance. In this environment, there is a natural tendency to safeguard the names of good freelancers and contractors for one's own accounts. However, there is also the likelihood that, by sharing this information, the firm's overall success would increase and everyone would benefit.

Alan Martin started the law firm 30 years ago with fellow UCLA graduate Harold Schofield, now deceased. Martin knows how the freelancing system works. The problem is that each attorney squirrels away the names of the people that he or she thinks is really excellent. There is no sharing among attorneys of the talent pool. Second-rate people may be used on a case because the names of the first-rate people are known to only one or two attorneys. If a partner hires a poor freelancer, and the verdict on a case goes against the interests of a client, the client may be inclined to look for new legal help and M&S profits and reputation may suffer.

Martin wants to establish some sort of centralized repository for this information. Too much time is wasted searching for people with particular skills or knowledge that may already be known to some of the partners. The central repository could also contain comments on the performance of the freelancer or contractor on prior occasions and other relevant data. Perhaps some sort of scoring system could be developed so that freelancers and contractors could be rank ordered. That way only the best people would be used to assist the attorneys on cases.

The partners are not happy with this idea. One of the ways they enhance their own reputations is by using highly capable people to research their cases and by getting competent experts to testify for them. Sharing these resources with the other partners may mean their favorite people will be unavailable when they most need them. On the other hand, a central repository might help them to find new resources for assistance that they did not previously know about. Therefore, with somewhat mixed feelings, the partners respond to a memo sent out by Martin asking them to list the resources they would like to have in a central database.

The following fields were identified by summarizing the memo responses: Name, Skill, Hourly Rate, number of hours employed for each quarter of 2001, and Phone Number. Martin reviewed the suggestions and added a field to store a text comment about each freelancer in a simple rating system format, "excellent", "good", "ok", or poor. These details could be input by the last partner for whom the freelancer worked.

Martin does not know if free form text can be attached to everyone's record in the database, but he knows that any software that does not have this capability is limited. At least with a 3x5 note card system, short notes can be attached to each person's record.

Parts of this database have been identified in the data table M&S in SOLVEIT.MDB. Create a new Access database and import this object now.

Tasks:

There are seven tasks in this case:

1. Complete the design of the table to store the rating system devised by Martin. Be sure to devise a way to record free-form text comments, remarks, or more descriptive ratings from the attorneys.

2. Fabricate and enter hours worked for the existing freelancers or contractors. Enter data for three new freelancers or contractors such as private investigators (PI), process servers (PS), legal researchers (LR), or expert witnesses (EW). Enter data for at least the first three freelancers in the comments field. Make up the name of the partner who is contributing the remarks.

3. Print the entire table. Create a query, and then print out a listing showing only the last name and comment fields.

4. Design and create a report to list all the freelancers and contractors with just the following fields: Last_Name, Hourly_Rate, and the total number of hours worked in 2001.

5. Produce and print a report to list all process servers who charge more than $100.00/hour. Include in this report the total number of hours this group of freelancers worked for M&S in 2001. Print the report.

6. There are several areas where this system can be enhanced and improved. Make a list of all of the improvements you would make, and then pick one and implement it in the database.

*7. Currently with the comments in a Memo field, no analysis or data manipulation can be performed using the ratings of the freelancers. There may also be conflicting opinions on the merits of any one freelancer if they have worked for more than one partner. Devise a method to accommodate these differing opinions in such a way that meaningful analysis can be performed

Time Estimates (excluding task marked with an *)
Expert: 45 minutes
Intermediate: 1.25 hours
Novice: 2 hours

Tutorial for Database Case 2 Using Access 2002

In the previous case you learned to use Table Design view to change the structure of a table by adding new fields and setting field properties, and how to use Datasheet view for adding and editing records. This case introduces the *memo* data type and *report design*. Start Access and open the database you used for the Case 1 tutorial (CONTACTS.MDB or FRIENDS.MDB) to practice the skills you will need for this case.

Using Memo Fields

Memo fields are used in tables to store free form text and notes. You use a memo field to store descriptive or narrative information and even large documents. A memo field can hold up to 65,536 characters of text. Unlike DOS-based database programs such as dBase, creating, entering, and saving data in an Access memo field is a very simple procedure. Because of their unstructured nature, memo fields cannot be *indexed* or *sorted*, but they can be searched. (We will look at indexing, sorting, and searching in later cases.)

1. In the FRIENDS or CONTACTS Database window, click Tables on the Objects bar and double-click either the ADDRESS or FRIENDS table to open it in Datasheet view. Click the Design View button ![icon] or select VIEW/DESIGN VIEW.

2. Let's add a new field to the end of the existing table. The name for the new field will be COMMENTS and the data type will be Memo. (Review the tutorial for Case 1 if you are unsure how to add new fields and select data types.) Notice that the Field Size cell in the Field Properties pane does not appear when you select the memo data type. Save the changes to the table structure by clicking the Save button or selecting FILE/SAVE.

3. Return to Datasheet view by clicking the Datasheet View button ![icon] or by selecting VIEW/DATASHEET VIEW. Scroll or Tab over to the new COMMENTS field and enter

text for each record to describe their relationship (e.g. Personal or Professional friend, family member, or a specific familial relationship) Press the down arrow key on the keyboard to move to each new record. (Remember that as you move to a new record, Access automatically saves the data.)

Printing Memo Fields

Memo fields can be printed like any other field in a table or query. To create a query that will select only certain fields in the table including the memo field:

1. In Datasheet view, press [F11] to view the Database window. Click *Queries* on the Objects bar. Click the *New* button on the Database window toolbar. In the New Query dialog box, select Design View if necessary and click OK. In the Show Table dialog box, with the FRIENDS table selected, click *Add* and then *Close*.

2. In the FRIENDS field list, select the Last_Name and Comments fields and drag them to the design grid. Release the mouse button when the selected fields symbol is over the first Field cell.

3. Click the *Run* button or select QUERY/RUN to display the data in the Last_Name and Comments fields (Figure 5-9).

4. Click the *Print* button or select FILE/PRINT to open the Print dialog box and click OK to print the query. Select FILE/CLOSE and click *No* when a warning dialog box asks if you want to save the changes to the design of Query 1. This will return you to the Database window without saving the query.

Figure 5-9:

LAST_NAME	COMMENTS
Drucker	Professional
Whitney	Personal
Sitkin	Professional
Skalek	Professional
Salione	Personal
Fabian	Professional
Kohlman	Father-in-law
Tedesco	Grandfather
Zito	Professional
Peterson	Personal
Nelson	Professional
Buckley	Sister
Roberts	Brother
Thompson	Personal
Parker	Professional
Jones	Professional
Kaufman	Personal
Timko	Professional
Emerson	Personal
Hicks	Professional
Williams	Professional

Creating Reports in Access

A more polished look can be achieved by creating an Access report. *Reports* are the database objects in Access that are specifically designed for printing. Reports can be based on tables and/or queries, and are used to provide subtotals and grand totals for numeric fields and to produce summaries of information contained in the database, mailing labels, and presentation quality display of your data. Report Wizards speed up the creation, display, and printout by providing a series of dialog boxes to help you determine the data you want the report to contain and a group of popular style templates from which to choose.

The items on a report that contain the data for display and printing are called *controls*. Different types of controls are used to display data of the various data types. Controls are used to display data from fields and the labels that identify this data, to display the results of calculations, for report headers and footers that will print identifying information at the top and bottom of every page of the report, and for group footers that identify a particular group of related data. Report controls can also be used to include graphs, pictures, and other Access objects.

1.   With the Database window on the screen, (press the [F11] key to display it if necessary) click *Reports* on the Objects bar and then *New* on the Database window toolbar. In the New Report dialog box, click the list arrow ⏷ on the *Choose the table or query where the object's data comes from* box. Select FRIENDS (See Figure 5-10). This action tells Access that the record source for the report will be the FRIENDS table.

Figure 5-10

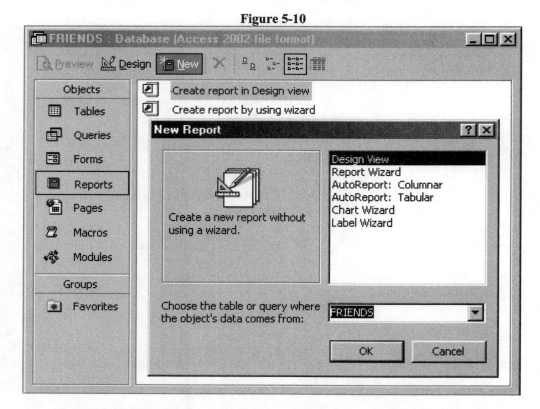

2.   The New Report dialog box enables you to create a new report in Design View or with the Report Wizard, two different types of AutoReports, or reports using the Chart Wizard

or the Label Wizard. Click each one to read a brief description of the type of report each one will create. Select *Report Wizard* and click the *OK button* shown in Figure 5-10.

3. The first Report Wizard dialog box opens. Here you can choose the fields that you want to display in the report and decide the order in which you want them to display. Select four fields: Title, First_Name, Last_Name, and City, for inclusion in the report. With the

   Title field selected in the *Available Fields* box, click the ![>] button to add it to the *Selected Fields* box (refer to Figure 5-11). Next, select the First_Name field in the

   Available Fields box and click ![>] again to add it to the list of selected fields. Follow the same procedure to add the remaining two fields as shown in Figure 5-20. (If you accidentally add the wrong field to the report, select the unwanted field and click

   the ![<] button to return it to the Available Fields box.) When you have finished, click the *Next* button.

Figure 5-11

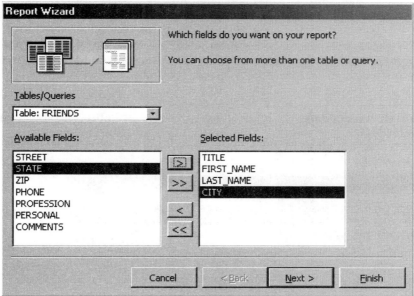

4. The second of the six report Wizard dialog boxes opens. Here you can add grouping levels for the data in your report based on one or more fields. Data can be grouped by City, for example, so that all contacts that live in a particular city will be grouped together in the report. Click *Next*. In the third dialog box you can impose a sort order on the data in the report based on one or more fields. Select City in the first sort order list box. Click *Next*.

5. In the fourth dialog box, you can choose the layout for the report. Option buttons are provided to choose either *Portrait* or *Landscape* orientation for the report and either a *Columnar*, *Tabular*, or *Justified* layout. Select the *Tabular* layout if necessary, make sure the *Adjust the field width so all fields fit on a page* check box is selected, and click *Next*.

6. In the fifth dialog box, you can select a style for your report. Select *Corporate* if necessary and click *Next*.

7. In the final dialog box, you can enter a title for your report. By default Access enters as the title the name of the table or query that serves as the record source for the report, in this case, FRIENDS. Type: *Report of My Friends.*

8. Click the *Finish* button. Access will generate the report and open it in Print Preview. Note that the records are displayed alphabetically by City according to the sort order selected in the Report Wizard. Click the *Print* button on the Print Preview toolbar or select FILE/PRINT to open the Print dialog box and click OK to print the report. Close the report.

How to Use Reports to Display and Print Selected Fields.

You can change the record source for an existing report thereby changing the records the report displays. For example, you can change the record source for the Report of My Friends report to the second query created in the tutorial for Case 1 (e.g. TutelQuery2). This query filtered out all records in the FRIENDS table that did not have the title MR.

1. With the Database window on the screen, click *Reports* on the Objects bar, if necessary. Select Report of My Friends, if necessary. Click the *Design* button on the Database window toolbar to open the report in the Report Design view window (see Figure 5-12).

Figure 5-12

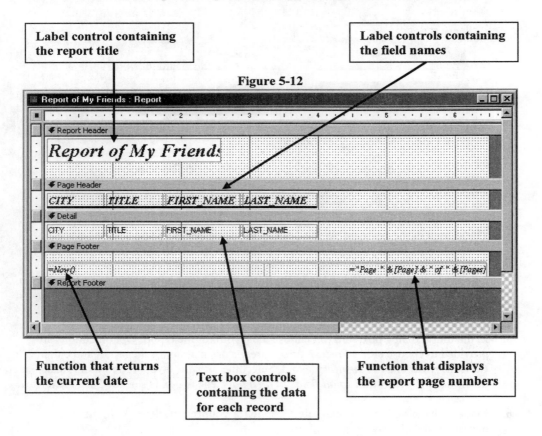

Label control containing the report title

Label controls containing the field names

Function that returns the current date

Text box controls containing the data for each record

Function that displays the report page numbers

Figure 5-13

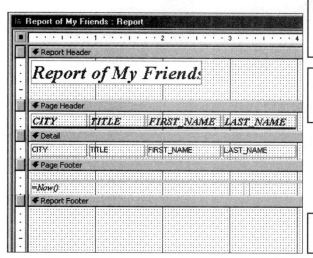

Report Header: Contains controls, such as the title, that print once at the beginning of the report

Page Header: Contains controls, usually the identifying labels, that print at the top of each page

Detail: The heart of the report which contains all of the records specified in the record source for the report

Page Footer: Contains controls that print at the bottom of each page

Report Footer: Contains controls that print at the end of the report, often calculated controls that display a grand total, grand count, or another function that summarizes the data in the report

(As Figure 5-13 shows, the Report Design view window is divided into sections. The **Report Header** prints once at the beginning of the report. It generally contains the title for the report. The **Page Header** prints at the top of every page in the report and contains the labels or column headings. The **Detail** section contains the records that are being displayed in the report. The **Page Footer** prints at the bottom of each page and often contains calculated controls that display the current system date and time and the page number and total number of pages in the report. The **Report Footer** prints once at the end of the report. It often contains calculated controls that summarize or total the data contained in the report. Additionally, group headers will be automatically added to a report in which records are grouped based on like values. You can add group footers to include summary information about the group such as a *Count*, *Sum*, or *Average*. We will look at report groups in a later tutorial.)

2.   Click the *Properties* button ▣ on the Report Design toolbar to open the property sheet for the report. Report properties define the data source for the report as well as its overall appearance.

3.   Click the *Data* tab on the property sheet if necessary. Click in the *Record Source* property settings box and click the list arrow ▾ to open a list of the available data sources in the FRIENDS database. Select the second query you created in the Case 1 tutorial (e.g. Tute1Query2) to change the record source for the report. (See Figure 5-14.)

Figure 5-14

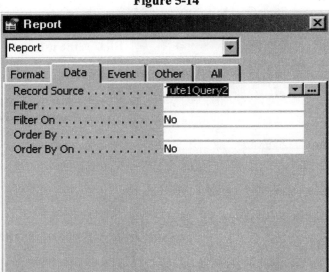

4.   Close the property sheet (Click the ☒ in the top right corner.)

5.   Click the Print Preview button 🔍 or select FILE/PRINT PREVIEW to view the new report. A reduced data set displays based upon the criteria set up in the query, but the sort order based upon the City field and the report style selected in the Report Wizard remain.

6.   Click the *Print* button to print the new report.

7.   Select FILE/SAVE AS to open the Save As dialog box. Type: *Tute2Report2*, in the top text box and click *OK*. Close the report and the FRIENDS database.

Using Expressions in Reports

Expressions are used to create calculated controls for a report. Calculated controls are used to display the results of expressions which can be built using Access functions, mathematical operators, raw values, and any values contained in the fields in the report. For example, the expression **=[UnitCost]*[Quantity]** will multiply the contents of the two fields with these names and display a single value as the result. A *function* is a predefined formula that helps to simplify the process of building expressions. For example the function *Sum* will add all of the values specified. The *Now* function in the Page Footer section, shown in Figure 5-12, returns the current date as stored in your computer's system clock.

You can create calculated controls using expressions in one of three ways.
- By typing an expression directly in a text box control
- By entering an expression in the Control Source property for a control
- By using the Expression Builder to help you to create the expression.

To learn and practice the skill of creating calculated controls using expressions, we will use the first method and the sample table HARDWARE provided on SOLVEIT.MDB. First create a new empty database (e.g.HARDWARE.MDB) and then import the HARDWARE table.

1. Open the HARDWARE.MDB database. (If you still have tables or reports open from the Friends database, save and close them and close the FRIENDS database.)

2. Double-click the HARDWARE table to open it in Datasheet view. There are four fields: Invoice, Item, UnitCost, and Quantity. Press [F11] to view the Database window.

3. Click *Reports* on the Objects bar and use the Report Wizard to create a new report using the HARDWARE table as the record source. Include the fields Invoice, UnitCost, and Quantity. Sort the records by Invoice number, use the Tabular layout and the Corporate style, and give the report the title: *Calculating Total Cost*. Click *Finish*. The report is generated and opened in Print Preview.

4. Click the [Close] button on the Print Preview toolbar to switch to Report Design view.

Changing the Report Margins

5. Widen the working area for your report by extending the margins. Position the mouse pointer over the right margin of the report area. When the horizontal resizing pointer appears (refer to Figure 5-15), drag to the right to widen the report area to the 7-inch mark on the horizontal ruler.

Figure 5-15

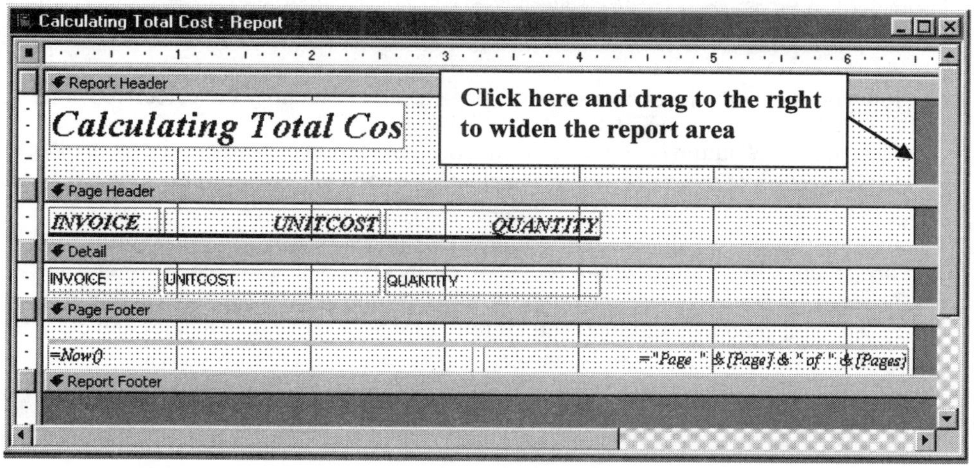

6. A calculated control contains an expression and displays the result of that expression when the report is opened. To practice creating a calculated control, multiply UnitCost by Quantity. Since this calculation will use the values in two existing fields to calculate a new value, we must create a control to display the new value.

7. Click the *Toolbox* button 🛠 on the Report Design toolbar to open the Toolbox if necessary. Click the *Text Box* button [ab] in the Toolbox. Click once with the Text Box

pointer at the 4-½-inch mark on the horizontal ruler in the Detail section of the report. An unbound text box control and a label control to identify it are added to the report. The label caption (*Text 11*) will vary depending on the number of controls on the report. Click the label control to select it and press the [Delete] key on the keyboard. You will add a label for the calculated control to the page header later.

8. Unbound controls are not linked to any existing field in the record source or sources for the report. They are used to display the results of calculations, text, or graphics. Click inside the unbound text box to get a blinking insertion point (called an *I-beam*). Type: **=UnitCost*Quantity** and press the [Enter] key. Access automatically adds the correct syntax for you by enclosing each field in square brackets. Access is not case sensitive, so it does not matter if you enter your field names in upper or lower case. You must, however, spell them correctly including the correct spacing!

Note:
If the field names contain spaces, you must enclose them in square brackets because Access will not recognize them as field names (e.g. [Time to Market]).

All expressions in Access must begin with an = sign. The asterisk is used to denote multiplication. A listing of other operators and functions used in Access is presented at the end of this tutorial.

9. You have now created a calculated control. The Detail section of your report should resemble Figure 5-16.

Figure 5-16

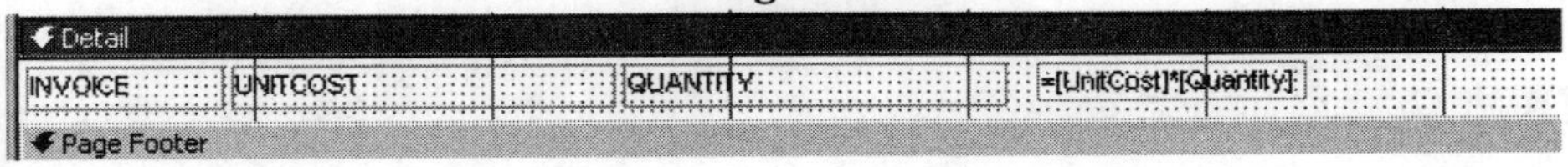

10. Now you will add a label control to the page header to identify the calculated control. Click the *Label* button [Aa] on the toolbox. Click the Label pointer once in the Page Header section of the report at the 5-inch mark on the horizontal ruler. Type: TOTAL.

11. Double-click the calculated control to open the property sheet for the control. Click the Format tab. Click in the *Format* property settings box. Click the list arrow and select *Currency* on the list. Close the property sheet, switch to Print Preview, and print the report. Your report should look similar to Figure 5-17. Save the changes and close the report.

Figure 5-17

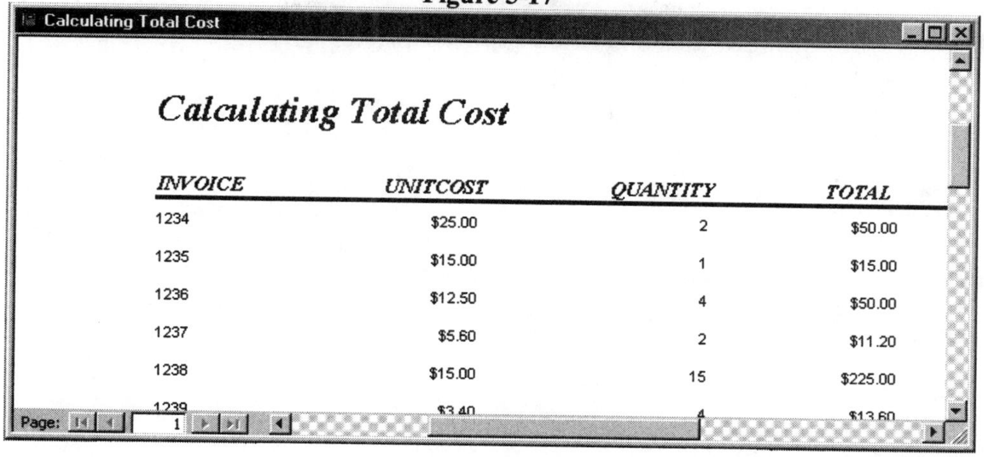

Calculations in Queries

A more rapid way of achieving the same result is to create a query that includes the calculated field that you want to display in the report and then to use the query as the record source for the report.

1. In the HARDWARE database window, click *Queries* on the Objects bar. Double-click *Create query in Design view*. Add the field list for the HARDWARE table to the Select Query window and close the Show Table dialog box. Drag the 3 fields Invoice, UnitCost, and Quantity to the design grid.

2. In the fourth Field cell, type: **TOTAL: =[UnitCost]*[Quantity]**. Your query window should look like Figure 5-18.

3. Click [icon] to run the query. Save the query as *CalculatingTotalCost* and create a report using the query as the data source for the report.

Expressions can play many roles in Access and can be used in virtually every type of database object. For example, you can use expressions in Table Design view to define default values for fields. In queries, expressions can be used to create calculated fields and criteria. The table below lists only those likely to be used in *Solve it!* For a more complete list, consult the *Office Assistant*, or search the Help facility using the term *operators*.

Figure 5-18

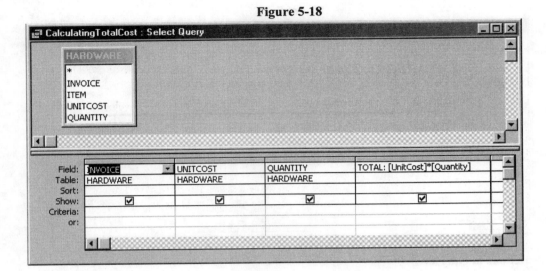

Operators in Access

An operator in an expression describes the type of action that the expression should perform, or how a comparison between two values should be carried out. Access has four kinds of operators: Arithmetic and Text, Comparison, Logical, and Miscellaneous. The table just below classifies, lists, and explains these operators. For a more complete list of operators, consult the Access 2002 Help facility.

Arithmetic and Text	
^	Raise one number to the power of the other (exponentiation)
*	Multiply two numbers
/	Add two numbers
+	Divide two numbers
-	Subtract two numbers
Mod	Divide two numbers and return the remainder
&	Concatenate: join two strings of text
Comparison	
< and <=	Less than; less than or equal to
> and >=	Greater than; greater than or equal to
= and <>	Equal to: not equal to
Logical	
And	Both comparisons are True
Or	One comparison or the other is True
Xor	One comparison or the other is True , but not both
Not	The comparison is not True
Miscellaneous	
Like	Text matches a pattern (Use with wildcard symbols ? and *)
Is	Comparison is True (e.g.: is Null)
Is Not	Comparison is not True (e.g.: not Null)

Functions in Access

A *function* in Access performs a calculation on data and returns the result of the calculation. There are over 100 functions available in Access in eight different categories. The table below lists only those likely to be used in Solve it! For a complete list, consult the Office Assistant or search the Help files using the keywords *functions reference*.

Date/Time	
Date	Returns current date
Now	Returns current date and time
Logical	
IF	Tests and returns a value based on whether an argument is True or False
Choose	Selects a value from a list based on the content of its argument
Aggregate	
Avg	Average
Count	Count how many
Sum	Sum total

The Access Form and Report Toolbox

The buttons displayed in the table below appear in the Toolbox used to create labels, text boxes, option buttons, etc. for forms, subforms, and other Access objects.

Select Objects — Use to select a control, section, or form. Click this tool to unlock a toolbox button that you've locked down.

Control Wizards — Turns control wizards on or off. Use control wizards to help you create a list box, combo box, option group, command button, chart, subreport, or subform.

Label — A control that displays descriptive text, such as a title, a caption, or instructions on a form or report. Access automatically attaches labels to the controls you create.

Text Box — Use to: Display, enter, or edit data in a form's or report's underlying record source, display the results of a calculation, or accept input from a user.

Option Group — Use along with check boxes, option buttons, or toggle buttons to display a set of alternative values. For example, you can use an option group to specify whether an order is shipped by air, sea, or land.

Toggle Button — Use as a stand-alone control bound to a Yes/No field, an unbound control for accepting user input in a custom dialog box, or part of an option group.

Option Button — Use as a stand-alone control bound to a Yes/No field, an unbound control for accepting user input in a custom dialog box, or part of an option group.

	Check Box	Use as a stand-alone control bound to a Yes/No field, an unbound control for accepting user input in a custom dialog box, or part of an option group.
	Combo Box	Combines the features of a list box and a text box. You can type in the text box or select an entry in the list box to add a value to an underlying field.
	List Box	Displays a scrollable list of values. In Form view, you can select from the list to enter a value into a new record or to change the value in an existing record.
	Command Button	Use to perform actions, such as finding a record, printing a record, or applying a form filter.
	Image	Use for displaying a static picture on a form or report. Because a static picture is not an OLE object, you can't edit the image inside Microsoft Access once you've added it to a form or report.
	Unbound Object	Use to display an unbound OLE object, such as a Microsoft Excel spreadsheet, on a form or report. The object remains constant as you move from record to record.
	Bound Object	Use to display OLE objects, such as a series of pictures, on a form or report. This control is for objects stored in a field in the form's or report's underlying record source. A different object displays on the form or report as you move from record to record.
	Page Break	Use to begin a new screen on a form, a new page on a printed form, or a new page of a report.
	Tab Control	Use to create a tabbed form with several pages or tabbed dialog box (such as the Options dialog box on the Tools menu). You can copy or add other controls onto a tab control. Right-click on the Tab control in the design grid to modify the number of pages, the page order, the selected page's properties, and the selected tab control properties.
	Subform/Subreport	Use to display data from more than one table on a form or report.
	Line	Use on a form or report, for example, to emphasize related or especially important information.
	Rectangle	Use for graphic effects such as grouping a set of related controls on a form, or emphasizing important data on a report.
	More Controls	Adds an ActiveX control (such as the Calendar control) to a form or report. ActiveX controls are stored as separate files.

Source: http://www.microsoft.com/access/productinfo/commandsummary/toolbartoolbox.htm

Database Case 3

Norton Furniture

Problem:	Develop an automated Bill of Materials
Management Skill:	Plan Coordinate
Access Skills:	Creating Queries Sorting (tables, queries, reports)
Data Table:	Norton

Richard Dattner, Production Manager of Norton Furniture, walked out of the Chief Executive Officer's office muttering to himself. He had just left a meeting between Troy Callen, the CEO; Hank Bosch, the Chief Financial Officer; and Wendy Tang, the Purchasing Officer. They had more or less ordered him to computerize the bill of materials (BoM) and purchasing systems. He argued that such an instruction was easier given than implemented. They had finally compromised on automating a section of the factory's assembly facilities as a pilot project. The pilot project would provide an opportunity to improve the design of the new system and measure the benefits before moving to complete implementation in the entire factory.

Norton, based in Spokane, WA, had experienced steady sales for its range of quality household furniture until the early 1980s when less expensive imports of similar quality began to capture significant market share. Costs had to be reduced, and senior management decided that increased production volume was needed before their household furniture products could regain competitiveness in such a capital-intensive industry. These increased volumes would provide economies of scale in materials purchases and enable a new, more efficient plant to be purchased. The increased volume would be obtained by entering the high-end commercial office furniture market. Norton's quality hardwood tables would be particularly suitable in such a highly discriminating market. In addition, a range of desks was developed. The strategy proved fruitful; Norton's business products were acclaimed in executive offices and boardrooms across the country. The strategy, together with a continuous improvement program initiated at the same time, reduced production costs, and gains occurred in both the household and business markets.

Management found that production scale had outpaced the manual, paper-based production control system, which proved inadequate for market intelligence, activity-based costing, and for efficient production administration.

Dattner entered his own office, considering how to start the process. Even if his budget permitted a full-blown Materials Requirement Planning system, the jump would be too large for Norton. He decided that creating an in-house system on a PC/Windows-based database would be the most suitable solution, since Caldwell and Bosch were not specific about what computer platform to use and future requirements were unclear. This approach would provide the necessary flexibility for incremental development and expansion. His knowledge of PC applications being limited, Dattner rang the Business School at the University of Seattle. The Placement Office at the university referred him to Megan Gates, a first-year MBA student seeking a summer internship in a manufacturer. Gates agreed to drive over to Spokane the following day.

Although from a fine-arts background, Gates had taken an Information Systems course in her graduate program and was keen to learn about production systems. Dattner explained what was required in the preliminary stages. Currently, the BoM for each product type was recorded on paper and used exclusively in the production area. Dattner was sure that a BoM could be constructed for use by both production and the purchasing department. Currently, the purchasing department used a separate list of components, which often resulted in difficulties in attributing supply costs to particular product lines.

A BoM, Dattner explained, was a list of materials, sub-parts, and quantities used in a finished product. Typically, the list would be arranged to represent the sequence of fabrication and assembly, and highlighted manufacturing dependencies. For the pilot project, this would not be needed because of the relative simplicity of the production sequence.

Gates decided to use the company's range of senior executive tables and desks for the pilot project, and run the new system parallel with the existing system. In this way, Norton could refine and cost out the system before committing to a complete implementation. This range had four products: two tables, the Swanborne and the Swanborne Deluxe; and two desks, the Director and the Executive. These four products were made of 15 different components, excluding taper screws.

The design for each product was very similar. The Swanborne tables were made of six legs supporting four 5.5' beams and five 3.75' beams, which in turn supported two 6'x 4' tabletops which were laid end to end. Eight 3' and four 2' struts were added for additional strength and aesthetic considerations. The other two products in this range, Director and Executive, were personal desks which have four legs, two 5.5' beams, three 3.75' beams, four 2' and 3' struts and a single table top. Director desks have three drawers, while the Chairman has six. The Swanborne Deluxe table and Executive desk also have leather tops; two pieces for the Deluxe and one piece for the Executive.

Norton's designers decided to use bolts to join the tables for strength and reliability rather than the mixture of bolts, nails, and adhesives used by their competitors. Two 1.5"x 8" bolts are used for each leg, each 5.5' beam and each 3.75' beam. Two 1"x 6" bolts are used in each 2' strut and 3' strut. For each bolt, a matching nut and spacer are used. Each product has differing levels of carved detail and finish.

Norton manufactures the tops and legs, and purchases the struts from Titan Timbers, the leather from Luxury Leathers, and the hardware from Ironmongers.

Gates listed each of the components as a record in a PC/Windows-based database table, with the number used for each product listed in separate fields. The number of each component currently in inventory and the unit cost also needed listing.

This partial bill of materials is supplied for you in the data table NORTON on SOLVEIT.MDB. Create a new Access database and import this file now.

Tasks: There are seven tasks in this case:

1. (a) Complete the supplied bill of materials by adding fields to represent inventory holdings (UNITS_IN_STOCK) and unit costs (UNIT_COST) of the materials, and by

fabricating the appropriate data. (b) Also add new part codes, quantities used, and the other information for the bolts, nuts, and spacers. Note that the PART_CODE field is made up of a letter (representing the supplier: N for Norton, T for Titan Timbers, L for Luxury Leathers, and I for Ironmongers) followed by four numbers. (c) Print out the completed table.

2.   Managers in a number of functional areas have heard of Gate's progress and have requested information from the computerized BoM. Sales managers want to know the total amount, in dollars, of the materials costs in each product type so that they can more easily set appropriate prices for these products. Accounting managers want to know the total dollar value of each component type in each table or desk. Dattner wants an estimate of the investment in dollars in inventory holdings of the component types and a total dollar value of inventory holdings. Gates is certain that these needs can be furnished within a single report.

(a) Create a report to satisfy these needs and (b) print this report.

3.   Rubric Corporation, a regular and valued customer, has ordered tables for their new Albuquerque office. They require 3 Swanborne and 42 Director tables. CEO Callen and Tang from Purchasing want a detailed Materials Requirement report for this order, showing the number of each component required for each of the two products ordered, a total components required field, and the amount held in inventory. Create and print the report.

4.   (a) Create a query that filters out the parts that have adequate supply in inventory to create the Directors tables. (b) Create and print a report to show this information. Include all necessary fields.

5.   Wendy Tang has heard rumors that Titan Timbers is having financial difficulties. Callen is worried by these rumors and the implications this may have for the Rubric contract. Print out a listing of the components supplied by Titan Timbers, sorted by PART_CODE, to facilitate the investigation.

6.   Engineering and Design wants a list of the components, sorted by value. (a) Create a query and (b) print the resulting listing.

*7.   Suggest any improvements or additions to the Bill of Materials, as it currently exists. Could the BoM be extended to encompass other aspects of Production Management or any other associated domains?

Time Estimates (excluding task marked with *):

Expert: 1 hour 45 minutes
Intermediate: 2.5 hour
Novice: 4 hours

Tutorial for Database Case 3 Using Access 2002

Creating Queries with Multiple Criteria

In the Tutorial for Case 1, we looked at creating queries for viewing and printing certain fields in the FRIENDS table, and fields that met simple selection criteria. In this tutorial, we will look at constructing more complex queries using logical operators.

1.   Open the practice database FRIENDS.MDB, and create a new query following the instructions given in the Tutorial for Case 1. Include the fields Last_Name, Zip, Profession, and Personal in the query.

Figure 5-19

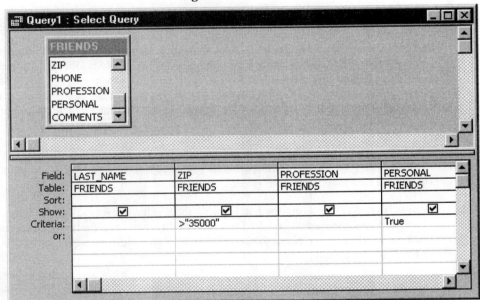

2.   The *Criteria* and *or* cells in the design grid allow for multiple conditions involving the logical operators "AND" and "OR". Conditions entered in the Criteria cell are "AND". Let's say you wanted a listing of all Personal friends with ZIP Codes greater than 35000. In the Criteria cell of the design grid (see Figure 5-19), type *>35000* in the Zip field and enter *True* in the Personal field.

3.   Click the Run button [image] on the Report Design toolbar or select QUERY/RUN to run the query. Results should show that there are seven records in the FRIENDS table, which match the criteria.

4.   Click the Design View button to return to the Query Design view window.

5.   Now try using the *OR* operator by deleting *True* from the **Criteria** cell in the **Personal** field, and entering it in the **or:** cell on the next line down (see Figure 5-20). In this instance, we are searching the table for people whose ZIP code is greater than 35000 *or* people who are

personal friends. Run the query again. This is a less stringent condition, and the resulting dynaset should show that there are seventeen records, which match the chosen criteria.

6. Print your queries by clicking the *Print* button, or selecting FILE/PRINT to open the Print dialog box. Save your query (e.g.: *Tute3Query1*), and close it

Figure 5-20

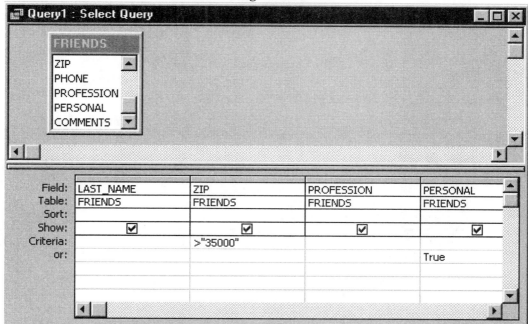

Sorting Tables in Access

It is often useful to sort a table by one or more fields. For instance, you may find it helpful to sort the records in your table alphabetically by Last Name, or to sort records in chronological order, or by some numerical order. There are several ways of sorting data in Access. A quick sort on a single field in either ascending or descending order can be achieved in Datasheet view, or you can sort on multiple fields in either the Query Design view or in a Report.

To Sort on a Single Field

1. In the FRIENDS Database window, click *Tables* on the Objects bar, and then double-click the FRIENDS table to open it in Datasheet view. Let's say you would like to sort the records alphabetically by Last Name. To do this, move the mouse to the Last Name field selector until the ↓ arrow appears. Click to select the Last Name column (see Figure 5-21).

2. Click the Sort Ascending button ![A Z↓] or select RECORDS/SORT and SORT ASCENDING so Access will sort the records in alphabetical order. Close the table saving the change to the design when prompted. (Clicking the *Sort Descending* button will sort in reverse order). *Warning: this is a dynamic sort and cannot be saved.*

Figure 5-21

TITLE	LAST_NAME	FIRST_NAME	STREET	CITY	STATE	
Mr.	Drucker	Peter H.	345 Warren Road	Hudson	New York	12305
Mr.	Whitney	Craig	25 Wood Lake Road	Morris	New Jersey	25059
Mr.	Sitkin	Howard W.	17 Morace Street	Springvale	New Hampshire	49492
Dr.	Skalek	William F.	8 Yorkshire Place	Teatown	South Dakota	39285
Mr.	Salione	Phillip	35 Truesdale Ave	Phoenix	Arizona	35842
Mr.	Fabian	James T.	36 Palmer Court	Chicago	Illinois	30928
Mr.	Kohlman	Frank	35 Miller Drive	Milwaukee	Wisconsin	49740
Mr.	Tedesco	George R.	346 Skytop Drive	Spokane	Washington	35828
Mrs.	Zito	Helen K.	64 Albany Post Rd.	Dana	Maryland	35080
Mr.	Peterson	Jack S.	54 Elmor Ave	Barston	Ohio	39897
Mr.	Nelson	Robert M.	1 Franklin Ave.	St. Louis	Missouri	34097
Ms.	Buckley	Denise	23 Georgetown Rd.	Chicago	Illinois	30928
Mr.	Roberts	James	567 Ridge Rd.	Columbus	Ohio	56778
Mr.	Thompson	Howard	799 Tucker Ave.	Blakeley	Wisconsin	35899
Ms.	Parker	Gina	640 Palm Tree Lane	Phoenix	Arizona	35899
Mr.	Jones	Timothy	89945 Marydale Lane	Starkey	New Hampshire	49478
Mr.	Kaufman	William	7654 Flamton St.	Milwaukee	Wisconsin	49788
Dr.	Timko	Rebecca	34 Salem Ave.	Spokane	Washington	35829
Mr.	Emerson	Douglas	789 Carmichael Ave.	Boston	Massachusetts	12345
Mr.	Hicks	Kevin	3407 Nathrop Dr.	Chicago	Illinois	30987
Mrs	Williams	Emily	678 National Pike	Baltimore	Maryland	22345

Record: 1 of 21

Sorts-within-Sorts

You can sort by multiple fields in a query to achieve a sort within a sort. This is analogous to a telephone directory where entries are first alphabetized by Last Name and then by First Name.

1.　　　Click *Queries* on the Objects bar, select *Tute1Query2* and then click the *Design* button on the Database window toolbar to open the query in Design view.

2.　　　Let's sort the Title field and then, within this, the Last Name field in ascending order. Before we do this, first delete *Mr* from the **Criteria** cell in the Title field. Then click in the **Sort**: cell in the Title field and select *Ascending order*. Repeat this action for the Last Name field. Your screen should now look like the one shown in Figure 5-22 on the next page.

Figure 5-22

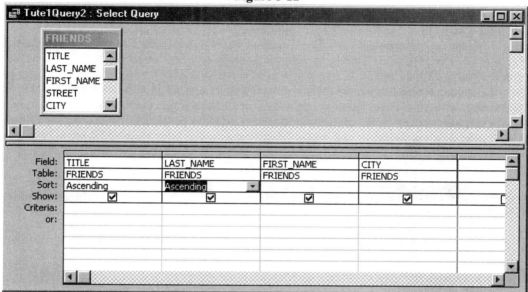

Click the *Run* button, or select QUERY/RUN to view the results of your query. The records should be sorted first by Title (i.e. *Dr.* before *Mr.*, *Mr.* before *Ms.* or *Prof.*), and then within each Title grouping, in ascending Last Name order.

4.   Save your query with a new name by selecting FILE/SAVE AS, and typing in a new name (e.g.: *Tute3Query2*). Close the query and press [F11] to return to the Database window if necessary.

Sorting Data in Reports

When you print a report, you usually want to order the records in a particular way. For example, if you were printing a list of suppliers, you may wish to sort the records alphabetically by company name. When you are setting up the parameters for a new report using the Report Wizard, Access enables you to specify the sort order. If you change your mind after the report has been created, you can use the Sorting and Grouping tool in Report Design view.

The Sorting and Grouping tool allows you to sort by up to 10 fields and expressions, and you can sort on the same field or expression more than once. For example in a five-character field, you could apply an ascending sort to the first three characters, and a descending sort to the last two characters.

Let's repeat the query sort we have just performed in Report Design view. (We could, of course, simply change the record source for the report to the query we have just created to achieve the same results).

1.   With the FRIENDS Database window on the screen, click *Reports* on the Objects bar and select the *Report of My Friends* report created in the Tutorial for Case 2. Click the *Design* button to open the report in Design view.

2.   Click the Sorting and Grouping   button on the Report Design toolbar, or select VIEW/SORTING AND GROUPING to open the Sorting and Grouping dialog box.

3.   Click in the first cell in the Field/Expression column. Click the list arrow and change the field from *City* to *Title*. Press the down arrow key on the keyboard to move to the next Field/Expression cell. Click the list arrow and select *Last Name*. Note that the default Sort Order is ascending which is perfect for our needs. Your screen should now resemble Figure 5-23.

Figure 5-23

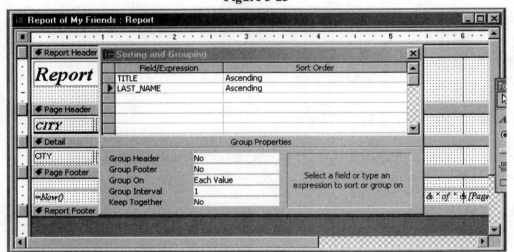

4.   Click the Print Preview button or select FILE/PRINT PREVIEW to see the effect that imposing the sort order has had on the report. Print your report.

5.   Save the report with a new name (e.g.: *Tute3Report1*) by selecting FILE/SAVE AS from the menu. Close the Report of My Friends report and exit Access by choosing FILE/EXIT from the menu.

Database Case 4

Clifford's Pharmacy

Problem: Summarize and analyze data from a transaction processing system for government reporting requirements

Management Skills: Organize
Control

Access Skills: Queries
Sorting
Data Reduction
Reporting

Data Table: CLIFFORD

Richard Clifford, the owner and pharmacist of Clifford's Pharmacy in Portland, OR, was going through his daily mail and came across a letter he had been expecting from the state government. The letter informed him of new regulations and reporting requirements for certain categories of drugs.

The Oregon state government had begun an initiative to restrict the growing use of addictive and dangerous drugs. One of the first steps involved identifying the type and amount of these drugs sold by each pharmacy in the state. The state then intended to analyze this data and identify any regional trends.

The new regulations had been discussed at a recent meeting of Richard's local chapter of the Pharmacy Guild, the state professional body for pharmacists. Most pharmacists agreed that the new controls were a good idea, but the thought of yet another record-keeping chore was not attractive.

Three years ago each of the members of Richard's Pharmacy Guild had installed a personal computer with software to manage the pharmacy prescription process. When a customer wanted a prescription filled, the pharmacist entered his or her personal details (if a new customer) and the drug and dosage requirements prescribed by the doctor. The system produced three outputs: a label to affix to the medication, a repeat prescription if required, and a detailed receipt for the customer for insurance purposes. For regular customers, the software could check whether new medication would interact adversely with any existing medication.

The letter from the government specified that usage information was required for only six classes of drugs: sedatives, analgesics, anti-hypertensives, diuretics, anti-inflammatory drugs and anti-depressives. At any given time, Richard's pharmacy stocked around 100 drugs in these target groups.

The government required each pharmacy to submit a quarterly summary report indicating the usage of each drug issued in the six target classes during this period. Total usage of these six classes was also required. The government would conduct random cross checks with drug company delivery records to check the accuracy of the reporting. Severe penalties were specified for non-compliance.

The table below shows a sampling of the codes assigned to drug classes used by Richard's pharmacy prescription program. Use this to identify the drug codes of interest to the government.

DRUG_CODE	DRUG_CLASS
A1	Steroids
A2	Diuretic
A3	Anti-hypertensives
A4	Analgesics
G7	Anti-diarrhoea
G8	Birth Control
G9	Sedatives
P1	Anti-inflammatories
P2	Anti-malaria
P3	Antibiotic
P4	Anti-depressives

ChemTech, the firm that had provided the computerized prescription system, had also attended the Pharmacy Guild's meeting. They said it would take many weeks to change the current system to meet the government's requirements. They quoted a very high fee, and a three-month delay before conversion would be possible. They could, however, immediately deliver an add-on program that would convert each quarter's prescriptions into a generic data format, which could be readily used by various Windows-based database packages.

For a low cost solution, ChemTech recommended that each pharmacist purchase a Windows-based database package and use it with the conversion program to perform the government's usage analysis.

The database package also could have other purposes. Many of the pharmacies stocked a range of gift lines, vitamins, and fashion accessories, and used a manual-card system to keep track of their inventory and suppliers in these areas. Using a database to automate this side of the business was another attractive idea.

Richard felt confident that he could design a database program to meet state government needs. The job could be performed on the pharmacy's personal computer on weekends when the store was closed. Richard estimated that he used only two or three of the drugs on the target list on any given day. He also believed that some of the information required by the government would be useful for his business. For example, it would be handy to know how much he sold of each company's drugs.

One problem still bothered Richard. Each drug company supplied medication in different tablet sizes. The strength of each tablet also varied in terms of milligram dosage. The government needed its usage statistics to be reported in milligrams (mgs). Fortunately, the pharmacy prescription system recorded both the number of tablets and their strength (in mgs) used for each prescription. To satisfy the government's requirements, Richard needed only to multiply the number of tablets by strength to get total milligram usage.

Part of the data table produced by the conversion program for a quarter's of prescriptions issued by Clifford Pharmacy has been saved as an Access table called CLIFFORD on SOLVEIT.MDB. Create a new empty database, and import this table now.

Tasks: There are six tasks in this case:

1. Design a query to filter out all of the drugs **not** of interest to the state government.

2. Design a summary report to present to the state government each quarter. Include only the total drug usage and the sub-total usage for each Drug Code. The report should be sorted by Drug Code. Do not include the individual prescription records.

3. Print this report.

4. Richard would like to discover which drug companies produce the drugs he sells under each Drug Code. Design and produce a report that presents all the quarter's transactions sorted by Drug Code. Within each Drug Code, sort alphabetically by Supplier. Include all appropriate fields including Drug Name and Supplier.

5. Richard has been frustrated by the slow delivery of supplies by Roche. The Roche sales representative is coming to visit next week and Richard will raise the subject. Richard would like to prepare for the visit by finding out how much of Roche's products he actually uses. Create and print out a report of all the prescriptions Clifford Pharmacy dispensed when the drug was provided by Roche. He would like this list sorted by Drug Code with sub-total usages included for each class.

*6. ChemTech has extended their pharmacy system. The new system is compatible with several Windows-based database packages including Access. The system is menu driven, and the pharmacist just selects which operation is required. Menu options include, "Enter a New Customer" and "Fill Prescription." The system has four main data files: customer, drug information, inventory, and transaction records.

The customer enters the store and gives the prescription to the pharmacist or shop assistant. The pharmacist goes to the computer and checks whether the customer is on file. If not, customer details are entered; otherwise, the customer's record is located by the system. Prescription details are then entered. A check automatically occurs to ensure that the new drug does not interact with any medication currently used by the customer.

The pharmacist then fills the prescription, the inventory level for that drug is adjusted downwards, a sticky label prints out, and a record is added to the transaction database. The transaction database is just a log of every prescription issued. A repeat script is printed if required, and a detailed customer receipt printed for insurance purposes.

Draw a data flow diagram (first-level only) describing ChemTech's new system. Include the major processes, data files, data flows, system outputs and people involved in the system. Identify all the fields in each of the data files.

At the end of each week, a number of management reports are produced. Suggest what you think these reports will be, and what fields they are likely to contain.

Information on producing data flow diagrams is contained in most information systems texts. Our reference is: *Essentials of Management Information Systems: A Contemporary Perspective,* K.C. Laudon & J.P. Laudon, 1996, Prentice Hall.

Time Estimates (excluding task marked *)

Expert: 30 minutes
Intermediate: 1.5 hours
Novice: 2.5 hours

Tutorial for Database Case 4 Using Access 2002

How to Create Record Groups in Reports

For many reports, sorting the records isn't enough; you may also want to divide them into groups. A *group* is a collection of records that share a common characteristic, such as the same Product Number or the same ZIP Code. In Access, a group consists of a group header, a series of detail records, and a group footer.

Grouping enables you to separate records of groups visually, and to display introductory and summary data for each group. For example, the report extract shown below groups sales by date and calculates the total amount of sales for each day.

Data Grouped by Date			
Delivery Date:	**Invoice No.**	**Company**	**Sale Amount**
11-Nov-2001			
	10423	Hungry Macs	$1,323.34
	10425	Barnacle Jill	$2,457.40
	10426	Blue Rooster	$161.18
	10428	Hot Chipps	$741.88
Total for 11-Nov-2001			$4,683.80
14-Nov-2001			
	10441	Chicken 'n' Chips	$1,074.20
Total summarises the Group			Sales sorted by Invoice No.

Let's produce a report with groups using the FRIENDS database and the Report of My Friends report created in the Tutorial for Case 2. We want to group the report by State to produce a listing of friends sorted alphabetically (ascending order) by state. For friends in the same state, we want to sort these alphabetically by Last Name. Before we can do this, we need to make some modifications to the existing FRIENDS table. Open the practice database FRIENDS.MDB.

1.   With the FRIENDS Database window on the screen, click *Tables* on the Objects bar, and double click the FRIENDS table. Add the five new records shown in Figure 5-24 to the table, making sure that some of the state names you enter in the State field duplicate those of existing records (see Figure 5-49). To speed up this

procedure, just enter the new records with the Title, Last Name, First Name, Street, City and State fields.

Figure 5-24

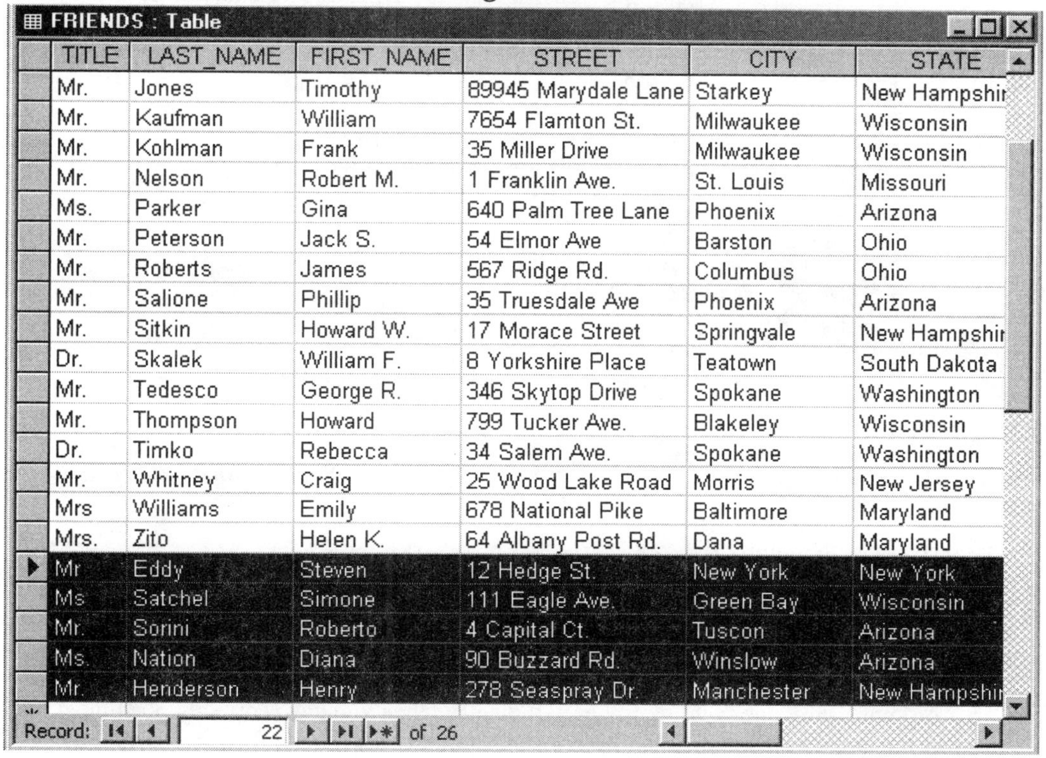

TITLE	LAST_NAME	FIRST_NAME	STREET	CITY	STATE
Mr.	Jones	Timothy	89945 Marydale Lane	Starkey	New Hampshir
Mr.	Kaufman	William	7654 Flamton St.	Milwaukee	Wisconsin
Mr.	Kohlman	Frank	35 Miller Drive	Milwaukee	Wisconsin
Mr.	Nelson	Robert M.	1 Franklin Ave.	St. Louis	Missouri
Ms.	Parker	Gina	640 Palm Tree Lane	Phoenix	Arizona
Mr.	Peterson	Jack S.	54 Elmor Ave	Barston	Ohio
Mr.	Roberts	James	567 Ridge Rd.	Columbus	Ohio
Mr.	Salione	Phillip	35 Truesdale Ave	Phoenix	Arizona
Mr.	Sitkin	Howard W.	17 Morace Street	Springvale	New Hampshir
Dr.	Skalek	William F.	8 Yorkshire Place	Teatown	South Dakota
Mr.	Tedesco	George R.	346 Skytop Drive	Spokane	Washington
Mr.	Thompson	Howard	799 Tucker Ave.	Blakeley	Wisconsin
Dr.	Timko	Rebecca	34 Salem Ave.	Spokane	Washington
Mr.	Whitney	Craig	25 Wood Lake Road	Morris	New Jersey
Mrs	Williams	Emily	678 National Pike	Baltimore	Maryland
Mrs.	Zito	Helen K.	64 Albany Post Rd.	Dana	Maryland
Mr	Eddy	Steven	12 Hedge St.	New York	New York
Ms	Satchel	Simone	111 Eagle Ave.	Green Bay	Wisconsin
Mr.	Sorini	Roberto	4 Capital Ct.	Tuscon	Arizona
Ms.	Nation	Diana	90 Buzzard Rd.	Winslow	Arizona
Mr.	Henderson	Henry	278 Seaspray Dr.	Manchester	New Hampshir

Record: 22 of 26

2.   Press F11 to return to the Database Window.

3.   Click *Reports* on the Objects bar, and select the *Report of My Friends* report you created in Tutorial 2. Click the *Design* button to open the report in Design view.

4.   Click the Sorting and Grouping button, or select VIEW/SORTING AND GROUPING to open the Sorting and Grouping dialog box.

5.   Click in the first cell in the Field/Expression column and change the primary sorting criterion from City to State. In the Group Properties section at the bottom of the dialog box, click in the Group Header box and change the default property setting to *Yes*.

6.   Click in second cell in the Field/Expression column immediately under State. Click the list arrow and select Last Name as the secondary sort criterion. Leave the Group Header for Last Name set to *No*. Accept the default ascending sort order for both fields. The settings in the Sorting and Grouping dialog box are displayed in Figure 5-25.

Figure 5-25

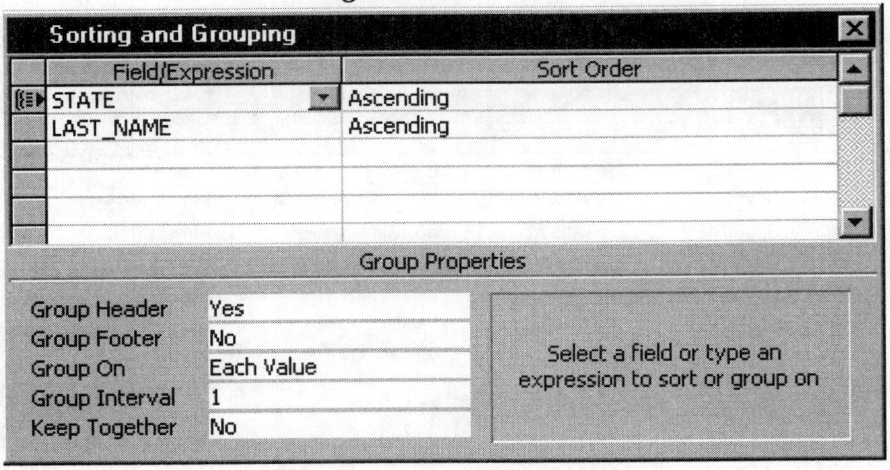

7.　　Exit the Sorting and Grouping box by clicking on the ⊠ box in the top right hand corner, and return to Report Design view. You should notice that a blank *State Header* area has been added to the report design.

8.　　Select VIEW/FIELDLIST or click the *Field List* button ▤ on the Report Design toolbar to activate a scrollable field list for the FRIENDS table, if not already activated. Select the State field in the field list. Drag the State field to the State Header and position it against the left margin. Two boxes, a label box and a text box, are inserted. Select the label and delete it. (You must use the move handle in the upper-left corner of the label to move it from on top of the text box first. A pointer with one pointing finger will display when you have correctly positioned the mouse over the move handle. Click the label to select it and press [Delete] on the keyboard)

9.　　Double click the State text box to open its property sheet. Click the *Format* tab, if necessary. Scroll down the list and change the *Font Size* property to *14* and the *Font Weight* property to *Bold*. Close the property sheet and resize the text box to suit the changes. Your screen should look similar to Figure 5-26.

10.　　Click the *Print Preview* button or select FILE/PRINT PREVIEW to see the effect that the changes have had on the report. Return to Design view and increase the size of the State text box if necessary to accommodate the lengths of the state names. When you have completed the change, return to Print Preview If your report appears in *Landscape* orientation, select FILE/PAGE SETUP from the menu to open the Page Setup dialog box. On the *Page* tab, change the orientation to *Portrait*. Print the report.

Your report should display the FRIENDS records grouped alphabetically by State, and within each group, ordered alphabetically by Last Name.

11.　　Save the report with a new name (e.g.: *Tute4Report1*) by selecting FILE/SAVE AS from the menu. Click the *Close* button [Close] on the Print Preview toolbar to return to Report Design view.

Figure 5-26

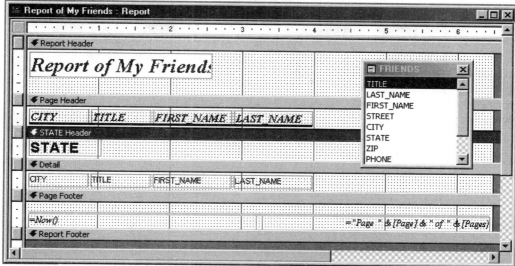

Calculating Group Summary Statistics

You often will want to ask questions about groups of data such as "How many orders did we receive this month?" or "What's the average price of all the products in our Toothpaste category?" You can perform calculations on groups of records in reports or queries. The following table shows some of the types of *functions* (calculations) you can use with Access (refer also Access Tutorial for Case 2)

Use This Type of Calculation	To Find
Sum	the total of values in a field
Avg	the average of values in a field
Min	the lowest value in a field
Max	the highest value in a field
Count	the number of values in a field (not including null values)

Let's use the *Count* function to count the number of friends we have in each State, and display that number at the end of each group in our report.

1.   In Report Design view, click the Sorting and Grouping button or select VIEW/SORTING AND GROUPING to reopen the Sorting and Grouping dialog box.

2.   Click in the first cell in the Field/Expression column where State is entered as the group to sort by, and then click in the Group Footer property settings box and change the default to *Yes*.

3.   Exit the Sorting and Grouping box by clicking the ⊠ box in the top right hand corner, and return to report design view. You should notice that a blank *State Footer* section has been added to the report design.

4.   Select VIEW/FIELDLIST from the menu or click on the *FieldList* toolbar button (displayed at right) to activate the scrollable field list for the

FRIENDS table if necessary. Select the Last_Name field in the field list. Drag the Last_Name field into the State Footer and position it. Use the move handle to move the label from on top of the text box and delete it.

5.   Double click the Last_Name text box in the State Footer to open its *property* sheet. On the *Data* tab, edit the *Control Source* property to include the Count calculation (see Figure 5-27). Be careful with the syntax here and with the entering of round and square brackets. When you use a function, you must enclose the expression on which it is being performed in parentheses. All field names must be enclosed in square brackets, as learned previously. Close the property sheet.

Figure 5-27

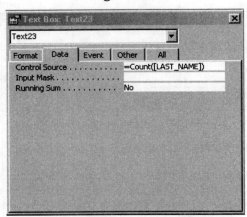

6.   Click the Print Preview button or select FILE/PRINT PREVIEW to see the effect of this change on your report. Results should resemble Figure 5-28. Print your report.

Figure 5-28

Report of My Friends

CITY	TITLE	FIRST_NAME	LAST_NAME
Arizona			
Winslow	Ms.	Diana	Nation
Phoenix	Ms.	Gina	Parker
Phoenix	Mr.	Phillip	Salione
Tuscon	Mr.	Roberto	Sorini
			4
Illinois			
Chicago	Ms.	Denise	Buckley
Chicago	Mr.	James T.	Fabian
Chicago	Mr.	Kevin	Hicks
			3
Maryland			
Baltimore	Mrs	Emily	Williams

7.   Save the report with a new name (e.g.: *Tute4Report2*) by selecting FILE/SAVE AS from the menu. Press [F11] to return to the Database Window.

Deleting Records in Access

To delete a record in an Access table, highlight the record row intended for deletion, and press either the [Delete] key or select EDIT/DELETE. Access will ask you to confirm your action. Click the OK button to proceed with deletion of the record.

Database Case 5

Waterford University

Problem:	Develop an admissions database
Management Skills:	Coordinate Decide
Access Skills:	Queries Finding Records Sorting and Grouping Reporting
Data Table:	WATERFORD

The Graduate School of Business (GSB) at Waterford University began operations the mid-1960s. Since that time it has grown to become one of the most competitive and well respected schools of management in the United States. Waterford has particularly strong faculty in the Marketing and Information Systems areas.

Andrew Ulrich has been Dean of Admissions at the GSB for over thirty years, and he feels it is time for a change. The business of running the admissions program has become so politicized, argumentative, and chaotic that he is considering resignation. Before he resigns, he has promised to himself and his boss, Tom Davenport, president of Waterford, that he will build a new admissions system. He could use your help.

The Office of Admissions gathers applications and supporting documentation from a number of sources. Each student submits a completed application form and an essay. Faculty who have worked with the students at their undergraduate institution submit references. The undergraduate university also submits transcript verification forms. The College Board also submits data on GMAT scores. Miscellaneous information on student ethnicity, age, and sex is also collected to meet various legal requirements and reporting standards.

The Alumni group has made it very clear that they want admissions to treat the children (though not more distant relatives) of alumni with special care.

All of this information is collected by the Admissions Office staff and summarized on an Admissions Sheet. The Admissions Sheet is the first piece of paper in the bulging folders kept on each student. The essays and outside faculty references are graded on a 1-5 scale (with 5 being the highest score) by faculty committees.

This procedure was developed in the mid 1970's when the school had 600 or so applicants for 200 positions. Today the school has 5,000 applicants for about 400 positions. Although the Admissions Office (AO) staff has doubled in size (to eight full-time people), the workload is still heavy, and the process is breaking down as older, experienced personnel retire.

The procedure for processing the Admissions Sheet is one source of the problems. Because the data arrive from different sources at different times, the AO clerks have to go back to each student folder many times to enter and update the information.

Students, parents, faculty, institutions, and alumni call frequently to see if certain information has been received. Sometimes clerks pull the sheet to answer queries and then the sheet is lost. New sheets have to be coded up in this case.

A number of data quality problems have emerged. For instance, more and more students are claiming that their GMAT scores are wrongly recorded. Changes from the University Board are submitted with growing frequency, but AO staff is often so pressed for time that sometimes these record changes are not made. Other data quality problems involve the undergraduate grade point average, address errors, and majors. Students move, change majors, and their GPAs change. The current system should be able to keep track of these changes.

The existing system does not appear to support the group decision-making process, which is at the heart of admissions. A small group of ten faculty and three Admissions Officers make all the decisions on the Admissions Committee. Each member of the Admissions Committee takes a different look at the data, wants the data organized differently, and feels frustrated when this is impossible. One result is that committee members spend too much time arguing over the decision criteria and weightings, and too little time searching for appropriate candidates. For instance, some faculty are interested only in GPA and GMAT scores and want to see the applicant pool sorted first by GPA, and then by GMAT. Other faculty are more oriented towards GPA and references and do not even want to see the GMAT.

Administrators want to make sure that, within accepted academic criteria, the alumni's children get a special hearing. There is little opportunity to find those candidates who do well on all the criteria. All in all, the manual resorting of lists and list compilation is a tedious process characterized by long delays and mistakes.

All of these problems have produced a political dimension: no one is happy with the existing system and everyone blames the Admissions Office. As Dean of Admissions, Andrew Ulrich is now under attack from many sides. The AO staff is also unsatisfied, even a bit surly at times, because of the long hours they must spend each spring compiling lists, up-dating files, and meeting last minute deadlines.

Rather than rely on the Administrative Computing Center (which is already extended beyond capacity), Andrew has decided to build a PC-based admissions database.

A sample of the admissions database (WATERFORD) has been created for you on SOLVEIT.MDB as an Access table object. Create a new Access database and import the WATERFORD table now.

Tasks: There are six tasks in this case:

1.   There are two typical faculty requests which the system must provide: one list of
        applicants sorted by GPA and GMAT scores, and another list for other professors who
        want the students listed by GPA and references. Include only the essential fields in each
        report. For example, for the report sorted by GPA and GMAT scores, the professors need
        only the student's name, school and scores. Create queries for the following:

        (a) A listing of all the applicants for professors on the admissions committee who want to
        see the applicants listed by decreasing GPA scores. Students with the same GPA should
        be sorted by decreasing GMAT scores.

        (b) A second listing showing the applicants sorted by decreasing GPA. Students with the
        same GPA should be sorted by decreasing reference scores. Print out the results of both
        listings.

2.   The AO clerks absolutely insist on having rapid access to students' complete records on
        the basis of Last Name only. That is, they want to type the last name of the student into a
        PC and have the complete record appear on the screen. Because so many people call in
        checking on student applicant files, this capability would save an enormous amount of
        time. Using the WATERFORD table, identify the Access sequence of commands that
        would enable the AO staff to do this.

3.   Ulrich wants a report or listing of just the applicants who are children of alumni. He will
        use this list as a crib sheet in committee deliberations. Whenever a candidate is settled
        on, he will check his list of alumni applicants to see if that person is on the list. If not, he
        will suggest an equally well-qualified alumni applicant. Thus the alumni applicants
        should be sorted by decreasing GPA. Students with the same GPA should be sorted by
        decreasing GMAT scores.

        It is advisable, since 5,000 applicants will be in the final database, to make two lists here.
        One list is alphabetical, permitting quick look-ups; the second list would arrange students
        by GPA and GMAT. (a) Create a query to display this information, and (b) create a
        report to print out the results.

4.   A small group of professors is concerned that the business school is loading up with
        Natural Science majors. They would like to ensure that students from Liberal Arts and
        Social Science backgrounds are considered as well. The non-science students tend to
        have better GPA scores than GMAT scores (because of an alleged quantitative bias in the
        GMAT test), and they tend to have better recommendations.

        This group of faculty would like a report that plays to the strengths of the non-science
        majors. Create a report, which lists applicants by college major, showing name, GPA,
        and reference scores. Students of the same major should be sorted by GPA.

*5.   There is an on-going dispute among Admissions Committee members about the
        comparative strengths of the Social Science (Business and Psychology), Liberal Arts

(English and History), and Science majors (Math, Physics and Engineering). Filter out these three groups and calculate their average scores on all quantitative variables. Then compare the groups in a one-paragraph statement.

*6.   There are number of ways this database system could be improved to better meet the needs of Waterford. List the ways the system could be improved. Pick one of these improvements and implement it in the database.

Time Estimates (excluding tasks marked with *):

Expert: 1 hour
Intermediate: 1.5 hours
Novice: 3.5 hours

Tutorial for Database Case 5 Using Access 2002

Indexing in Access

If you often search a table or frequently need to sort records by a certain field, you can speed up these operations by assigning indexes to your fields. Access uses indexes in a table in the same way as you would use an index in a book: to find data, it looks up the location of the data in the index.

In Access, you create an index on a single field by setting the Index property. The table below lists the possible settings for Indexed properties.

Index Property Setting	Definition
No	Do not create an index for this field (the default)
Yes (duplicates OK)	Create an index for this field
Yes (no duplicates)	Create a unique index for this field

If you create a unique index, Access will not allow a value that already exists in that field to be entered in the same field for another record. Primary key fields (see the Chapter 4 Tutorial) are automatically indexed by Access, to help speed up the execution of queries and other operations. Up to 32 indexes can be assigned to a single table or query; each index can contain up to 10 fields. Fields with Memo or Counter data types cannot be indexed.

You want an index only if it speeds up the execution of queries, searching, or sorting. A Last Name field is a good candidate for an index since the values stored in it vary greatly, and it is often used to find specific records.

1.   Open the practice database FRIENDS.MDB. With the FRIENDS Database window on
      the screen, click *Tables* on the Objects bar. Select the FRIENDS table and click the
      Design button on the Database Window toolbar to open it in Design view.

2.   Add a new field before the TITLE field. The Field Name for the new field will be *ID*,
      and the Data Type will be *AutoNumber*. Right-click the ID field and select *Primary Key*
      on the shortcut menu.

3.   In the Field Name column, select the Last_Name field. In the Field Properties pane, click
      in the *Indexed* property settings box. Click the list arrow and select *Yes (Duplicates OK)*
      to set the index for the Last_Name field. Click the Save button or select FILE/SAVE.
      Your Design view window should look like Figure 5-29.

Figure 5-29

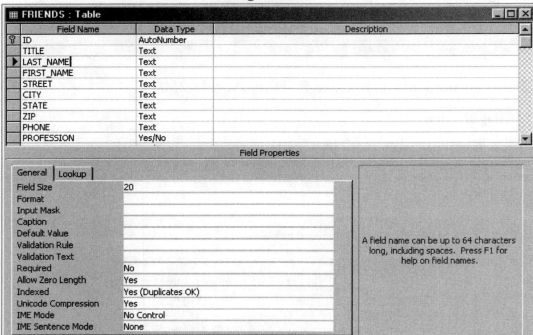

4.   To view and/or edit existing indexes, open the Indexes window by clicking the
      Indexes button (displayed at right) on the Table Design toolbar or by selecting
      VIEW/INDEXES (see Figure 5-30).

Figure 5-30

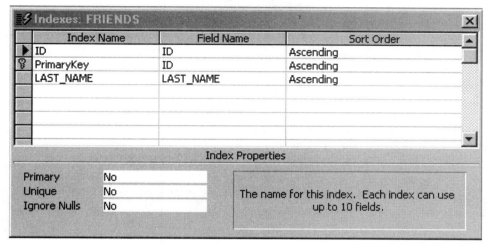

5.   Change indexes or index properties as needed. To delete an index, highlight the intended row and press the [Delete] key. This removes only the index, not the field itself. For Help on index properties, press [F1] with the Indexes window open.

6.   Close the Indexes window by clicking on the ☒ box in the top right hand corner.

Creating Multiple-Field Indexes

If you often search or sort by two or more specific fields at the same time, you may need to create a multiple field index. For instance, if you often set criteria in the same query for LastName and FirstName fields, it makes sense to index both fields. When you sort a table by a multiple field index, Access sorts first by the first field listed in the Indexes window. If there are records with duplicate values in this field, Access then sorts by the second field listed.

Multiple field indexes are created in the Indexes Window by including a row for each field in the index, but including the index name in the first row only (see Figure 5-31). Access treats all rows as part of the same index until it reaches a different Index Name. To insert a new row between existing indexes, click the row *below* the location of the row to be inserted. Then press the *Insert* key.

To create a multiple field index in the FRIENDS table:

1.   Reopen the Indexes window. Click in the Field Name cell directly below the one containing the LAST_NAME field. Click the list arrow and select FIRST_NAME on the list. Ascending is automatically selected as the sort order.

2.   Close the Indexes window. Save the changes.

Figure 5-31

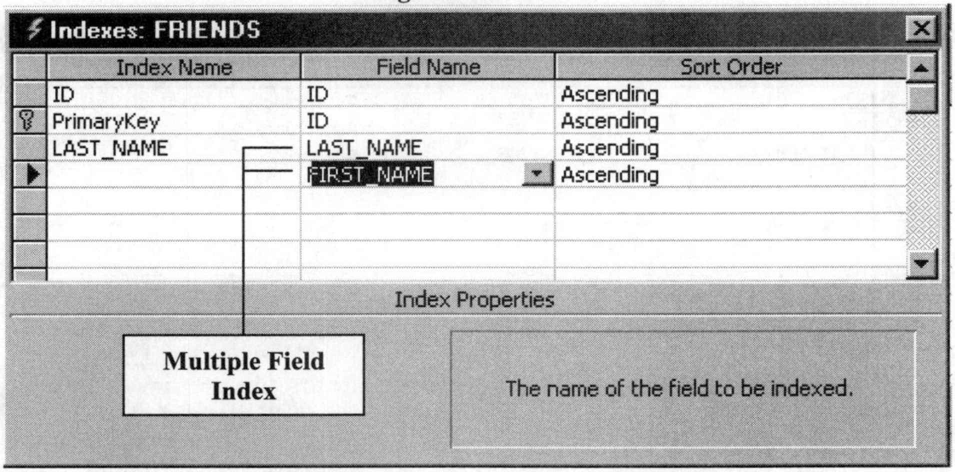

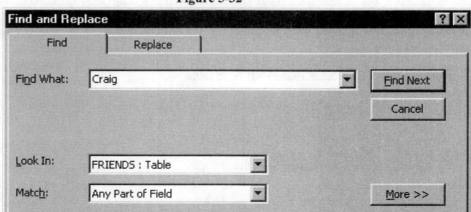

Forward and Backward Searching in Access

When you want to find a specific record or certain values within fields, you can use the *Find* command to go directly to a record. *Find* can be used with most Access objects. To use *Find*, select EDIT/FIND to open the Find and Replace dialog box (see Figure 5-32). The Find and Replace dialog box enables you to search and replace text within a field.

Type the text you want to locate into the *Find What* list box. For added flexibility, *Find* enables you to enter word stems, and wildcard symbols. Similar to DOS, a question mark (?) stands for any single character in the same position as the question mark. The asterisk (*) stands for any number of characters in the same position as the asterisk. The pound sign or number sign (#) stands for a single numeric digit in the same position as the sign.

Choose between seaching across fields or a single field, and whether to search forwards or the whole file. Practice using *Find* with your FRIENDS table.

Figure 5-32

Database Case 6

Acoustic Designs 1

Problem:	Develop a mailing list database
Management skills:	Organize Control
Access skills:	Database Design Queries Reports Linking Tables
Data Tables:	ACOUSTIC_A ACOUSTIC_B

Acoustic Designs is a medium-sized company based in Nashville, TN. The business was established in the early 1980s by Trevor and Brad Knox, and grew out of a hobby the two brothers shared in music and electronic circuitry. The company has two distinct business divisions. The Acoustic Design side of the business designs, manufactures, and retails a range of audio equipment at the high end of the market. This business includes custom-built sound systems, the famous Acoustic Design valve amplifier, which is eagerly sought by audiophile buffs around the world, and high performance ribbon speakers. This side of the business is high margin and very successful, and is managed by Trevor Knox.

Acoustic Design's main customers are audio retailers, and music production houses such as EMI, Warner Music, and Polygram Records. Every six months, Acoustic Design distributes a product catalog to its 3,500 customers.

Brad Knox manages Melodia, the other division in the company. Melodia is a lucrative mail-order business that locates and purchases rare and hard-to-find sound recordings through contact agents around the world. Many of these items are sourced from the estates of deceased musical performers. Music areas include classical, opera, jazz, rock, country and western, folk, soul, reggae, and ethnic (Asian and African). The business currently carries around 15,000 titles in this area, which are held in audio CD, vinyl record, tape, or video format. These are sold to audio retailers and music production houses throughout the world. Melodia currently has around 12,000 customers on its mailing list and, Acoustic Design, distributes a catalog of new and current offerings on a biannual basis.

The existing Melodia mailing list presents a difficulty for Brad Knox. While the marketing side of Acoustic Design has been handled by a PC-based database package for some years, Knox has been unsure how to go about integrating the Melodia mailing list into this system, although he knows this could make good business sense. Knox suspects that at least 25% of the customers on his mailing list are also customers who regularly purchase from Acoustic Design.

The Melodia mailing list has been steadily growing since the mid 1980s, when this side of the business was formed. The mailing list originally was kept on a series of 3 x 5 cards that recorded customer mailing and music interest details. This method soon became unwieldy as the list grew. In the late 1980's, Melodia outsourced the data management of its list to Source Right Computer Services. Source Right provides data entry and maintenance services, and produces mailing label printouts for Melodia whenever a catalog mailing is required.

Knox has several problems with the bureau method. He has recently received an invoice from Source Right requesting its usual quarterly payment of $2,500 for maintenance of his mailing list. Knox has been concerned about the escalating costs of using Source Right for some time and no longer believes their services are worthwhile. He also believes that the bureau method does not give him control of his data.

The current mailing list is not a database. In the 1980s, Source Right created the original list as a long sequential file organized alphabetically by customer last name, and has continued to maintain it in this format. Knox is not happy with this structure, which he feels is inflexible, and cannot provide information vital to the management of his business. For example, he cannot easily obtain information about the music interests of his customers for targeted mailouts. A simple query like *Print a list of all Australian customers with an interest in Opera* requires a special programming task by Source Right, a lengthy delay before Knox receives the information, and incurs an additional charge for Melodia. More complex queries are simply impossible.

The structure of the current mailing list also complicates updating existing data or checking whether a customer is already on the list. Knox knows that a large portion of his mailing list probably is out of date. He has noticed that the number of return-to-sender envelopes Melodia receives has rapidly increased as customers move addresses or contact names change. The present system makes it difficult to incorporate these changes. Meanwhile, Melodia is incurring a lot of unnecessary mailing-associated expenses. Knox has also noticed that some of these returns have been sent to the same customer several times. This means that there is a level of data duplication in the mailing list. From current indications Knox suspects the duplication may be as high as 20 percent

Another inherent problem with the current system is that, if there are 45 customers at a large music company like Warner Music, the name and address of the company is repeated 45 times! If the name of the company were to change (as is common in the music business) the new name would need to be re-entered 45 times!

Knox is frustrated by the deficiencies of his current mailing list. Although Melodia is profitable, Knox suspects it could be more so if he had the right information when he wanted it and was able to do targeted mailings with ease. He has decided that the only way to get what he wants is to build a parallel mailing list system from the ground up. After consulting with his brother, Knox has purchased a Pentium IV computer and the same relational data base package used by Acoustic Design. Once the new mailing system is working satisfactorily, he plans to dispense with Source Right's services. At a later stage, he will consider integrating his system with that of Acoustic Design.

The existing mailing system has the right information, but it is not stored efficiently and is not easy to interrogate. The existing system has the customer's name, primary music interest (MusIntA), secondary music interest (MusIntB), organization name, address, city, state, country, and ZIP code. The music interests of customers are coded using an internally developed schema.

To make storage and updating of the mailing list more efficient, Knox wants the data stored in two tables, with one containing the names of the customers and the other containing the name and addressing details of the company they work for. Whenever a mailing list is required, the two tables could be joined and the results printed. Knox needs your assistance in developing this project.

The Access data tables on your *Solvelt!* Diskette, ACOUSTIC_A and ACOUSTIC_B, provide the overall design and sample data for the new mailing system. These tables form the basis of this case.

Tasks: There are six tasks in this case:

1. Link the two tables ACOUSTIC_A and ACOUSTIC_B on the Org field. It may be helpful to print out the structure of these tables first. Then print out the results of this join.

2. Create a report for marketing purposes that list all customers separated into alphabetical organizational groups. The fields describing reading interests and address are not needed. Each group should contain one organization with the records sorted alphabetically by last name within these groups.

3. Design this report as a professional document. Include a title, group headings, and any other useful features you think of. Print the report.

4. Design a custom label with four lines of information that can be used as a mailing label.

5. Melodia has recently obtained some rare Soul and Jazz sound recordings. Print a report of all USA customers with one of two music interests (i.e. 64 or 77) in these areas, as either their primary or secondary music interest. Be careful with the Boolean logic in this problem.

*6. The current system uses codes (e.g. 64, 77) for data in the music interest fields. The user of the system and recipients of its reports must know what these codes mean. Devise a way to include the meaning for these codes into the database. You will need to make up meanings for each of the music interest codes (e.g. 64 is Jazz Music and 77 is Soul Music).

Make sure that the method you devise does not include data redundancy. It would be poor database design to have the meanings for these codes repeated (redundantly) throughout the database. With your new table structure, produce a report of customers, their organization and music interests which does not include codes.

Time Estimates (excluding task marked with *):

Expert: 45 minutes
Intermediate: 1.5 hours
Novice: 3 hours

Tutorial for Database Case 6 Using Access 2002

In this case, you will learn two important new skills: joining table files (creating relationships), and creating labels in reports.

Joining Tables

In many earlier database applications, the joining of tables is a procedure that would require you to generate programming code. Access allows you to do this simply via the menu or toolbar, and to run the results of the join in a query (or a report). Access will also generate the SQL (Structured Query Language) programming code for the procedure, so that you can see the effect of your actions.

Before you can join two tables, there must be a related field in both tables. While the field names do not have to be the same for the join to work, the two fields must contain matching data in the records. For this procedure, we will be using the FRIENDS database, and a second practice table BUSDRESS. The latter contains the last names and business addresses of persons in the FRIENDS database.

1. Open the practice database FRIENDS.MDB. Import the BUSDRESS table from the SOLVEIT.MDB database file using FILE/GET EXTERNAL DATA and then the IMPORT command or by clicking the *Import* button (displayed at right) on the Database toolbar. Review the tutorial in Chapter 4 if you are unsure about importing external files. BUSDRESS is a table contained within the SOLVEIT master database. FRIENDS.MDB should now have two tables, and look similar to Figure 5-33.

Figure 5-33

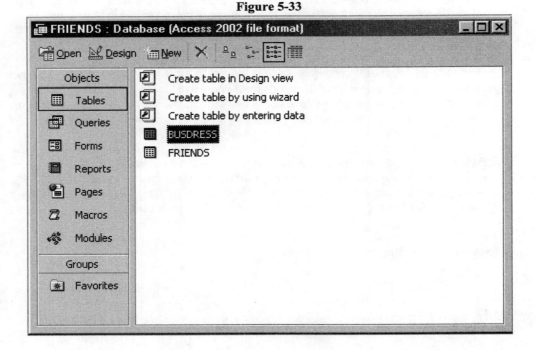

2. In the Database window, double-click the FRIENDS table to open it in Datasheet view. Resize the table so that only the first three columns including the Last_Name field are showing and resize the ID field to its best fit. Then open the BUSDRESS table. Compare the two tables, noting that both LastName fields contain identical data. Remember that the field names themselves do not have to be the same. Close the tables in turn by double clicking the control menu icon ▦ in the top left corner of each table. Save the change to the layout of the FRIENDS table.

3. Click the *Relationships* button (displayed at right) on the Database toolbar to open the Relationships window. Add both tables to the window and close the Show Table dialog box. Now we will create a relationship between the two tables. This will speed up the execution of the query we will create in a moment. Table relationships were last discussed in the tutorial for Chapter 4.

4. Select the LastName field in the BUSDRESS table. Drag the field symbol over to the Last_Name field in the FRIENDS table and release the mouse button. The Edit Relationships dialog box opens. Click the *Create* button. Access generates a dynamic link (line) between the two known as an *equi-join*. An equi-join selects all the records from both tables that have the same value in the selected field.

5. Your Relationships window should look similar to Figure 5-34.

Figure 5-34

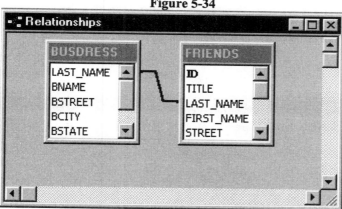

6. Save the relationship by choosing FILE/SAVE.

7. Close the Relationships window. (You are now ready to create a query to generate the effect of the joining action.)

8. In the Database window, click *Queries* on the Objects bar. Double-click *Create query in Design view*.

9. In the *Show Table* dialog box, select the BUSDRESS table and click *Add*. Repeat this action for the FRIENDS table. Click *Close*. Notice that Access has remembered the table relationship, and has immediately established a join between the two Last_Name fields.

10. Select VIEW/SQL VIEW to see the equivalent of this action in the Access Basic programming code:

SELECT
FROM BUSDRESS INNER JOIN FRIENDS ON BUSDRESS.LAST_NAME = FRIENDS.LAST_NAME;

Select VIEW/DESIGN VIEW to return to Query Design view.

11.   In the query window, select and drag the following fields down into the Field row of the design grid.

From FRIENDS	From BUSDRESS
Title	BStreet
First_Name	BCity
Last_Name	BState
	BZip

Finally, click in the *Sort* cell for the Last_Name field, and choose Ascending order. Your query window should now look similar to Figure 5-35.

12.   Select VIEW/SQL VIEW again to see the effect this action has had on the Access Basic programming code:

SELECT FRIENDS.TITLE, FRIENDS.LAST_NAME, FRIENDS.FIRST_NAME, BUSDRESS.BSTREET,
BUSDRESS.BCITY, BUSDRESS.BSTATE, BUSDRESS.BZIP
FROM BUSDRESS INNER JOIN FRIENDS ON BUSDRESS.LAST_NAME = FRIENDS.LAST_NAME
ORDER BY FRIENDS.LAST_NAME;

Figure 5-35

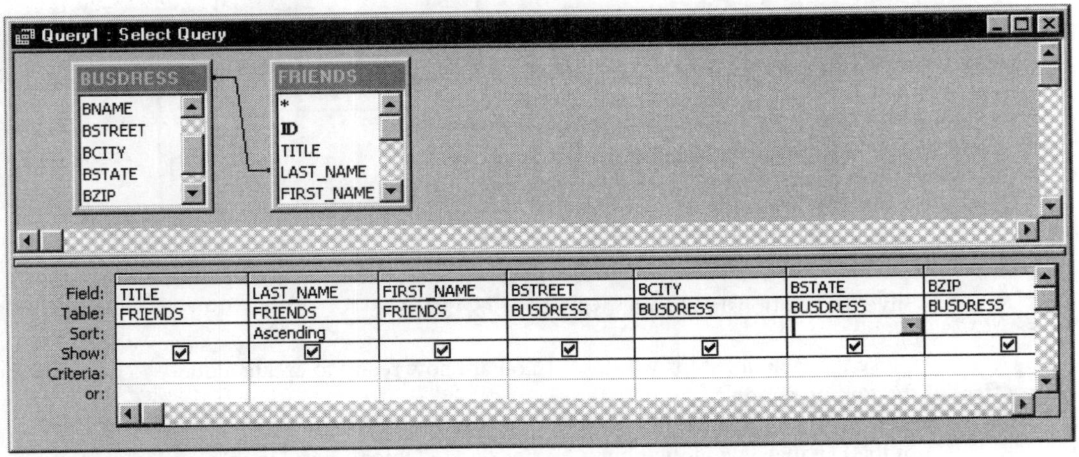

13.   Click the *Run* [button] button and view the resulting dynaset. Access has matched and merged the business address data in the BUSDRESS table with the name data in the FRIENDS table to create a composite display containing non-duplicative data from both (see Figure 5-70).

14.   Print the query if you wish to, or use as the basis for a new report.

15.   Save the query (e.g.: *Tute6Query1*) as shown in Figure 5-36, then close it.

Figure 5-36

| FRIENDS | | | | BUSDRESS | | |

Tute6Query1 : Select Query

TITLE	LAST_NAME	FIRST_NAME	BSTREET	BCITY	BSTATE	BZIP
Ms.	Buckley	Denise	786 Rice Street	Cleveland	Ohio	43203
Mr.	Drucker	Peter H.	345 Ohio St.	Cleveland	Ohio	34203
Mr	Eddy	Steven	873 Dupont Ave.	St. Paul	Minnesota	55444
Mr.	Emerson	Douglas	67 Thistle Way	Detroit	Michigan	45577
Mr.	Fabian	James T.	98 Kansas Street	Burlington	Vermont	94532
Mr.	Henderson	Henry	8956 Front Street	Springvale	California	75893
Mr.	Hicks	Kevin	458 Southmont Drive	Catonsville	Maryland	21228
Mr.	Jones	Timothy	10050 Baltimore Pike	Baltimore	Maryland	21042
Mr.	Kaufman	William	567 Ridge Road	Baltimore	Maryland	21044
Mr.	Kohlman	Frank	856 Irvine Road	Irvine	California	54323
Ms.	Nation	Diana	1098 Cornridge Drive	Ellicott City	Maryland	21117
Mr.	Nelson	Robert M.	75 Yorktown Circle	Yorktown	New York	58964
Ms.	Parker	Gina	459 Palm Drive	Springvale	California	75834
Mr.	Peterson	Jack S.	900 Lake Drive	Detroit	Michigan	45563
Mr.	Roberts	James	900 Lake Drive	Detroit	Michigan	45563
Mr.	Salione	Phillip	459 Palm Drive	Springvale	California	75834
Ms	Singer	Simone	7893 Gregory Avenue	Irvine	California	75945
Mr.	Sitkin	Howard W.	4523 8th Avenue	Hartford	Connecticut	34120
Dr.	Skalek	William F.	57 Morris Drive	Seattle	Washington	45026

Record: 1 of 26

Joined with

How to Create Labels in Access

A report designed to print names and addresses on labels is a common feature of most database applications. Access includes a Label Wizard which can be used to create mailing labels with sizes to match most common commercial adhesive labels. Let's use the practice database FRIENDS.MDB to create a simple three-line address label.

1. Open FRIENDS.MDB. Click *Reports* on the Objects bar. Click *New* on the Database Window toolbar. In the New Reports dialog box, click the list arrow on the *Choose the table or query where the object's data comes from* list box and select the *FRIENDS* table.

2. Select *Label Wizard* and then click *OK*.

3. In the first Wizard dialog box, accept the default label type and dimensions. Click the *Next>* button.

4. On the second screen, select the font, font size, font weight and text color you want for the label. Click the *Next>* button.

5. Choose fields for your label:

First Line
Select *Title*, and click the button to enter it onto the prototype label. Press [Space bar] on your keyboard.
Repeat this action with the *FirstName* field. Press [Space bar].
Select *Last_Name*, and then click . Press [Enter].

Second Line
Select *Street*, and then click . Press [Enter].

Third Line
Select *City*, and then click . Add a comma (,) and press the [Space bar].
Repeat this action with the *State* field. Press the [Space bar].
Select *Zip*, and then click .

Your screen should now look like the one in Figure 5-37. Click the *Next>* button.

Figure 5-37

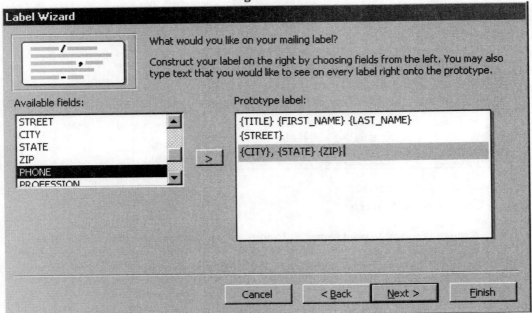

6.   In the next Label Wizard dialog box, select the Last_Name field to sort by. Click the *Next>* button.

7.   In the last Wizard dialog box, choose a name for your report (e.g.: *Tute6Report1*). Click the *Finish* button, and Access will generate your labels and display them in Print Preview.

8.   Send your labels to print, close the report, and exit Access.

Database Case 7

Kingsolver Contractors

Problem:	Develop a payroll system
Management Skill:	Control
Access skills:	Select Queries (calculated fields) Append Queries Reports (wizards)
Data Tables:	CONTRACT 1_MONTH 2_MONTH 3_MONTH

After twelve years working for a general contractor, Martin Kingsolver started his own road construction firm, Kingsolver Contractors, in 1994. For a start-up firm, Kingsolver had done extremely well. In 2001 the company showed gross revenues of $15 million and a net profit of $950,000.

Before starting his own company, Martin had gained a sound understanding of the road building and public sector market working as an estimator for a general contractor in Boston, MA. He developed a network of contacts among local government officials and learned the procedures and pitfalls of responding to government contract solicitations. Fortunately, the local economy grew very rapidly as major corporations, government agencies, and related housing created a boom market for road construction.

The key to Martin's success has been in keeping permanent employee numbers low, relying on sub-contractors, and keeping his capital costs down by renting or leasing heavy equipment. Automated tools have also played an important role.

About 80% of Kingsolver's business is in road construction. Kingsolver responds to government agency solicitations for bids on construction projects. Kingsolver and other firms prepare competitive proposals and then offer bids. A large part of the bid preparation process (especially the design, cost estimation, and technical specification) is aided by using a proprietary decision support system (DSS) written for the road construction industry. The DSS runs on a Pentium IV PC in Kingsolver's office.

Payroll and personnel—along with other office administrative tasks—are somewhat more chaotic. There are only five full-time employees (Martin, two engineers, and two office staff). However, about 40 sub-contractors work for the firm during a typical monthly payroll period. More than 400 individuals will work for the firm in a year.

Currently, one of the office staff spends 80% of her time keeping track of the firm's part time and full time employees. Originally Martin had considered outsourcing his payroll, but this proved far too expensive an option. Martin is convinced the answer lies in building a simple in-house personnel system to handle employee wages and related payroll information.

Last year, the situation became serious when the Internal Revenue Service (IRS) audited the firm's books. The IRS wondered why Kingsolver had more than 400 employees but showed very low tax withholdings. Martin explained that most of the employees were short-term, part-time workers and/or sub-contractors. In recent times the IRS has taken a dim view of employees being declared as "contract workers" because federal tax is not withheld for contract workers, so the IRS has trouble collecting taxes from them later.

While Kingsolver's contract workers appeared legitimate, examination of the records found a number of errors in withholding statements for regular employees who were part-time workers. For 35 part time workers, no withholding was deducted or submitted to the IRS because of clerical errors. The IRS has given Martin one year to straighten out the records.

Martin has decided that a PC-based database system would be ideal for a small payroll system. He wants you to design such a system for a sample quarter. Employees are paid monthly.

A sample of the employee database showing the ID number, name, and address can be seen by opening the CONTRACT table in the SOLVEIT.MDB database. For each monthly payroll period, a monthly file is created. Three hand-calculated files for the first quarter have been built for you in Access: 1_MONTH, 2_MONTH, and 3_MONTH.

Tasks   There are five tasks in this case:

1.   Combine the three individual monthly reports (i.e.: 1_MONTH, 2_MONTH, 3_MONTH) into a single data table representing the first quarter.

   Hint: Use an append action query to do this. You should end up with 45 records in a single, new data table.

2.   (a) Develop a query that will calculate the gross, pay, federal and state withholdings, FICA, and resulting net pay for all employees in the first quarter. Set federal withholdings at 17.4% of gross, FICA at 2.7% of gross, state withholding at 8% of gross, and calculate net pay as gross pay minus all deductions. (b) Use this query to create a report that shows the gross pay, all deductions, and net pay for all employees for the quarter.

3.   Develop a payroll report that shows just the firm's grand totals for the quarter for gross pay, all the deductions, and net pay.

4.   Develop a report that shows for each employee the earnings and deductions for the quarter, giving subtotals by employee. At the bottom, the report should also show firm totals.

*5.   Produce a report for the IRS for the first quarter that shows the employees' name, address, all deductions, and net pay.

   You will need the CONTRACT table in the SOLVEIT database to do this task. This table contains the names and addresses of Kingsolver's employees.

Time Estimates (excluding task marked with *):

Expert: 1.5 hour
Intermediate: 2.5 hours
Novice: 4+ hours

Tutorial for Database Case 7 Using Access 2002

Copying and Pasting Table Structures

Using the Database window, you can create an empty copy of an existing table (i.e.: field structure only), as a first step in merging records from a number of different tables to a single table. Let's practice this by creating an empty copy of the FRIENDS table:

1) Open FRIENDS.MDB. In the Database window, select the FRIENDS table.
2) Select EDIT/COPY.
3) Select EDIT/PASTE.
4) In the Paste Tables As dialog box, give the table a new name (e.g.: Tute7CopyTable)
5) In the Paste Options section, select the Structure Only option button and click OK.

Access creates an empty table with an identical field structure to the FRIENDS table.

Action Queries

When you create a new query with the Simple Query Wizard or in Design View, Access generates a Select query by default. *Select queries* retrieve and display data from tables according to specified criteria. We have used Select queries for *Solve it!* database cases 1 to 6. In contrast, *Action queries*, which are constructed within the Select query window, actually alter data in tables. Action queries can be used to add, delete, or change data, and to create new tables from existing records. For example, a Delete action query is used to delete obsolete records from a table. Access uses four types of action queries. A brief description of each type appears in Figure 5-38, and the graphical objects that identify them in the database appear in the menu shown in Figure 5-39. In this tutorial, we will concentrate on *Append* action queries. Other Action query types will be covered in later tutorials.

Figure 5-38

Types of Queries
Access query types include:

Select queries select a group of records from one or more tables.

Action Queries
The following action queries change the data in your tables:

Make-table queries create a new table from all or parts of other tables.

Delete queries delete records from one or more tables.

Append queries add a group of records to a table.

Update queries make changes to data in a group of records.

Figure 5-39

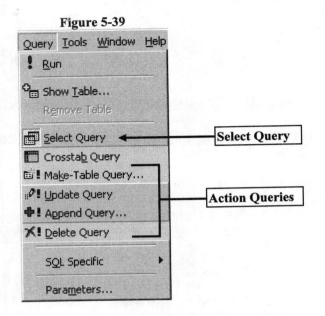

Append Queries

Append queries copy all or some records from one table and add them to the bottom of another existing table. This is especially useful if you use separate tables to manage certain data (e.g.: you keep payroll data on a month by month basis and need to merge it every financial quarter). Append queries are also handy for storing historical data. For instance, in an Orders table, completed orders could be separated from active, uncompleted orders to prevent the Orders table from becoming too large, and to provide a backup for future reference.

When data is appended, the tables involved in the query do not need to have the same structure, but the data types of the appended fields **must** match. (The exception is Counter data types, which may be appended to Long Integer data types). When records are appended to a table, the records in the original table remain intact. Access does not delete the original records.

> **Note:**
> If two tables involved in an Append query have identical field structures, the * in the table field list can be used instead of the individual field names in the Field row of the design grid.

Let's use the FRIENDS table and the empty copy of the FRIENDS table (e.g.: TUTE7COPYTABLE) we created earlier in this tutorial to generate an Append action query.

1.   In the Database window, click *Queries* on the Objects bar and create a new query in Design View using the FRIENDS table.

2.   In the Query Design view window, select QUERY/APPEND QUERY. This will change the Select query into an Append query, and an *Append to:* row will be added to the design grid.

3.   In the *Append* dialog box, type: *TUTE7COPYTABLE* in the *Table Name* list box and click *OK*. This means that we are going to append records from the FRIENDS table to TUTE7 COPYTABLE.

4.   In the Append query design window, select and drag the ✳ symbol in the FRIENDS field list down to the first cell in the Field row in the design grid. This tells Access two things: that all FRIENDS fields should be included in the query, and that the field structure of TUTE7 COPYTABLE is identical to FRIENDS. Access immediately adds notation to this effect in the *Append to:* cell.

5.   Test the Append query before committing to its execution. One of the things to note about any Action query is that it **changes** table data in some way. For this reason, it is good practice to test the query before running it. Testing also allows you to check for errors in the query setup.

        To test your Append query, click the [▦ ▾] button. The resulting dynaset should display all the records in the FRIENDS table. Return to Query Design view and run the query. Access should append all FRIENDS table records to TUTE7COPYTABLE. A warning dialog box will advise you that you are about to append the number of rows selected by the query and that the action will be irreversible. Click *Yes* to append the records to TUTE7COPYTABLE.

6.   Save your query (e.g.: TUTE7APPENDQUERY) and close it to return to the Database window. Click *Tables* on the Objects bar and open TUTE7 COPYTABLE and check the contents.

Hint:
You will need to use both the Copy/Paste table structure sequence and Append queries to complete Task 2 of Case 7.

Database Case 8

Hildebrand Rentals Inc.

Problem:	Develop a transaction and fee checking system
Management skills:	Control Decide
Access Skills:	Forms Action Queries Macros
Data Table:	CARS

Doug Hildebrand punched the buttons on his hand-held calculator. Three months ago Hildebrand had been an independent rental-car dealer, based in Fargo, ND, when HiJaak Rentals, a medium-sized operator, offered him a sizeable sum for majority ownership of Hildebrand Rentals. HiJaak had recognized that the recent boom in the Fargo area was merely the start of sustained growth. HiJaak also had realized that the three existing rental agencies (two of them franchises of national dealerships) would provide intense competition for any start-up enterprise in the area. HiJaak decided to approach the single independent dealer with a partnership offer.

Doug was surprised and relieved when the HiJaak offer arrived. His 17-year-old dealership was straining under the pressure from the newly established national franchises that could offer some cut-price deals, one-way rentals, and arrangements with frequent-flyer schemes that he could not match. HiJaak had a cooperative deal with one of the key domestic airlines, and Hildebrand realized that when rental dealers' prices were very similar, customers made decisions based on issues like frequent-flyer points. HiJaak also could assist during temporary price wars. Faced with deciding between hard times as an independent dealer and receiving cash for losing control, Hildebrand accepted HiJaak's offer.

Hildebrand soon realized that the extra security offered by HiJaak came with additional obligations, like monthly reporting duties. These reports involved the calculations he was currently performing manually on his calculator. Hildebrand already had a computerized reservation and charging system, a necessity in his industry. However, his system could not provide the required reports. Although HiJaak was willing to supply its own software, Hildebrand was happy with his system. He knew that his system could write the details of transactions to an exportable file. With this knowledge, Hildebrand asked HiJaak to send one of its system programmers. HiJaak obliged by dispatching Jeanne Lind.

Jeanne examined a typical file on Hildebrand's system and found that it could be readily imported into any common database management system. Although not ideal, this solution would certainly prevent the need for Hildebrand to calculate his reports manually. Jeanne advised him to purchase a Windows-based database package and use it to meet HiJaak's monthly reporting requirements.

The senior managers at HiJaak need quarterly information in order to make informed decisions. They require the total revenue derived from each of the car model sizes over each month. Each transaction record contains certain information: a sequential code generated by the computer, date of transaction, model code (S=small, M=medium, L=large, X=sports, W=wagon), car registration, miles traveled, number of rental days, rental fee, and a logical field signifying whether the rental was "limited miles" or not. The customer usually can choose unlimited miles or a limit of 100 free miles with a lower base rate. For a limited-mile transaction, each mile above 100 miles would incur a per mile cost.

The CARS table supplied in the SOLVEIT2002.MDB database on the *Solve it!* diskette contains a partial list of transactions downloaded from Hildebrand Rentals reservation system.

Tasks: There are three tasks in this case:

1.   Doug Hildebrand wants Jeanne to develop a simple solution for him so he can check the accuracy of the transactions in the sample list against the paper records he has in his office. He wants the solution to include an entry screen where the user may enter the transaction code (e.g. S24155). The procedure then will display the record corresponding to the code, if it is valid. If the code is not valid, the user should be informed that the entry is invalid and be required to re-enter the code. The user also should be able to exit the system easily. The entry screen should have ample instructions for the user to use the system.

Hint: Create forms with command buttons to complete this task.

2.   To meet his reporting commitments, Hildebrand currently must manually calculate the revenue from each transaction. Thus he wants Jeanne to develop a procedure to calculate the fee for each transaction and place the result in the CARS table. The charges for each model type appear in the table below:

	Small (S)	Medium (M)	Large (L)	Sports (X)	Wagon (W)
Limited Rate ($)	$45.00	$50.00	$55.00	$60.00	$60.00
Additional cost per mile ($)	$0.55	$0.65	$0.75	$0.85	$0.80
Unlimited Rate ($)	$50.00	$55.00	$60.00	$65.00	$65.00
Depreciation Rate (%)	3.3%	3.2%	3.0%	3.5%	4.4%
Purchase Price ($)	$9200	$11650	$17800	$19250	$17100

Hint: First create a table to store the rate information for each car model type from the first three rows in the table above. Then create three update queries to complete this task. The first query will calculate the charge for customers who choose the Unlimited rate. The second query will calculate the charge for customers who choose the Limited rate and do not go over the 100 miles allotted. The third query will calculate the charge for customers who choose the Limited rate and exceed the 100 free miles. The last expression will multiply the limited rate by the number of days and add to that the total miles driven minus the free 100 miles multiplied by the additional cost per mile. You must enclose parts of an expression that must be performed first (i.e. addition and subtraction to override the order of operations) in parentheses. Each calculation will *update to* the CHARGE field in the CARS table.

*3.   HiJaak is becoming more demanding in its reporting requirements, adding to Hildebrand's workload. The company wants to know the depreciation of any car in Hildebrand's yard. The method of depreciation in the car rental industry is dictated by the Internal Revenue Service. The depreciation amount for each vehicle depends on the total distance traveled (read from the odometer), the rate of depreciation for the model type (i.e. small, medium, large, sports, wagon), and the purchase price of the vehicle. The IRS says the depreciation amount is defined as a fixed percentage (i.e. the depreciation rate) of the purchase price for every 6,000 miles the vehicle has traveled. Develop a procedure to calculate the amount of depreciation for each car based on the depreciation rates and purchase prices appearing in the table above. Enable the user to enter the registration of a particular vehicle and then calculate the depreciation on that car.

Hint: First create a table to store the depreciation and purchase price information for each car model type from the bottom two rows of the table above. Set the *Format* property for the depreciation rate field to Percent and the *Field Size* property to Single. Then create a Parameter query to complete this task. You first must create a calculated field to compute the depreciation. The expression will divide the depreciation rate by 100 and multiply the result by the purchase price multiplied by the odometer reading divided by 6,000. You must enclose parts of an expression that must be performed first (i.e. dividing the depreciation rate by 100) in parentheses. The parameter query will prompt the user to enter the car registration number.

Time Estimates (excluding task marked with *):

Expert: 1.5 hour
Intermediate: 2.5 hours
Novice: 4 hours

Tutorial for Database Case 8 Using Access 2002

Creating Forms in Access

Forms are used to view, enter, or edit data in a database and often are the most convenient way of performing these operations. Forms can be based on tables or queries and can display data on a record-by-record basis. As with reports, forms can be created using a Wizard. A series of dialog boxes enables the user to customize the way data will be organized and displayed. With one mouse click, you can switch from Form to Datasheet view, which is a tabular view of the same set of records.

An Access form, just like a report, is constructed from any number of controls: text boxes for entering and editing data; label controls to identify the text boxes; and other controls, list boxes, or combo boxes from which a user can select a value, and toggle buttons, option buttons, or check boxes for *Yes/No* fields. You can modify forms in various ways, including using colors to highlight important data, inserting graphics, and displaying messages to indicate when an incorrect value has been entered. You also can set up your form so that Access automatically inserts data for you, prints data on the click of a command button, and/or displays the results of calculations. Let's use the FRIENDS database to create a simple form.

Forms

1.   Open the practice database FRIENDS.MDB. Click *Forms* on the Objects bar and then click *New* on the Database Window toolbar. In the *New Form* dialog box, click the list arrow [▼] to the right of the *Choose the table or query where the object's data comes from* box and select the FRIENDS table. Select *AutoForm: Columnar* and click *OK*. This will automatically generate a form, using the last autoformat style used in the database that displays the fields in a single column. Access creates the form and opens it for you. The form shows the first record in your table (see Figure 5-40). Save and name your form (e.g.: FRIENDSSHOW). In a matter of minutes, you have created a form that can be used for viewing, editing, adding, and deleting records in the FRIENDS table.

Figure 5-40

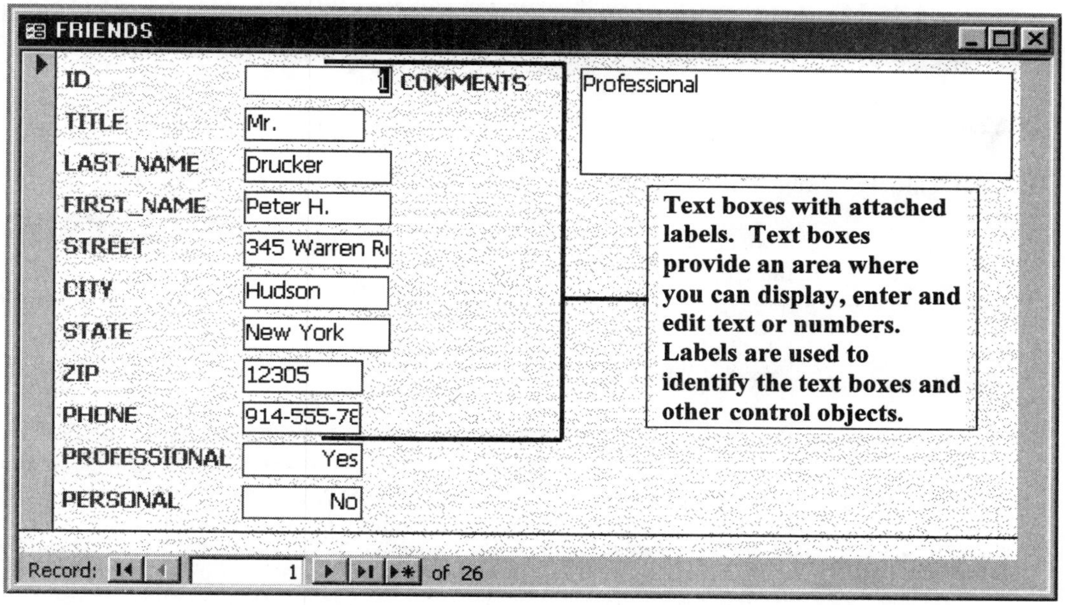

Access offers a number of other form wizard types:

*   **AutoForm:Datasheet** - which displays fields in datasheet format

*   **AutoForm:Tabular** - which displays each record as a row of fields.

*   **Chart Wizard** - creates a form that displays graphs.

*   **Form Wizard** - creates a form based on user-selected fields from more than one record source. This wizard supports a variety of form display formats.

*   **Pivot Table Wizard** - creates a form with a Microsoft Excel pivot table - a feature which enables analysis and summarization of data in lists and tables.

Or you can create your own form in the **Form Design view** window. You also can use forms with Macros, which are discussed later in this tutorial.

Three Ways of Viewing a Form

Access offers three quick and easy ways of viewing a form. You will need to use each of these when designing and using forms. To switch views, simply click on the appropriate toolbar button.

Design View	• Use for customizing the appearance or changing the structure of forms, and for adding and modifying controls
Form View	• Use for viewing, entering and editing record data
Datasheet View	• Displays the underlying table or query dynaset on which the form is based

You can also use the *Print Preview* button to see how a form will look when printed.

Remember: *Right click* means to click the right hand button of your mouse once.

Double click top left means to click the Control menu icon such as ▦ , ▦ , or ▦ in the top left corner of an open window.

Creating a Form in Design View

As the name suggests, you start with a blank form and use the toolbox to add controls in Form Design view. You use the tools in the toolbox to add all of the text boxes, labels, combo boxes, list boxes, check boxes, and other controls required for your form. For this reason, blank forms often have no initial connection to an underlying query or table. *Hint: You will need to create a form in Design view by adding unbound controls to a blank form for Task 1 of Case 8.*

To create a blank form:

1. Click *Forms* on the Objects bar in the Database window. Double-click *Create form in Design view*. Access immediately opens a blank form in Design view. The initial form will contain only a Detail section. Forms use the same type of sectioning as Reports. Review the Access tutorial for Case 2 for an explanation of report sections.

Let's create a simple customized form using the FRIENDS table. The form is designed to lookup and display specific FRIENDS records based on their ID numbers (**Note**: Your FRIENDS table will need to contain an ID field set to Autonumber field type). *Hint: The criteria used could just as easily be product numbers or transaction codes.*

1. Select VIEW/FORM HEADER/FOOTER to add a form header and a form footer to your new form. Click ⚒ to open the Toolbox, if necessary. Next, click the *Label* button (displayed at right) and use the label pointer to click in the form header section of the form. Type a heading for the form (e.g.: *Friends Lookup*). Change the label size, font, font size, and font color as you see fit. If necessary, increase the size of the form header by positioning the pointer over the top edge of the Detail section bar and dragging downward with the vertical resizing pointer.

2.   Click the *Text Box* button (displayed at right), and then click in the *Detail* section of the form to create an unbound text box and label for the form. *Right click* the label and select *Properties* on the shortcut menu. On the *Format* tab in the property sheet, change the *Caption* property to: *Search for a Friend*. Close the property sheet and resize the label so that it displays all of the text.

3.   R*ight-click* the unbound text box and select *Properties* on the shortcut menu. Select the *Data* tab. Locate the *Validation Rule* property, click in the settings box, and type: *>=1 And <=200.*

Note: The ID numbers in the FRIENDS table must be greater than or equal to 1 and less than or equal to 200. This will allow you to enter up to 200 names in the table but will catch typing errors that include letters, negative values, or numbers greater than 200. It creates a valid ID number range. (Right click and select Zoom if you need more room to type).

4.   Press the down arrow key on the keyboard to move to the *Validation Text* property settings box. Enter a message that will display in an error dialog box if a user enters invalid data. (e.g.: You must enter values between 1 and 200. Click OK and Reenter).

5.   Click the *Other* tab. Change the *Name* property for the text box to FriendID. In the *Status Bar Text* property settings box, enter: Enter an ID number. *Double-click* the Control menu icon in the *top left* corner to close the property sheet and return to Design view.

6.   Save your form (e.g.: FRIENDS LOOKUP). Next, we will create three *command buttons*: One that links FRIENDS LOOKUP through an event procedure to the FRIENDSSHOW form and displays the relevant record, one that Exits FRIENDS SHOW so that FRIENDS LOOKUP displays, and one to exit FRIENDS LOOKUP.

Using Control Wizards in Forms   **Control Wizards Button**

The Access Control Wizards will help you to create complex controls for your forms by taking you step-by-step through the creation process. Control Wizards are available for creating option groups, list boxes, combo boxes, and command buttons. Command buttons can be created to start many different types of actions or sets of actions. These are referred to by programmers as *event procedures.* An *event* is a particular action that triggers a procedure such as clicking a command button in a form or report. A *procedure* is a unit of programming code designed to accomplish a specific task.

You will not have to directly do any programming because the Command Button Wizard will write the Microsoft Jscript or Visual Basic Scripting Edition code for you. You can create command buttons that will automate many frequently used activities associated with forms and reports, such and opening and closing objects, linking fields between objects, printing individual records, going to specific records, or updating data.

1.   Let's create the first of our command buttons. Click the *Control Wizard* button on the toolbox if necessary. Click the *Command Button* button (displayed at right) and then click in an empty section of the *Detail* section in the FRIENDS LOOKUP form.

The first of several Command Button Wizard dialog boxes opens. Make these choices as you proceed through the dialog boxes:

1) In the *Categories* box, select *Form Operations*
2) In the *Actions* box, select *Open Form*
3) Click Next
4) Select FRIENDSSHOW as the form to open.
5) Click Next.
6) Choose to *Open the form and find specific data to display.*
7) Click Next.
8) In the FRIENDS LOOKUP box, select the FriendID text box.
9) In the FRIENDSSHOW box, select the ID field.
10) Click Next.
11) Select the *Text* option button and type: *Show Record*, as the text to display on the button.
12) Click Next.
13) *Type: Show Record*, to name the button.
14) Click Finish to generate the command button.

2.   Save the changes to the FRIENDS LOOKUP form.

3.   Right-click the Show Record button and select *Properties*. Click the *Event* tab. Scroll down the list to the *On Click* property. Notice that Access has added an Event Procedure for this property. Click in the On Click property settings box and then click the ⊡ *Build* button. The Code window in the Visual Basic Editor opens displaying the code for the event procedure for the Show Record button (see Figure 5-41). *Double click top left* to close the Visual Basic Editor and return to Design view. (Note: Double-click the Control menu icon for the Visual Basic Editor, not for the Code window.)

Figure 5-41

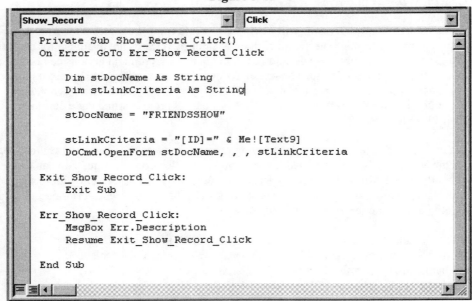

```
Show_Record                    ▼   Click                      ▼

    Private Sub Show_Record_Click()
    On Error GoTo Err_Show_Record_Click

        Dim stDocName As String
        Dim stLinkCriteria As String

        stDocName = "FRIENDSSHOW"

        stLinkCriteria = "[ID]=" & Me![Text9]
        DoCmd.OpenForm stDocName, , , stLinkCriteria

    Exit_Show_Record_Click:
        Exit Sub

    Err_Show_Record_Click:
        MsgBox Err.Description
        Resume Exit_Show_Record_Click

    End Sub
```

4.   **Time to Test:** Close the property sheet and switch to Form view. Notice that the text you entered for the *Status Bar Text* property displays in the Status bar. Enter an ID number between 1 and 26 (or whatever the last record number is at present in your FRIENDS table), and click the Show Record Button. The sequence works, but there is no easy or immediate way to run the procedure again, or to exit from FRIENDS SHOW. We need to add an Exit button to both the Friends Lookup form and the FRIENDS SHOW form. Use the Close button to close FRIENDS SHOW.

5.   Return to Design view in the Friends Lookup form. Use the Command Button Wizard to create another command button in the *Detail* section to Exit the form. Select the *Form Operations* category and the *Close Form* action, use the Exit picture on the button, and name the button *Close Form*. Reposition the command button as necessary, save the changes, and close the form.

6.   Open FRIENDS SHOW in Design view. Add a command button under the Comments field to close the form. Use the text *Close Form* on the button and name the button *Close Friends Show*. Reposition the command button as necessary, save the changes, and close the form.

7.   Open the Friends Lookup form in Form view. Enter 10 in the Search for a Friend text box. Click *Show Record*. Click the *Close Form* button to close FRIENDS SHOW. Click the Exit button to close Friends Lookup.

8.   Reopen Friends Lookup in Form view and test the procedure several times. Also enter an ID not in the valid range to make sure the validation procedure is working. With two simple forms and three easy to generate command buttons, we have created a robust, easy-to-use FRIENDS lookup program.

Macros in Access

A *macro* in Access is a set of actions that automate common tasks such as opening a table or printing a report. Macros help you to work smarter and save time without having to learn programming. Macros are simple to create, and Access offers a choice of around 50 different macro actions which include (see also Figure 5-42 on the next page):

- Opening and closing tables, forms, and reports
- Opening a form and finding records related to another form
- Automatically printing reports upon opening a particular database
- Checking or improving data validity

Figure 5-42: An Access Macro in Action

You can press a command
button on a form ...

Print Monthly Sales

Macro: Print Monthly Sales

Action	Comment
▶ OpenReport	

Action Arguments

Report Name	1992 Orders
View	Print
Filter Name	
Where Condition	Datepart("m",[Date])=Datepart("m",Now())

... to run a macro that opens a report. The macro then ...

... finds and prints
sales data for the
current month.

The great thing about macros is that they can handle tasks that would often require extensive programming skills in other database packages, and the more you use them, the more you learn about the underlying principles of programming. Macro actions often involve *arguments*. These are simply parameters, which govern how an action is executed. If you have problems choosing macro actions or specifying arguments, press the [F1] key to open the Help file on the selected action or argument.

Let's create a simple macro using the practice database FRIENDS.MDB. This macro will open the FRIENDS table and display only records whose Zip code is greater than 35000. It will also filter out all records where the State is not Arizona, before returning to the full FRIENDS table record set.

1.   Open FRIENDS.MDB. Click *Tables* on the Objects bar in the Database window and double click the FRIENDS table. Switch to Table Design view, and change the Zip field to the Number data type. Save the change and close the FRIENDS table.

2.   Click *Macros* on the Objects bar in the Database window and then click *New*. The Macro Builder window opens. Click in the first blank cell in the *Action* column. Click the list arrow ▾ to display a list of all available Macro actions. Scroll down this list and select *OpenTable*. (Read the information box at bottom right of the window for an explanation of what this action does). In the *Comments* column, type a short description of the action (e.g.: Opens the FRIENDS table).

3.   In the *Action Arguments* panel at the bottom of the window, click in the *Table Name* box. Click the list arrow ▾ and select the FRIENDS table.

4.   Click in the next empty Action cell and select *ApplyFilter* on the list. In the *Comment* column, type a short description of the action (e.g.: Only display records where the Zip code is greater than 35000).

5   In the Action Arguments section, click in the *Where Condition* box and type: **[FRIENDS]![ZIP] >35000**

6.   Click in the next empty Action cell and select *ApplyFilter* on the list. In the *Comments* column, type a short description of the action (e.g.: Within this reduced record set show records only from Arizona).

7.   In the Action Arguments section, click in the *Where Condition* box and type: **[FRIENDS]![STATE]= "Arizona"** (see Figure 5-43).

(**Note:** Additional records were added to the FRIENDS table in the Tutorial for Case 4. If you did not do this tutorial, you will need to add the 5 new records to the FRIENDS table shown in Figure 5-24.)

Figure 5-43

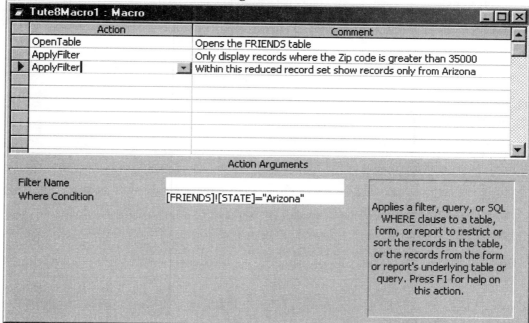

8.   Save your macro by clicking the *Save* button or selecting FILE/SAVE. In the *Save As* dialog box, give your macro a name (e.g.: TUTE8 MACRO1) and click *OK*.

9.   Execute the macro by clicking the *Run* button, or selecting MACRO/RUN. As the macro runs, it first opens and displays all of the records in the FRIENDS table. The first filter is then applied and only records where the Zip code is greater than 35000 are shown. The second filter then is then applied, and the record set is further reduced to records where the Zip code is greater than 35000 AND the State is Arizona.

10.   Close the dynaset and the Macro Design window and return to the Database window.

Use Macros When:	• performing tasks such as opening and closing tables or forms, or running reports
	• your application involves custom menus and submenus for forms
	• your application is basically simple and uncomplicated, and does not require debugging procedures

Update Queries in Access

Update queries are a type of action query, which modify data according to specific criteria such as increasing **all** car rental rates or **certain** product prices by 15%. Update queries are created in much the same way as other queries, except that a new value is specified for a particular field. Like all other types of action queries, update queries save time and effort, but must be used carefully because they actually change the data in the underlying table. Let's use the sample data table HARDWARE to create a simple update query. HARDWARE is included in SOLVEIT.MDB.

1.   Open the HARDWARE.MDB database you created in the Tutorial for Case 2. If you did not create this database, create a new empty database and import the HARDWARE table provided on SOLVEIT.MDB. Open the HARDWARE table and browse the records of the table, particularly noting the data in the UnitCost field (see Figure 5-44).

Figure 5-44 (Before Update)

HARDWARE : Table			
INVOICE	**ITEM**	**UNITCOST**	**QUANTITY**
1234	Shovel	$25.00	2
1235	Rake	$15.00	1
1236	Rack	$12.50	4
1237	Nails	$5.60	2
1238	Rake	$15.00	15
1239	Screws	$3.40	4
1240	Shovel	$25.00	1
1241	Hinges	$2.50	6
1242	Widgets	$1.60	12
1243	Nails	$5.60	3
1244	Rake	$15.00	6
1245	Screws	$3.40	3
1246	Hinges	$2.50	4
1247	Widgets	$1.60	5
1248	Rack	$12.50	2

Record: 1 of 15

2.   Create a new query in Design view using the ITEM and UNITCOST fields from the HARDWARE table. Select QUERY/UPDATE QUERY to turn the Select query into an Update query and add an *Update to* line to the design grid.

3.   In the *Update to* cell for the UNITCOST field enter the expression *[Unitcost]*1.15*. This expression will multiply the current value in the UNITCOST field by 115%, thereby increasing the prices of all items in the HARDWARE table by 15%.

4.   In the *Criteria* cell for the Item field, type: Rake. This tells Access to limit the update of the Unitcost field to only those records, which contain the word *Rake* in the Item field. Click the Datasheet View button to make sure that only invoices for rakes are being selected for updating.

5.   Return to Design view and save the query (e.g.: TUTE8QUERY1). Run the query. Click *Yes* to update the three rows containing the unit cost for rakes. Close the query. Open the HARDWARE table and notice the changes made to the UnitCost field (see Figure 5-45). All invoices for rakes have been increased by 15%.

Figure 5-45
(After Update)

The three invoices for rakes have been updated. The unit cost per rake is now $17.25, a 15% increase from the original $15.00 price

Parameter Queries

You can also create a parameter query which will prompt the user to enter criteria each time the query is run. For example, instead of entering "Rake" as the criterion in the ITEM field you could enter: [Enter an Item]. When the query is run, the Enter Parameter Value dialog box will open prompting the user to "Enter an Item" (see Figure 5-46 on the next page). The text that will serve as the prompt is enclosed in square brackets in the criterion expression. In this way the query can be saved and rerun each time a price increase occurs. As is, the query will increase the price of any product entered by the user by 15%, but the expression can be modified to accommodate larger or smaller percentage increases. Parameter statements can be used with all types of queries - select and action.

Solve it!

Figure 5-46

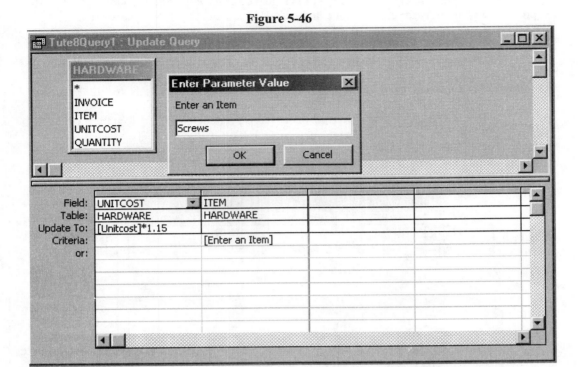

Database Case 9

Buena Vista Hotel

Problem:	Design a hotel reservation system.
Management skill:	Control
Access Skills:	Forms Screen Design Macros Queries Functions
Data Tables:	ROOMS VISITORS BOOKINGS

Linda O'Hara settled down at her office desk with the accounts and reservation book and started the monthly chore of calculating the month's takings at the hotel she owns and operates jointly with her husband, Mike. When the Buena Vista Hotel in Port Arthur, TX, was bequeathed to Linda by her grandparents, Linda and Mike faced the decision of whether to manage or sell the hotel. As recent MBA graduates of the University of Texas at Austin, the couple prepared a complete business plan, as if they were deciding to purchase the business.

Linda found that while the 23-room hotel was profitable, it was experiencing steadily declining rentals. After talking with owners of nearby hotels, Linda discovered that up to 70% of hotel business in the area came from repeat business. Despite this, Buena Vista had no list of past customers, either regular or otherwise, and records of past capacity utilization were patchy. In addition, the current booking and reservation system was manually based. Even so, Linda and Mike thought the business had great potential, given a more modern management approach. They believed that, after a few years of successful operation, there would be enough funds to expand the hotel. They decided to go ahead with running the hotel.

Linda contacted one of her Operations professors from UTA, who suggested the reservation and booking system was amenable to computerization. The professor recommended a PC-based database management system for tracking the usage of rooms, automatically establishing a history of customers, and recording a transaction list whereby revenues could be easily calculated. The list of past guests could then be used for mail-outs to remind potential repeat customers of the attractions of Port Arthur and, particularly, the Buena Vista Hotel.

Linda and Mike were excited at the prospect of owning and managing a business at such an early age. However, managing the hotel and its staff was a full-time responsibility, and they did not believe they could develop the required database system themselves. They contacted the Career Placement Office at UTA, which directed them to Ricardo Martin, a first-year MBA student and an IS major, proficient in PC database systems. Ricardo agreed that he could develop a simple menu-driven program to record guests booking in and out of the hotel.

Linda and Mike hired Ricardo to develop the management system. Ricardo decided that several data tables would be necessary for the hotel's reservation system. These would be:

1.   a list of rooms and their features (ROOMS),
2.   a list of past guests and their details (VISITORS),
3.   a list of transactions of each guest's stay (BOOKINGS)

In addition, a lookup table, ROOMS LOOKUP, would be generated from the ROOMS data table to provide a list of currently available rooms. Ricardo believed appropriate options on a menu would be:

1.   Registering a guest.
2.   Checking out.
3.   Listing vacant rooms.
4.   Exit the program.

Ricardo explained that he intended to use these different options to operate the three data tables, using customer name as the common field. For example, when a guest arrived, the hotel receptionist would select Option 1 from the menu. The vacant rooms would then be displayed from the ROOMS LOOKUP table. The receptionist would enter the guest's name and offer a room choice to the guest. Once the choice was made, the ROOMS table would then be amended to show the details of the new guest, his/her room number, and the room rate. The program would then check to see whether the guest had visited before by consulting the VISITORS table. If the guest was a newcomer, further details such as address would be entered and added to the VISITORS table. This new data would eventually build a significant guest list and be a valuable marketing tool.

The second option would be used at the end of a guest's stay. The relevant room in the ROOMS LOOKUP table would be changed to vacant status. Also, entries in the VISITORS, ROOMS, and BOOKINGS tables would be amended or updated to reflect details of the current visit. At the same time, a charge would be calculated by subtracting the current date from the date of arrival and multiplying the number of days stayed by the room rate.

The third option would enable the user to examine a list of vacant rooms at any time using the ROOMS LOOKUP table. The fourth option would simply exit the hotel reservation system.

You have been supplied with three of the four data tables needed to complete this case: ROOMS, VISITORS, and BOOKINGS on the SOLVEIT.MDB database. The fourth table ROOMS LOOKUP, should be created within the database package you are using. Open these tables now and examine their structure.

Tasks:

There are five tasks in this case:

1.   Create a form, appropriate command buttons, and macros to register a guest at the Buena Vista Hotel. This will require the use of the ROOMS and VISITORS tables supplied on the *Solveit!* disk. Include on your form all appropriate formatting, header information and instructional text.

2. Create a new table (ROOMS LOOKUP) that hotel clerks can use to look up a list of all vacant rooms, their rates, and features. This table will be based on some of the fields in the ROOMS table. Create a command button on the form you created in Task 1 that will allow access to this new table.

3. Create a procedure to check a guest out. This will involve appending a record to the BOOKINGS table from the ROOMS table, before deleting the relevant record from the ROOMS table. The BOOKINGS table should then be updated to calculate total charges owing. Be sure to use parameters for isolating specific records in this procedure.

4. Create a Main Menu form and appropriate command buttons to enable the user to choose from and use any of the four options described in the case. The four menu options should be displayed using forms, which all include an Exit procedure back to the main menu.

*5. Suggest and implement how the O'Haras can incorporate the following improvements:

- A mechanism to distinguish between guests of the same name.
- A future booking system whereby guests may reserve rooms ahead of time for peak periods.
- A checking system so other guests cannot stay in reserved rooms.

Time Estimates (excluding task marked with *):

Expert: 2 hour
Intermediate: 3 hours
Novice: 5 hours

Tutorial for Database Case 9 Using Access 2002

More About Forms - Main/Subform

A *subform* is a form embedded inside another form (known as the main form). Main or subforms are used to generate and display data from any two tables or queries that have a one-to-many relationship. The Main form will be based on the table that's on the "one" side of the relationship, and the subform on the "many" side of the relationship (e.g.: in Case 9, one guest can have many bookings).

The relationship between the two tables **must exist before** attempting to create the subform. In addition, the main form (the table on the "one side") should have a primary key, while the subform (the table on the "many side") needs to contain a field with the same name and data type as that primary key. Primary keys are usually unique identifiers. You will need to create primary key fields for some of the tables used in Case 9. Review the section *Creating Relationships Between Tables* at the end of Chapter 4 if you are unsure how to do this.

To create a Main/Subform:

1. Create a new empty database named VICTOR'S FURNITURE and import the CUSTOMERS, PRODUCTS, and ORDERS tables from the SOLVEIT.MDB database into it.

2. Open the Relationships window and add the three tables to the window. Select the CustomerID field in the field list for the CUSTOMERS table and drag it to the CustomerID field in the ORDERS table. Click the Enforce Referential integrity checkbox and then the *Create* button to create the one-to-many relationship between the two tables.

3. Select the ProductID field in the field list for the PRODUCTS table and drag it to the ProductID field in the ORDERS table. Click the Enforce Referential Integrity checkbox and then the *Create* button to create the one-to-many relationship between the two tables. The Relationships window is shown in Figure 5-47. Close the Relationships window, saving the changes to the layout of the window when prompted.

Figure 5-47

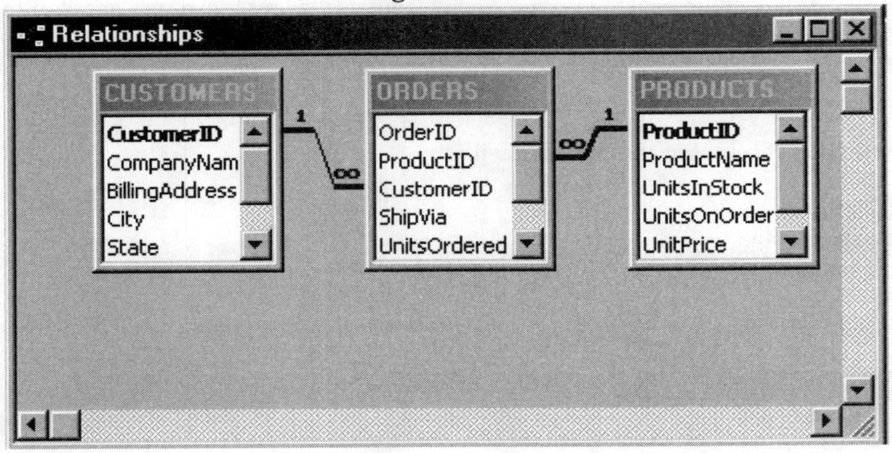

4. Click Forms on the Objects bar on the Database window. Double-click *Create form by using wizard.* In the first Wizard dialog box select the CUSTOMERS table and click [>>] to add all of the fields in the table to the form.

5. Click the list arrow on the Tables/Queries box and select the ORDERS table. Click [>>] to add all of the fields in the table to the form. Select ORDERS.CustomerID Click [<] to remove this field from the form. (This field is a duplicate. The CustomerID field has already been added to the form from the CUSTOMERS table). Click *Next*.

6. You want to view the data by CUSTOMERS with the customer data in the main form and the order data in the subform. Click *Next*.

7. Use the *Datasheet* layout. Click *Next*. Use the *Sumi Painting* style. Click *Next*.

8. Keep the default names for the form, CUSTOMERS, and subform, ORDERS. Click *Finish.*

9. Switch to Design view. Reposition the subform underneath the ORDERS label and increase its width to the 6-inch mark on the horizontal ruler. Save the changes and return to Form view. You can now view all orders placed by a particular customer in the subform. New orders can be entered in the subform.

10. Return to Design view and make any other changes as you see fit to the sizes or positions of the controls on the form, save them, and close the form. The form/subform is shown in Figure 5-48.

Figure 5-48

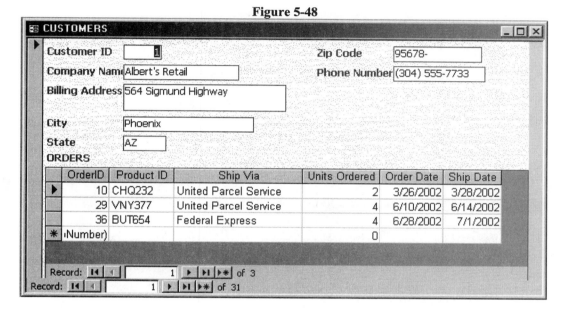

Delete Queries

Delete queries are a type of action query that remove records from a table according to some specified search criteria. Delete queries are created in the same way as other action queries. Begin by creating a select query, which contains field criteria such as parameter statements for isolating the records targeted for deletion. *Warning: A delete query always deletes **entire** records, not just the contents of specific fields.*

Choose QUERY/DELETE from the menu or click on the Delete Query toolbar button to turn the select query to a delete query. This action generates display of a *Delete:* row in the design grid. Test the query without committing to execution by using the Datasheet View button to preview the targeted records. Execute the query by clicking the *Run* button or selecting QUERY/RUN from the menu. *Warning: Delete queries cannot be undone, so test thoroughly before committing to Run.*

1. In the Victor's Furniture Database window, click *Queries* on the Objects bar. Double-click *Create query in Design view*. Add the ORDERS table to the Query Design window and close the Show Table dialog box.

2. Drag the * **(all fields)** symbol to the design grid. Drag the CustomerID field to the second column in the design grid. Clear the check box in the *Show* cell for the CustomerID field.

(You must clear the check box so that the CustomerID field is not included in the query results set twice.)

3. Type: *28* in the Criteria cell for the CustomerID field. This is the ID for a customer which has gone out of business.

4. Drag the ShipDate field to the design grid. Type: *Is Null* in the Criteria cell for the Ship Date field. This command will delete all unshipped orders (those with a blank ship date). Clear the *Show* checkbox to prevent the ShipDate field from appearing twice in the query result set.

5. Click the Datasheet View button to check that the correct records will be deleted. There is only one order for CustomerID 28 that has not yet shipped (see Figure 5-49).

6. Return to Design view and select QUERY/DELETE QUERY. The Sort and Show rows are replaced by the *Delete* row. Orders will be deleted **from** the ORDERS table **where** the CustomerID is 28 AND **where** the ShipDate field contains a null value, as shown in Figure 5-50. Run the query. A warning message box asks you to confirm the deletion of the row. Click *Yes*. Close the query without saving it. Close the database.

Figure 5-49

	OrderID	Product ID	Customer ID	Ship Via	Units Ordered	Order Date	Ship Date
▶	101	CCC92:	28	Airborne Express	6	6/24/2002	
*	‹Number)				0		

Record: |◄ ◄| 1 |► ►| ►*| of 1

Figure 5-50

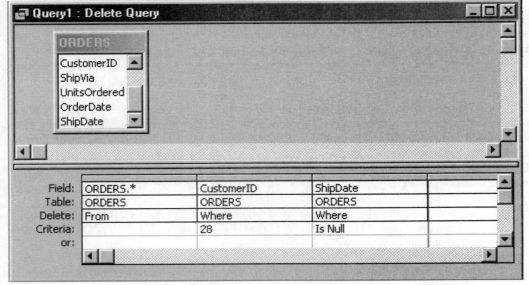

Functions in Access

A *function* in Access performs some sort of calculation on data and then returns the result of that calculation. There are over 130 different functions available in Access. Functions can be used in Macros or Modules, in Query expressions, or as calculated controls in Form or Report objects. Case 9 involves using two different types of functions:

Type of Function	Name of Function	Calculation Performed
Date/Time	DateDiff	Number of time intervals between dates
Domain Aggregate	DLookup	Finds/Looks Up and displays a Value

DateDiff

The *DateDiff* function is used to determine how many time intervals (e.g.: days, weeks, years) exist between two dates. In the following example, the DateDiff function is used to calculate the number of days between an Entry and Exit date at a parking garage. The result of this calculation is then multiplied by the Daily Parking Rate to give a total amount owing by the driver. Required syntax is exactly as shown.

In Case 9, the DateDiff function is used in an Update action query, to first determine the number of days a guest has stayed at the hotel, and then to calculate the appropriate charge.

———— Time Interval code for Days

DateDiff("d",[Entry Date],[Exit Date])*[Daily Rate]

DLookup

DLookup returns a field value from a domain (a specific set of records as defined by a table or query). The following example first looks up the Tax Rate in a table called *Personnel* where data in the *Skill* field of a table called *Staff* matches data in the Skill field of the Personnel table. The appropriate *Tax Rate* is then added to the Tax Rate field in the Personnel table. Required syntax is exactly as shown.

DLookup("[Tax Rate]","[Personnel]","[Skill]"=[Staff]![Skill]")

In Case 9, the DLookup function is used in a Set Value macro sequence to look up a room rate in the ROOMS LOOKUP table and add it to the Rate field in the ROOMS table, as part of the registration procedure.

More About Macros

The following macro actions may help in completing the tasks associated with Case 9.

MACRO ACTION	WHAT IT DOES
Close	Closes the current active window
Echo	Hides or shows the result of a macro while it runs
MsgBox	Displays a message box with informational or warning text
Open Form	Opens a specified Form object
Open Query	Opens a select query and/or runs an action query
Set Value	Sets the value for a control field or property on a form or report
Set Warnings	Turns off all system messages such as warnings while a macro is running

Database Case 10

Acoustic Designs 2

Problem:	Create a complete system
Management skill:	Control Organize
Access Skills:	Forms Macros Advanced Queries (Union)
Data Tables:	ACOUSTIC_A ACOUSTIC_B ACOUSTIC_C

This case is a continuation of Solve it! Database Case 6. Refer to this case for background information relating to Case 10. We recommend that you make a copy of the Case 6 files and save them as Case 10 before starting this case.

Brad Knox was feeling very pleased with himself as he gazed out of his office window at the busy Nashville streetscape. He had just finished his perusal of Melodia's financial performance figures for the 2000-2001 year. His mail order music company had performed stunningly last year, with sales improving by nearly 18%. Knox had also noticed that the costs associated with postage and packaging of his mail order catalogs and the maintenance of his mailing list had dropped significantly.

Knox believed that these results were largely due to the ability of the PC-based database mailing system his company had developed to provide carefully targeted mail outs for his various customer segments. Previously Knox had relied on blanket mailouts to all customers on his mailing list whenever he wanted to advertise new product offerings. Thanks to his new mailing system, his company was now able to tailor its mailouts so that catalogs were sent out only to customers with interests in the music areas which were relevant to his new products.

Knox now wanted to complete the development of his new system by adding some enhancements and new features. He began to jot down his main requirements.

(a) A system that is easy to use.

The new system worked well, but it required a thorough understanding of the database package it had been created in to operate effectively. Knox was the only one who knew how the system worked and what it did, and he currently maintained the system himself. He did not regard this as a productive way to spend his time, and wanted to pass over the operation and day-to-day maintenance of the system to his clerical staff.

Knox had to remember which query did what, and which report gave him the result formats he wanted. The system was efficient but it was not the kind of product you would want in the hands of untrained people. What was needed was a more robust and user-friendly version of the system.

Knox's objective is to produce a self-contained mailing system that could be operated by someone with little or no database knowledge. The system must be menu driven and modular in design. The menu should also execute automatically when the user opens the database, which contains the system (i.e.: the .MDB file). When a task option is selected from the menu, the menu will open the required object, and then execute that option. Each option should contain a facility to exit back to the menu.

(b) Integrate the Melodia mailing list with that of Acoustic Design.

Knox suspects that at least 25% of the customers on his mailing list are also customers who regularly purchase from Acoustic Design, his brother's side of the business (refer back to *Case 6*). While the marketing side of Acoustic Design has been handled by a PC-based database package for some time, the system is not menu driven and requires someone with a good understanding of databases to operate it. Knox and his brother would like to combine their mailing lists under one menu based system. They have agreed that while information unique to each of the businesses will be maintained separately, the names and addresses will be shared. Although the two divisions do business with many of the same organizations, Melodia's customer contact names often may be different than the ones used by Acoustic Design.

Brad Knox would like to test how well this procedure will work. His brother Trevor has provided him with a sample listing of Acoustic Design customer names. This is provided on the *Solvelt!* data table ACOUSTIC_C. Brad wants to combine this file with his own listing (ACOUSTIC_A). The result of this procedure should show no duplicate records. The combined listings will then be incorporated into a menu option on the new system.

Knox needs your help. He does not have the time or expertise needed to create the menu driven mailing system required and would like you to develop a prototype for him. Part of the job was completed in *Solvelt!* database Case 6, and you will need to use the database used in that previous case to complete Case 10.

Tasks

There are six tasks in this case.

1.   Create a Main Menu form and appropriate command buttons, which allow the user the following executable options. Call this form MAIN MENU.

     1. Add a new customer.

     2. Add a new company.

     3. Produce a complete mailing list.

     4. Exit the system.

Hint: Insert command buttons w/o the Control Wizards activated on the Main Menu form for the first three options: These options will not initially be active. Use the Command Button Wizard to set up an active Exit procedure for option four.

2. Create data entry forms for command buttons 1 and 2. Include Exit and Add New Record command buttons and test them thoroughly. Call these forms ADD CUSTOMER and ADD COMPANY.

3. Devise a procedure that will execute the Main Menu automatically whenever the database is opened.

4. Create a procedure that will combine the customer name tables of Melodia (ACOUSTIC_A) and Acoustic Design (ACOUSTIC_C). There are a number of names, which appear in both tables. Your aim is to produce a listing with no duplicate records. *Hint: Use a Union query to complete this task.*

    The combined file should then be joined to the ACOUSTIC_B table to give a full listing of the customers and their organizational details. This task can be accomplished with a Select query.

5. Create a report to display results for Task 4. The report should be sorted first by organization, and then by last name. Incorporate this report as Option 3 on the Main Menu form

    Hint: Use the existing report created for Task2/3 of Case 6 (Marketing Report), and simply change the record source for the report to the TASK4B query. Also change the title and the name for the report to Full Mailing List (Both the Caption property for the report and the Caption property for the title label.) Save the report with the new name: Full Mailing List.

*6. Extend the system even further to include the sales and number of sound recordings sold to each customer. Add the necessary fields and some sample data to the appropriate table. Then add a new option to the menu, which will calculate and display the total sales for Melodia and the average price per recording.

Time Estimates (excluding task marked with *):

Expert: 2 hours
Intermediate: 3 hours
Novice: 5 hours

Tutorial for Database Case 10 Using Access 2002

Advanced Queries - the SQL-Specific Query

SQL (Structured Query Language) is a simple programming language used for querying, updating and managing relational databases. When you create a select query or action query, Access automatically generates the equivalent SQL statement in the background. You can view or edit the SQL statement by choosing SQL View on the View menu in either the Datasheet view or Query Design view or by clicking the list arrow on the View button and selecting SQL View.

Some Access query types however, can only be created by writing an SQL statement. These queries are known as SQL-Specific queries. This group includes:

Union	•	*queries that combine fields from two or more tables or queries*
Pass-through	•	*queries that send commands directly to a database server*
Data-definition	•	*queries used to create or alter database tables in the current database*
Subqueries	•	*an SQL SELECT statement inside another select or action query*

SQL statements refer to expressions that define SQL commands such as SELECT, UPDATE or DELETE, and include clauses such as WHERE, GROUP BY and ORDER BY. SQL statements are typically used in the construct of queries and aggregate functions.

The Union Query

You will need to use the Union SQL-Specific query type as part of the requirement for completing Task 4 of Case 10. You can use UNION queries to combine the result sets of two or more Select queries into a single result set. You can also create Union queries that combine rows in two tables.

Using simple *SELECT ... FROM* SQL statements, *Union Queries* enable you to combine fields from two or more tables into one listing. In contrast, *Select queries,* which are based on a join, creates a dynaset only from those records whose related fields meet a specified condition. Commands and clauses commonly used in the creation of Union queries include:

> **SELECT** *fieldlist*
> **FROM** *tablenames* **IN** *database name*
> **WHERE** *search conditions*
> **GROUP BY** *fieldlist*
> **HAVING** *search conditions*
> **ORDER BY** *fieldlist*

Creating a Union Query

1.   In the Database window, click *Queries* on the Objects bar. Double-click *Create query in Design view* to open the Query Design view window, but do not add any field lists to the design grid. Union queries <u>do not use</u> the Query Window/QBE Grid for their construction.

2.   Select QUERY/SQL SPECIFIC/UNION from the menu. Access displays the Union Query window.

3.   Enter the appropriate SQL *SELECT....xx* statements needed for your Union Query. For example

        Let's create a simple UNION query that will combine rows from two tables. To complete this exercise you will use the Colby's Custom Camping database provided with your Solve it! files. The SQL statement you will construct will select the records of all customers and suppliers who live in the state of Connecticut.

   a.   Open *Colby's Custom Camping.mdb*. Click *Queries* on the Objects bar. Double-click *Create query in Design view*. Close the Show Table dialog box. Select QUERY/SQL SPECIFIC/UNION.

   b.   Type: (See Figure 5-51)

SELECT CustomerName, BillingAddress, City, State, ZipCode, PhoneNumber, CustomerID
FROM Customers
WHERE State = 'CT'

UNION SELECT CompanyName, BillingAddress, City, State, ZipCode, PhoneNumber, SupplierID
FROM Suppliers
WHERE State = 'CT'

   c.   Click the *Run* button. The query result set is shown in Figure 5-52. Save the query as *Tute10UnionQuery* and close it. Close the database.

        The number of fields in the field list of each Select and Union Select query must be the same. You will receive an error message if the number of fields is not the same

        The sequence of the field names in each field list must also correspond to the similar entity in the other field list. You will not receive an error message, but the result set may be incoherent.

        Commas are used to separate members of lists of parameters such as multiple field names as in the example.

        Square brackets are required only around field names which include a space or other symbols including punctuation. If fields from more than one table are included in a query, a period must separate the table name and the field name (e.g. Suppliers. [Company Name]).

        Be sure to include a semi-colon at the end of each statement (refer to examples below) to complete the required Access syntax. Note also the use of square brackets to enclose field names.

This punctuation is necessary if you are using field names composed of two or more words separated by spaces or punctuation.

Figure 5-51

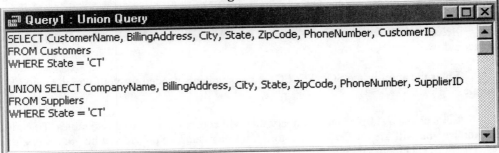

Figure 5-52

CustomerName	BillingAddress	City	State	ZipCode	PhoneNumber	CustomerID
Burke Lyrid Medical Supply	622 Lindale Rd.	Keedysville	CT	00675	6075553444	6
Carol Thompson	294 Bradford Rd.	Turner	CT	66844	5785552233	14
David Johnson	722 Blanchard Rd.	Greenfield	CT	10784	2045554378	3
Georgette Starr	34786 Richards Rd.	Michaelton	CT	10647	2045551093	13
Jim Smith	6887 Grant Ave.	Lawrence	CT	35509	7455557532	11
Peters Camping Supplies	74 Delaponte Ave.	Lawrence	CT	37856	5665559054	1
Steven O'Patrick	213 Singleton Dr.	Morristown	CT	11988	2045553355	8

Record: 14 ◀ [1   ] ▶ ▶I ▶* of 7

Here is another example of an SQL statement:

SELECT [Supplier Name], [City]
FROM Suppliers
UNION SELECT [Customer Name], [City]
FROM Customers;

Retrieves the names and cities of suppliers and customers from the Suppliers and Customers tables

SELECT [Supplier Name], [City]
FROM Suppliers
WHERE [Country] = "Brazil"
UNION SELECT [Customer Name], [City]
FROM Customers
WHERE [Country] = "Brazil"
ORDER BY [City];

Retrieves the names and cities of suppliers and customers located in Brazil, sorted by the City field

Note: Unless you specify otherwise, a Union Query automatically removes duplicate records from the resulting listing. If you want to show all records, including duplicates, add the word ALL after the word UNION in your statement. For example:

SELECT [Supplier Name], [City] FROM Suppliers **UNION ALL** SELECT [Customer Name], [City] FROM Customers;	*Retrieves the names and cities of suppliers and customers from the Suppliers and Customers tables, and shows all records including duplicates*

Task 1 of Case 10 requires you to create a merged file of the customer records of Melodia and Acoustic Design. Contrast the difference between omitting and including ALL in the Union Query you need to create to complete this task.

> <u>Caution</u>: Don't convert an SQL-specific query to another type of query, such as a select query. If you do, you'll lose the SQL statement that you entered. *You can however use an SQL-specific query as part of a select query.*

Creating an AutoExec Macro

You can create a special macro that runs automatically whenever you open a Microsoft Access database. For example, you may wish to open certain tables and forms every time you open a database.

To create a macro that runs whenever you open a database

1. Create a macro.
2. Add the actions that you want this macro to perform.
3. Save the macro. **Its name must be AutoExec.**

AutoExec macros can be used to create a custom workspace, import data from other databases, or to execute tasks that you want to perform every time the database is opened. To prevent the AutoExec macro from running, hold down the Shift key while opening the database.

Setting Startup Options

You can easily control many aspects of how an Access database looks and behaves when it opens without writing a macro or any Visual Basic code. You can set startup options to give your database a title and/or to program Access to open a particular form first when a user opens the database. Select TOOLS/STARTUP to open the Startup dialog box. Type the name you want for your application in the *Application Title* text box. Click the list arrow on the *Display Form/Page* list box and select the form you want to open first. You can also clear the check from the *Display Database Window* checkbox so that users will only be able to access the form or forms that you want them to, and will not be able to change the database structure in any way.

Other startup options include inserting a custom icon as the Control menu icon and choosing whether or not to display the Status bar. You can also decide if you want full menus to display in the database and whether or not you want users to be able to make changes to the menus or toolbars.

6

Internet Business Cases

The Internet and the World Wide Web have had an extraordinary impact on the conduct of business in the last decade. E-commerce—the use of the Web to conduct business transactions—has grown into a $70 billion business-to-consumer (B2C) marketplace by 2002 from a standing start of zero in 1995. The Web also enables a $700 billion trade in 2002 among businesses (B2B E-commerce). The Internet has also transformed the internal transactions of businesses by providing a powerful, inexpensive, standards-based communications infrastructure that can be used to support relationships with customers, vendors, and employees in the form of Extranets and Intranets.

In 2002, there are approximately 500,000 business firms connected to the Web worldwide. About 400 million individuals have Web access worldwide, and in the U.S. about 170 million people use the Web at home or at work. The size of the Web continues to grow at a torrid pace albeit slower than the earlier years of exponential growth. The Web contains about one billion pages of information. Searching through all this information and making sense out of it is a major challenge.

Aside from E-commerce and E-business, the Web has had an equally large impact on how business people gather and use information. For businesses the Web provides a storehouse of information on markets, competitor behavior, consumer research and behavior, and financial information. In the past much of this information could either not be obtained, or would be very expensive and require a team of researchers. Today business people can in a few hours conduct a Web search for product and service vendors, discover what their competitors are doing, research developments in government policy that effect the firm, and find out the latest financial information on their firm, or an entire industry.

In this chapter we focus on the business uses of the Web to conduct business research, competive intelligence, financial analysis, and market research. Table 6-1 describes the cases in this chapter.

Table 6-1 Web Cases

Name and Type	Description	Potential Web Sources
Case 1: FastSearch.com Web Portal Business Research	Search engine/travel and entertainment Web portal seeks to improve management environment by purchasing an internal corporate portal	BusinessMonkey mySAP.com Oracle Plumtree Software
Case 2: JobEden.com Competitive Intelligence	Online career placement startup assess the competition	Nielsen NetRatings CyberAtlas.com Internetstats.com Tagdata.com Monster.com Toptenlinks.com Jobweb.com
Case 3: Comprehensive Benefits Services Business Research	Health insurance and retirement plan administrator investigates Internet security and privacy issues	U.S. House of Representatives U.S. Senate Electronic Privacy Info Center Library of Congress
Case 4: Acadia Investment Advisors Financial Analysis	Financial advising firm helps a client choose a company in which to invest using financial ratios	SEC Edgar database Finance.Yahoo.com Hoovers.com Smartmoney.com
Case 5: Aperture, Inc. Market Research	Communications company researches the likelihood of a successful expansion of services	United States Census Statistical Abstract of the United States

Solve it!

We assume in this chapter that you are familiar with the Web and know how to use basic Web search tools. If this is not the case you can use the following tutorials available on the Web that describe the Internet and the World Wide Web:

Table 6-2 On Line Internet and Web Tutorials

Web Site URL	Description
http://library.albany.edu/internet	University at Albany Internet Tutorials—Links to basic tutorials about the Internet, Internet research, search engines, Web browsers, and software training.
http://www.findtutorials.com	Access to hundreds of free tutorials, low-cost online training courses, and IT jobs.
http://www.lib.berkeley.edu/TeachingLib/Guides/Internet/	University of California, Berkeley, Internet Guide—Internet tutorials to help college and university students learn how to search the Internet, create WWW resources, evaluate sites for academic value, compare Web browsers, find Internet and Web terms, etc.
http://www.wdvl.com	Web Developers' Virtual Library—Thorough, illustrated guide to Web technology including tutorials, and examples, and links to other resources.
http://www.davesite.com	Dave's Site—Includes a beginner's guide to the Internet and various other Internet-related guides.

The Web cases that follow generally do not require new software skills but focus instead on the use of the Web for management decision making in business. In most cases Chapter 6 tutorials will refer you to previous chapters to review earlier software tutorials as required. Where new software skills are required, they will be covered in the Chapter 6 tutorials.

Web Case 1

FastSearch.com Web Portal

Problem:	Prepare a report on Web portal technology and calculate the return on investment for a portal project.
Management skills:	Planning Deciding
Web skills:	Business research

File: Fastsearch_q.xls

FastSearch.com started as a simple search engine in 1994. Over the last seven years, it has expanded beyond its core business into providing a wide range of travel and entertainment services, in-depth content on sports, medical issues, and news in an effort to find a wider audience and to keep visitors at its site for longer periods of time. The longer visitors stay at its site, the greater the revenue for FastSearch. Companies and individuals now use FastSearch to find low-cost airline fares, discounted hotel rates, rental car information, and related travel information. Individuals often use the site to research entertainment packages at popular tourist destinations. Using FastSearch's unique reservation system, registered site users make reservations, buy tickets, rent rooms, reserve cars, buy entertainment packages, and make other travel arrangements all in one Web site visit.

As FastSearch has grown from fifteen employees providing a simple search service to a Web portal with 450 employees providing many services, the management team has become overwhelmed with information. The small management team must keep track of Web activity at its site including visitors, sales for each of its services, results of promotional campaigns, as well as weekly and monthly cost reports. Even though they are a Web services company, managers are overloaded with paper-based reports. Different managers need different types of reports, and each report requires data that the IT Department needs to provide on a routine basis. With so many employees, there is a growing demand for information on training, pensions, and benefits. As the customer base has expanded, it has become increasingly difficult to respond to customers seeking help with FastSearch's various service offerings, or to deal with customer complaints.

As a result, the costs of managing the firm have skyrocketed despite a long-term effort to keep the management head count down.

CEO Jeannine Toscana wants to move the firm towards a more uniform information management environment, one that would be more efficient and result in better service to customers, provide employees with more information on company activities and programs, and provide managers with a coherent online information environment. She is considering the development of an internal Web portal as a tool for organizing and accessing the companies critical management information.

A corporate *portal* is an internal Web site running on a corporate intranet that organizes the important management information for decision makers as well as general corporate information required by all employees. Portals provide a single point of access and a delivery vehicle for important corporate information. Users can customize and personalize the content they see to focus on just those pieces of information they are interested in and need in order to do their jobs. Portals also can be configured to call information from a variety of back-office legacy systems and present it to users in an easy to use Web environment.

Although the FastSearch technical development team could build such a corporate portal, this is not one of their core competencies and Toscana does not want to pull the technical team off more valuable Web site development work. Therefore Toscana is planning to purchase an off-the-shelf Web portal service from a firm that specializes in this technology.

CEO Toscana has given the job of designing and developing a successful corporate portal project to CIO Adam Wainwright. Wainwright supports the idea of purchasing a corporate portal from an outside firm that has experience with this technology rather than building it in house. He needs some help in identifying vendors in this area and background information on costs and benefits. As Wainwright's executive assistant, your first assignment is to use the Web to research corporate portal vendors and develop a report for the portal project.

Tasks

There are three tasks in this case.

1. Use a search engine like Google.com or Yahoo.com to find three Web sites of companies that sell corporate portal technology. Prepare a short report (3-5 pages) or PowerPoint presentation (5-7 slides) that describes the features of corporate portals, their benefits and costs. Many sites will include case studies of "success" stories. Be sure to include at least one successful case in your report. Include a section in your report or presentation that describes some of the potential risks and pitfalls of using this technology.

2. Wainwright has provided you with some initial estimates of the costs and benefits of the new portal for the next three years. These estimates are provided in the accompanying spreadsheet **fastsearch_q.xls**. He would like your help in analyzing the results.

Calculate the following:

(a) Total projected costs for each year, and the total costs for all years.
(b) Total projected benefits for each year, and the total benefits for all years.
(c) Depreciation. Assume a straight line depreciation over three years.
(d) Annual net benefits (nominal) for each year (benefits-costs for each year)
(e) Cumulative payback (nominal).
(f) The accounting rate of return for the next three years. The accounting rate of return is defined as:

$$\frac{(\text{total benefits- total costs- depreciation})/\text{useful life}}{\text{total costs}}$$

We will assume in this problem that the useful life of the portal is three years, that the depreciation is equal for each year, and at the end of the period the portal has no salvage value (the value is zero after three years).

(g) Prepare a brief statement arguing for or against this investment by the firm.

*3. Calculate the net present value of the investment in the portal technology. Assume a prime interest rate of 5%. You will need to calculate the present value of the annual net benefits. Hint: use Excel's NPV function to do this. The net present value is defined as the present value of annual net benefits minus the total investment cost.

On the basis of your results, do you recommend this investment? Write a paragraph describing the benefit of this investment for the firm.

Tutorial for Web Case 1

Search Engines on the Web

Search Engines are software programs that enable users of the Web to locate documents of interest through keyword searching. Most of them also allow the searcher to use Boolean logic (AND, OR, NOT operators) to refine searches. It is estimated that there are around 900 search engines available for use on the Web and most of them are free. Some of the most popular search engines are:

WORD-ORIENTED SEARCH ENGINES

Google
www.google.com

AltaVista
http://www.altavista.com

Web Crawler
http://www.webcrawler.com

Lycos
http://www.lycos.com
Excite
http://www.excite.com

SUBJECT-ORIENTED SEARCH ENGINES

Yahoo
http://yahoo.com

Each of these search tools work in different ways and often produce similar but different results. *Alta Vista* is a true keyword searching of document titles and text within documents, and is possibly the most comprehensive search engine of its type. Alta Vista tends to produce very large lists of search results. Therefore, be careful to narrow your search arguments when using keyword search engines. For instance, if searching for information on "security alarms," narrow your search by specifying "home," "business," "boat" or "automobile." What type of security alarm are you really looking for? If you are really looking for a wireless car alarm that will sound an audible alarm and then send a radio signal to your beeper, then your search argument on a keyword search engine should be something like "security alarm and automobile and wireless."

Other search engines like Yahoo! are more like yellow page directories and are put together by human editors assisted by input from Web site operators (some of whom pay for listing), and their own Web crawlers that search the Web for pages to index, as well as information provided by other software programs that record the "connectedness" of a site (how many sites link to this target site). The popular sites are very well connected because many sites have links to, for example, www.espn.com, the Web's most popular sports site. The result is a smaller, more targeted list of search results.

The most widely used search engine is Google. Google uses a combination of techniques including Web crawlers that index the word content of nearly 300 million Web pages, and connectedness. This means that search engines fail to index about 700 million pages (most of these pages are unpopular, not connected, or on internal Web sites that are difficult to access).

Different search engines produce some differences in results, especially for very specialized search topics. Researchers have found for instance that there is about a 60% overlap among search engines. Nevertheless, this also suggests that 40% of the pages found on one search engine will not be found on another search engine even using the same search argument.

Understanding the Financial Value of Information Systems

Businesses invest in information technology applications for a variety of reasons. In some cases the investment is undertaken to achieve growth in market share, in some cases simply as a requirement of staying in business, and in still other cases it is undertaken simply to achieve a return on invested capital. Sometimes all three motivations are important. Whatever the reason for investment, most businesses will perform a financial returns analysis. The two most common financial return calculations are the accounting rate of return (ROI) and net present value analysis.

Accounting Rate of Return

The accounting rate of return is defined as:

$$\frac{(\text{total benefits- total costs- depreciation})/\text{useful life}}{\text{total costs}}$$

For instance, in the example below the total benefits of an investment over four years are $450,000, total costs are $100,000, and depreciation of the investment is $50,000. The useful life is four years in this example. Using the formula above, the accounting rate of return is 75% over the life of the project.

Total Benefits	$	450,000
Total Costs	$	100,000
Depreciation	$	50,000
Useful life	4 years	

ROI=   75%

Net Present Value Analysis

The accounting rate of return does not take into account the time value of money, and the fact that the benefits you receive in future years will be worth less than their nominal or face value because of the opportunity cost of money and inflation. For instance, if I promise to pay you back $15 one year from now in return for a $10 loan from you to me today, you would have to take into account at least two facts. One, you will lose the $10 you loan me for one year and give up the interest you could have earned in a bank. Also, inflation will erode the value of money so the $15 I pay you next year will be worth less because of inflation.

In net present value analysis you need to understand, first, what is the value in today's dollars of a future set of payments (this value is called "the present value"). In net present value analysis, both the opportunity cost of an investment and the inflation factor are summed up and taken into account by the use of a "prime rate" or other bank rate to deflate the value of future payments.

The net present value is defined as:

Present value of total annual benefits - total investment cost

In Excel you use the net present value function (npv) to calculate the present value of total future annual benefits. [Unfortunately, the Excel npv function is misnamed and does not give you a true net present value but in fact returns the present value of a set of payments in the future]. To calculate the net present value, take the present value of future payments and subtract the total initial investment (usually made in today's dollars).

In the spreadsheet below there are future benefits of $100, $150, and $300 in the next three years. The initial investment is $300, and the interest rate is 6%. Is the investment worth it?

Benefits

Year 1		Year 2		Year 3	
$	100	$	150	$	300

Cost	$	300
Interest rate		6.00%
Present value	$	480

Net present value		$180

This investment is "worth it" because in today's dollars it has a net present value of greater than $0 and will return in fact $180 today's dollars in the future.

You can use the Function wizard to calculate the Excel NPV function. Follow these steps:

1. Click on the cell in the spreadsheet where you want the NPV calculation to appear.
2. Use the Insert/Function menu or the toolbar shortcut Fx
3. Select Financial functions
4. Select the NPV function
5. Fill in the Wizard information for the interest rate and the values of the annual payments. You can also enter cell references for these values if you think they might change.
6. Click OK

Web Case 2

JobEden.Com

Problem:	Analyze the online job search industry
Management skills:	Planning Deciding
Web skills:	Competitive intelligence
File:	JobEden_q.xls

Jobeden.org is a start up venture founded by a group of career-placement officers who have decided they would rather be entrepreneurs than employees. CEO Dan Minor and CFO Susan Mahoney—the two main founders—have approached an East Coast venture-capital firm, Steinmann Investing, to provide start-up capital for the Web site. Steinmann Investing believes JobEden could be profitable if the financials worked out. Steinmann is worried about the potential number of visitors, the revenue generated by employers who would pay for access to the site, and by potential operational costs.

The placement officers who started JobEden have great track records placing recent college graduates into the financial service and media industries in the New York Metropolitan area. Together the founding team of eight placement officers has a combined experience of more than 80 years in job placement and executive recruiting. Despite this experienced management team, Steinmann is cautious about investing in start-ups given the recent experience of so many failures among dotcoms.

Steinmann has requested that CEO Minor and CFO Mahoney do additional research on the financials of the online career-placement business. Specifically, the investors want a better idea of the overall size of the online job market, and the principal competitors; the levels of traffic at the competing Web sites; and a better idea of what JobEden's budget would look like based on the experience of a similar firm. The management team at JobEden has asked you to develop the information requested by the investors.

Tasks

There are three tasks in this case.

1. Using a Web search engine, identify Web sites that have information about the leading firms in the online job search industry. Build a spreadsheet of the top ten most frequently visited Web sites. A sample spreadsheet has been started for you in JobEden_q.xls. Sort the sites in terms of their unique visitors. In addition to visitors, find out how much revenue each of the top ten sites generate. Identify the major sources of revenue for online job search sites such as employer listing fees, advertising fees, and the selling of services to users. You may not be able to find this detailed information for all top ten sites.

Write a short report on your findings.

2. To understand the potential revenue and profit picture for the new company, the investors want you to look at a competitor's financial statements and calculate a series of standard financial ratios. Use HotJobs.com as the competitor. As a public company, HotJobs is required by the 1934 Securities Act to report its financial results and all other material developments at the company to the Securities and Exchange Commission (SEC). The SEC maintains a database of these filings called "EDGAR."

Go to www.sec.gov/edgar and select "Search for Company Filings." Then select "Search the EDGAR Archives." Enter the company name "hotjobs" into the text entry box labeled "EDGAR Search: Enter a Search String."

Search for the latest Hotjobs "10-K" filing which contains the last reported year of financial information. Select **the text** version of the 10-K.

Once you have the text version of the 10-K filing on screen, look in the table of contents for the location of consolidated financial statements (usually this section is called "Consolidated Financial Statements and Supplementary Data"). Scroll to a table that provides the consolidated statement of operations (the Income Statement).

Scroll down the document until you find a table called "HOTJOBS.COM, LTD. CONSOLIDATED STATEMENTS OF OPERATIONS (found in a section called "Consolidated Financial Statements and Supplementary Data"). Select with your mouse all the data from first row labeled "Revenues" to the last row labeled "Net Loss." Copy to the clipboard (or use CTRL+C). Open Excel, and paste into an Excel spreadsheet.

You will notice that the data you pasted spreads haphazardly across the worksheet and needs to be organized in columns. Also the first column of data will be highlighted in blue. Leave the blue hightlighting as is, and use the Excel Data Menu to convert the text data into Excel spreadsheet columns.

Click the *Data* menu, and then click the *Text to Columns* command to open the Convert Text to Columns Wizard. In Step 1 of the wizard, be sure that the *Fixed Width* option is selected, and then click the [Next] button. Generally, the default options of the Wizard work well.

Use the *Data Preview* window to scroll back and forth, and up and down, in the worksheet to see how the columns of numbers appears on the worksheet. Follow the instructions in the top half of the dialog box to add and delete lines to indicate where you want the columns to break. For example, the first break line should appear at the right side of the column that describes each financial category, the second line should appear at the right side of the first year of data, and so on.

When you have set all the break lines, click the [Next] button.

Select the *General* option button in the *Column data format* section near the upper right of the dialog box. Click the [Finish] button to close the wizard.

In the worksheet, delete extra columns and rows as needed to format your categories and data in related groupings and in an attractive format. Delete extraneous formatting symbols. Delete columns containing previous years of data-- you are interested only in the latest year's data.

Select just the financial data, and format it with the *Currency Style* button on the Formatting toolbar. Also on the Formatting toolbar, use the *Decrease Decimal* button to delete the two decimal places. Resave the workbook.

Use the Data/Text to Columns wizard to convert the pasted data into an Excel spreadsheet form. Accept all default selections. You will have to widen the columns to display all the information properly. Remove all extraneous formatting symbols and unneeded text.

Now calculate the following ratios:

Gross Margin (Gross profit /Total revenues)
Cost of revenues/Total revenues
Net Margin (Net income (or Net loss) /Total Revenues)
R&D or Product Development Expense/ Total revenues
Sales and Marketing Expense/Total revenues
General and Administrative Expense/Total revenues

Express all ratios as percentages and copy the formulas to previous years so that you end up with ratios for three years' worth of experience.

3. Mahoney also wants you to create a pro forma profit and loss statement for the start-up company. A pro forma profit and loss statement is used to project how much money the business should allocate to various activities. Assume the new company will have first year revenues of $15 million. Using the five ratios you calculated in Task 2, calculate how much JobEden.com would have to spend for product development, for sales and marketing, and for general and administrative costs, assuming total revenues of $15 million.

Tutorial for Web Case 2

This case assumes the reader has already mastered the use of search engines.

Using the EDGAR Database

EDGAR is major research tool for business and stock analysts as well as ordinary investors. EDGAR provides a treasure trove of information that companies are required to reveal to the public in order to ensure efficient and honest capital markets. Only public companies that sell stock to the public report to EDGAR. There are many different types of annual, quarterly, and event driven filings

To look up a public company, go to www.sec.gov/edgar and select "Search for Company Filings." Then select "Search the EDGAR Archives." Enter the company name "hotjobs" into the text entry box labeled "EDGAR Search: Enter a Search String."

Search for the latest Hotjobs "10-K" filing which contains the last reported year of financial information. Select the **text** version of the 10-K.

Once you have the text version of the 10-K filing on screen, look in the table of contents for the location of consolidated financial statements (usually this section is called "Consolidated Financial Statements and Supplementary Data"). Scroll to a table that provides the consolidated statement of operations (the Income Statement).

Scroll down the document until you find a table called "HOTJOBS.COM, LTD. CONSOLIDATED STATEMENTS OPERATIONS (found in a section called "Consolidated Financial Statements and Supplementary Data"). Select with your mouse all the data from first row labeled "Revenues" to the last row labeled "Net Loss." Copy the data to the Clipboard (or use CTRL+C). Open Excel, and paste the data into an Excel spreadsheet.

You will notice that the data you pasted spreads haphazardly across the worksheet and needs to be organized in columns. Also, the first column of data will be highlighted in blue. Leave the blue highlighting as is, and use the Excel Data Menu to convert the text data into Excel spreadsheet columns.

Click the *Data* menu, and then click the *Text to Columns* command to open the Convert Text to Columns Wizard. In Step 1 of the wizard, be sure that the *Fixed Width* option is selected, and then click the [Next] button. Generally, the default options of the Wizard work well.

Use the *Data Preview* window to scroll back and forth, and up and down, in the worksheet to see how the columns of numbers appear on the worksheet. Follow the instructions in the top half of the dialog box to add and delete lines to indicate where you want the columns to break. For example, the first break line should appear at the right side of the column that describes each financial category, the second line should appear at the right side of the first year of data, and so on.

When you have set all the break lines, click the [Next] button.

Select the *General* option button in the *Column data format* section near the upper right of the dialog box. Click the [Finish] button to close the wizard.

In the worksheet, delete extra columns and rows as needed to format your categories and data in related groupings and in an attractive format. Delete extraneous formatting symbols and unneeded text. Delete columns containing previous years of data—you are interested only in the latest year's data. You may have to widen the columns to display all the information properly.

Select just the financial data, and format it with the *Currency Style* button on the Formatting toolbar. Also on the Formatting toolbar, use the *Decrease Decimal* button to delete the two decimal places. Resave the workbook.

Display all financial ratios as percentages. In this case you are interested only in the most recent year's data, so you can eliminate the information from earlier years.

Pro Forma Profit/Loss Statements (Income Statements)

A profit and loss statement (P&L) is a statement that describes how much the revenue and operating expenses of a firm are. These statements are also called "Income statements." A "pro forma" P&L is a forecast based on best management judgment either for a new business or for a future year. Generally a profit and loss statement has the following categories of revenue and expenditures (the starred items are calculated by the user and are not usually a part of the 10-K statement):

Revenue:

Net sales	Gross sales revenue minus any returns
Cost of sales	The cost of physical products or services
Gross profit	Sales revenue minus cost of goods
*Gross Profit Margin	**Gross profit divided by net sales (%)**

Operating expenses

Marketing and fulfillment...............	Marketing and advertising costs
Technology and content..................	Research and development costs
General and administrative.............	Administrative costs, mostly labor
Stock-based compensation...............	Options programs for employees
Amortization of goodwill and other intangibles............................	Costs associated with purchases of other companies for prices higher than their book value
Total operating expenses..............	Total operating costs
Gain/Loss from operations......................	Gross profit minus cost of operations

*Net Margin

Gain/loss from operations divided by gross profit

Other Income/Expenses

Interest income..........................	Income from interest bearing accounts
Interest expense.........................	Expenses for short term loans
Other income (expense), net..............	Miscellaneous income
	Miscellaneous income

Net Gain/Loss

Gross profit minus operating expenses and other incomes/losses

Web Case 3

Comprehensive Benefits Services

Problem: Research Internet security and privacy

Management skills: Research analysis, Decision-making

Web skills: Business research

Comprehensive Benefits Services Inc. is a regional a firm in central New York that administers health insurance and retirement plans for the employees of small to midsize businesses. Comprehensive does not provide the services, but acts as an agent between businesses and health care providers and investment services.

Comprehensive has achieved moderate success in its seventeen-year history. The founders of the company believed that many businesses would prefer to outsource the legwork of researching and maintaining health and retirement plans rather than devoting human resources personnel to this work. Their theory was correct. However, the growth of the Internet has allowed Comprehensive to re-examine its services with an eye toward making the company even more successful.

Lucy Laviolette, Director of Customer Service for Comprehensive, has worked with the IT department for several years to make the company's Web site as helpful to customers as it can be. However, until now, that is all the Web site has been: a source of information. In the near future, Comprehensive will launch a new Web site that will allow customers to interact with their accounts online. Some of the new services will include enabling health insurance customers to submit requests for changing their primary care physician or for obtaining referrals. Retirement plan customers will be able to submit requests for changing their contribution amount or for adjusting the allocation of their investment to different funds.

Lucy realizes that this new venture carries a great deal of responsibility for the company. In order to make such transactions possible, customers will have to submit personal information such as name, address, phone number, policy or account number, and Social Security number. In order for the new services to be successful, customers must feel secure in Comprehensive's ability to protect their personal information. They also must trust that their personal information will not be used for any undesirable purposes. Furthermore, Comprehensive must consider their legal obligations in matters of privacy as it pertains to the Internet.

Lucy has determined that she can use the Web to investigate the current state of federal legislation concerning Internet privacy. She will compile details about relevant active legislation in an Access database so that the company can use it as a guideline in designing the new site and setting policy. She will also expand her research on privacy and prepare a report for the company's CIO that summarizes the advantages and disadvantages of existing and pending legislation to the company and to the consumer. The report will include legal proposals and the main trends in Internet privacy. Ultimately, Lucy will make a recommendation about how the company should respond to the issue of Internet privacy.

Tasks

There are five tasks in this case.

1.   Visit http://www.house.gov (The United States House of Representatives) and http://www.epic.org (Electronic Privacy Information Center) to find active bills on Internet privacy. The House site contains a link to the Library of Congress' THOMAS search facility, which will allow you to search for bills by topic. The EPIC site features Bill-Track, which tracks pending legislation on privacy and Cyber-Liberties in the current session of Congress.

2.   Use Microsoft Access to create a database of existing and pending legislation that is relevant to Internet privacy. The database fields you should use are law (or bill) number, law (or bill) name, proposing legislator (sponsor), and a brief summary of the law or bill. The summary field should use the Memo data type. Save the table.

3.   Enter the relevant legislation data you have found on the Web in the database table. (Note: If you prefer, you may skip ahead to Task 4 and create the form first so that you may use it to enter the data.)

4.   Once you have created the initial database table that organizes the data, create a form to facilitate entering additional data and a report for printing the data. Use all of the fields from the table in the form and in the report.

5.   Prepare a report or presentation for the Chief Information Officer that summarizes the advantages and disadvantages of various privacy laws to both the company and to the consumer. Also include recent trends in privacy legislation and its application. Present the views of a pro-privacy organization that you find on the Web. Finally, conclude your report or presentation by making a recommendation about how the company should approach the issue of privacy in creating its new Web site.

Tutorial for Web Case 3

This case requires you to use the Web to conduct business research. The table below lists URLs that will help you complete the research tasks.

URL	Description
http://www.house.gov	United States House of Representatives
http://www.senate.gov	United States Senate
http://www.epic.org	Electronic Privacy Information Center
http://www.epic.org/privacy	EPIC Privacy page
http://www.cdt.org/privacy	Center for Democracy & Technology
http://thomas.loc.gov/home/c107query.html#keyword	Library of Congress bill search

Previous tutorials you may find useful for this case:

Database Case 1 (page 95)
Database Case 2 (page 106)
Database Case 8 (page 158)

In this case you are required to place data found on Web pages in an Access database table. You can transfer data by keying it into the table manually or by using copy and paste techniques. To copy and paste data from a Web page into a database table, use the mouse to drag over the piece of data, such as a bill number or description, on the Web page. Once the piece of data is selected (highlighted in blue) use the Copy command on the Edit menu in the browser to copy the selection to the Clipboard. You may also use Ctrl+C to execute the copy command. Then switch to Access, click in the appropriate field, and use the Paste command on the Edit menu in Access (or Ctrl+V) to paste the copied data.

Web Case 4

Acadia Investment Advisors

Problem:	Prepare a financial analysis of two publicly held companies based on data from Web sources.
Management skills:	Planning Deciding
Web skills:	Financial analysis

Acadia Investment Advisers (AIA) is a financial advising firm in White Plains, New York. Acadia encourages clients to invest for long-term capital gains. Clients may call, visit, or use AIA's Web site to get advice about stocks they want to buy. Rick Langella, who owns Langella Contracting, a developer of office space, wants to invest in an office furniture company. Rick believes that the long-term market for office space construction in the country is quite strong and he believes that this demand for office space will lead to demand for office furniture.

But Langella knows very little about how to analyze potential office furniture investments. He has retained AIA to do some financial research for him on two of the leading office furniture companies in the United States: Open Plan Systems Inc. and Steelcase, Inc. Rick would like to invest in one of these companies but does not know which one is the better investment.

- *Open Plan Systems* sells and rents restored and refurbished workstations and office cubicles. The company buys used workstations from end users and brokers and rebuilds them to customer specifications. Open Plan Systems sells its products through its own sales offices and through independent dealers and has been trimming costs recently. The company's chairman, Anthony Markel, owns 13% of the company and the company is publicly traded.

- *Steelcase, Inc.* is the world's largest manufacturer of office furniture, and makes everything from file cabinets to whole office furniture systems. Steelcase also remanufactures office furniture and offers office-furniture-related services. Steelcase sells over 500 products through over 750 dealers in over 100 countries; however, in 2001 Steelcase has laid off some workers. Although publicly traded on the NYSE under the symbol SCS, descendents of the company's founders control over 65% of the voting shares.

To make sound recommendations to Langella, AIA's analysts will examine two key financial documents of the two companies—the *income statement* and the *balance sheet*, which were first introduced in Spreadsheet Case 3. From that case, recall the following types of financial statements:

- Income statements (also called operating statements) summarize the income, expenses, and profits (or losses) of businesses for a period, usually a year, quarter, or month.

- Balance sheets identify the assets, liabilities, and shareholders' equity of a firm at a particular point in time. The difference between assets and liabilities is net worth or equity (literally what the organization is worth net of all other factors).

As you did in Spreadsheet Case 3, you will need to calculate a number of financial ratios based on the financial statements of these two companies. Before doing this case, review the descriptions and formulas that appear in Spreadsheet Case 3 for the following ratios:

- Current Ratio
- Quick Ratio (or "Acid Test")
- Total Assets Utilization
- Debt Ratio
- Return on Total Assets (ROA)
- Return on Equity (ROE)
- Profit Margin
- Price/Earnings Ratio

Tasks

There are two tasks in this case:

1. Obtain the financial statements of the two companies Open Plan Systems and Steelcase and import the statements to an Excel spreadsheet. Go to the Security and Exchange Commission's Web site (www.sec.gov) and obtain the data from each company's latest 10-K filing. **Follow the directions for capturing the data at EDGAR and pasting into an Excel spreadsheet given in the Tasks section for Web Case 2.**

Copy and past the income statement and balance sheet, one at a time, for the first company—Open Systems Inc.—onto a blank Excel worksheet. Copy the Income statement first, and the consolidated balance sheet second. Place the balance sheet below the Income statement in your spreadsheet. Immediately save the worksheet with an appropriate file name (e.g., *WebCase4 Open Plan.xls*).

Repeat these steps for Steelcase. Create a new spreadsheet file *WebCase4 Steelcase.xls*.

2. Below the bottom of the financial statements, calculate the first seven financial ratios outlined above for each company. Look up the most current price/earnings ratio on the Web for both companies and enter it into the spreadsheet manually.

In a few paragraphs, write an analysis of both companies. Based on the information provided in this case, which firm has the strongest set of ratios? Which would make the better investment? Review the financial statements of both companies for any items that might help explain their financial condition. Include a table of your financial ratios for both companies as supporting evidence.

You may also use financial content Web sites like *Finance.Yahoo.com, Bigcharts.com, Hoovers.com, Smartmoney.com*, etc. to find additional information on these companies. The 10-K statement also contains very insightful sections on firm strategy, operations, and future prospects.

Tutorial for Web Case 4

Web Case 4 requires skills for obtaining financial data from the SEC EDGAR database which are covered in the Tutorial for Web Case 2. The new skill in this case is learning how to read a typical consolidated balance sheet that is a part of the 10-K statement.

Consolidated Balance Sheets

A balance sheet describes the assets and liabilities (debts) of a firm. Because the assets must equal the liabilities, the statement is called a "balance" sheet. Generally an SEC 10-K balance sheet contains the following types of information:

Summary Balance Sheet Data
Assets

Cash and cash equivalents equivalents............	Cash or immediately available funds
Marketable securities...	Usually stock in other companies
Other assets	Real estate and office equipment
Total assets............	

Liabilities

Current liabilities (short term debt)	Payments required in the current year
Long-term debt..........	Usually long term bonds
Stockholders' Equity	Shares issued to stock holders

Along with information on the SEC 10-K income statement, you can calculate the ratios required in this case.

Web Case 5

Aperture, Inc.

Problem: Analyze the communications market

Management skills: Data analysis, Strategizing

Web skills: Market research

Aperture is a regional communications company serving six states. Aperture provides a number of communications services, the main ones being local and long distance telephone service, cellular phone service, and cable television. The company has known for some time that it has the infrastructure in place to add Internet service to its stable of services. Until now, it has resisted this move due to a saturated market. However, a number of local and regional Internet service providers have gone out of business in the last two years, leaving a gap in the marketplace.

Aperture's CEO wants to approach an entrance into the Internet service market very cautiously. Aperture's Marketing Director, Alex Charles knows he needs to consult hard statistics in order to make the proper recommendations to the CEO.

Alex's first goal is to determine whether Aperture should even consider expanding its services in the first place. For this, he intends to research the growth of Internet usage since it became a common tool for both business and home users. He wants to know if Internet usage will continue to increase or if it will plateau in the near future.

Next, Alex must devise a marketing strategy, assuming that Aperture will choose to introduce an Internet service brand. He has already given this task some thought and has determined that Aperture should begin by targeting its existing customers. Since Aperture phone service users and cable subscribers are already familiar with the company, they would likely trust Aperture as their first Internet service provider or as an alternative to their current provider. Targeting existing customers initially would allow Aperture to build a customer base for its Internet brand quickly and at a lower cost than if the company tried to target the general public. Including all of its services, Aperture already has a database of 4.5 million customers. Acquiring a database of names that large is an expense the company could avoid for now.

Going further, Alex would like to determine which segment of Aperture's existing customer base should be targeted most aggressively with promotional material for a new Internet service. He has already narrowed down the choices to cellular customers and cable subscribers who are more technically saavy. He has found no data indicating a significant growth in landline telephone use. And people who have only landline telephone service are far less likely than cellphone users to want Internet service. Alex's approach will be to target the customer base that is showing more growth in recent years. He believes that if people are already embracing technology products or services, they are more likely to continue spending money on technology.

The result of Alex's research will be a full-scale report to the CEO that includes an outline, statement of goal, presentation of the facts, and concluding statements. Hard statistics will be introduced in written arguments and illustrated with spreadsheets and charts.

Tasks

There are seven tasks in this case.

1.   Go to relevant government Web sites to find statistics on Internet usage. Be certain you can answer these questions: Has the number of Internet users increased consistently over the past few years? Has the number of people using the Internet at work increased during that time? Has the number of people using the Internet at home also increased? How about "intensity of use" or hours using the Internet?

2.   Transfer the statistical data you have found into a spreadsheet file either by copying and pasting it from a Web page or by keying it in manually. Some online resources will also allow you to download data tables directly into an Excel file. If you wish to cut and paste data from online sources into an Excel spreadsheet, consult the instructions in Web Case 2 first.

3.   Display the Internet growth data you have found in the form of a chart in the spreadsheet file.

4.   Go to relevant government Web sites to find statistics that track the number of cellular phone subscribers and the number of cable television subscribers over the last several years. Be certain you can determine which is the more promising market based on the criteria set up by Alex.

5.   Transfer the subscriber comparison data you have found into a separate worksheet in the same spreadsheet file you used for the Internet growth data. Display the subscriber data in the form of a chart.

6.   Search the Web for companies or services that sell mailing lists. Determine what the approximate cost would be to acquire a list of potential customer names equal to the number of customers Aperture already has (4.5 million). Decide whether you can use this figure to fortify the position of targeting existing customers first.

7.   Write a report for the CEO as described above (include an outline, statement of goal, presentation of facts including your spreadsheets and charts, and concluding statements). Do not forget to cite your statistical sources.

Tutorial for Web Case 5

A great source for statistics like the ones required for this case is the U.S. Census. The Census Web site can be found at *http://www.census.gov*. From the Census home page, you can access the *Statistical Abstract of the United States* (*http://www.census.gov/statab/www/*). From the Statistical Abstract home page, pay particular attention to the *USA Statistics in Brief* and *Frequently Requested Tables* links in the section titled *"Selected features from the Statistical Abstract."* Also, the Pew Foundation Internet and American Life Project conducts regular surveys on Internet usage (www.pewinternet.org).

Use of the suggested sources is not mandatory, but they are stable sources that provide accurate user-friendly data. As a whole, U.S. government sites are very useful for this type of research. Another source you may want to consider is the U.S. Department of Commerce's National Telecommunications & Information Administration report titled *"Falling through the Net: Defining the Digital Divide."* The document and accompanying charts can be found at *http://www.ntia.doc.gov/ntiahome/fttn99/contents.html*.

Previous tutorials you may find useful for this case:

Spreadsheet Case 1 (page 21)
Spreadsheet Case 5 (page 44)

NOTES

NOTES

NOTES

NOTES

NOTES

NOTES

NOTES

NOTES

NOTES

NOTES

NOTES

NOTES

AC 51   TT 1130-1¹⁰

BL 71   TT 8→9¹⁵

HU 44   TT 2-3¹⁵

BA 25   TT 9³⁰/10⁴⁵ AC ⚤

EG 13   TT 2-3¹⁵ ⚤ ⚤ (BU)

　　　　　　EG 13

　　　　　　PE.

AC 52

BL 72

HU